There and Back Again

There and Back Again

An Actor's Tale

Sean Astin
with Joe Layden

St. Martin's Press ❧ New York

www.stmartins.com

ISBN 0-312-33146-0
EAN 978-0312-33146-7

First Edition: October 2004

10 9 8 7 6 5 4 3 2 1

The making of the *Lord of the Rings* film trilogy was the greatest personal and professional experience of my life. This book is dedicated to Peter Jackson, Fran Walsh, and the entire cast and crew. Without their courage, creativity, and professionalism, I would never have been able to learn so much about myself. The thoughts and experiences related in this book are from my heart and try to answer, in as thoughtful a way as possible, the many questions that people have asked me over these past few years. I will forever be grateful to my wife, Christine, as well as to my daughters, Alexandra and Elizabeth, for their enduring love and support. *The road goes ever on....*

There and Back Again

CHAPTER ONE

I sensed from the very beginning that *The Lord of the Rings* had the potential to be something extraordinary. Not merely extraordinary in the way that, say, *Raiders of the Lost Ark* was extraordinary—as pure, cinematic adventure, a thrill-ride of the highest order—but as something even more. I'm talking about epic filmmaking not seen since the days of David Lean or John Ford. I knew that the director, Peter Jackson, was a man of prodigious talent and vision, an artist capable of creating a film that might one day be mentioned in the same breath as Lean's desert classic *Lawrence of Arabia*. *The Lord of the Rings*, I thought—I hoped—could be like that: Oscar-caliber art on par with the best films ever made.

How did I know this? Well, sometimes you just get a gut feeling. It's as simple as that. As a journeyman actor I've survived by seeing an opportunity pop up on the radar screen, guessing kind of intuitively what the odds are of success, and then determining whether I want to be part of that project. Sometimes, for practical, real-world reasons, I've made decisions knowing full well what the cycle would be, and that my association with a given film might even have a minor negative impact on my image or marketability. As in any field, you calculate the odds and make a choice, and then you live with it. You can only wait so long for Martin Scorcese to call; sometimes you have to take the best available offer. I've done any number of low-budget movies in which my participation was based primarily on the following logic:

All right, it's a week out of my life or six weeks out of my life, the money is pretty

good, and I don't have to audition. Let me take a look at the script. Does my charac-
ter have a banana sticking out of his ass? No? No banana? Well, then, how bad can
it be? It's a third-tier knockoff of a Die Hard *movie, but the morality is reasonably*
intact; the violence is kind of sophomoric, but not gratuitous, and for the most part
everyone keeps their clothes on. Most important of all, is anybody in the business ever
going to see it? Not likely. Okay . . . where do I sign?

Ah, but old movies never really die, do they? Not anymore. Thanks to video and DVD, the Internet, and late-night cable television, they live on forever, seeping inevitably into the public consciousness whether they deserve to or not. Case in point: a cold winter day on the south island of New Zealand, back in 1999. One of many days on the set of *The Lord of the Rings* when things weren't going quite as planned. The kind of day where the scene called for filming six hundred horses on the top of a windswept deer park, so the crew was furiously washing away snow with fire hoses to make it look like it wasn't wintertime—resulting, of course, in a veritable sea of mud. In New Zealand we traveled almost everywhere in four-wheel-drive vehicles, so thick and persistent was the slop. At times it felt like what I have read about soldiers fighting in the trenches in World War I. We couldn't go anywhere without getting muck splattered all over us. On our shoes, our clothes . . . our capes. (We were hobbits, remember?) No hyperbole or disrespect intended, but there were times when it almost felt as though we were part of a military operation. It was that rugged, that spartan, that precise. Mountainside locations looked almost like battlefields, dotted with tents and armies of workers. The general, of course, was Peter Jackson.

Well, on this one particular morning I saw Peter sitting in his tent with a bemused look on his face. Now, protocol on movie sets often dictates that directors, even those as approachable and thoughtful as Peter, be given space in the morning hours—it's a time for preparation, not long conversations. But, as I approached, planning to offer no more than a cheery "Good morning," Peter began to nod ever so slightly. With his unruly hair, stout frame, and generally disheveled appearance, Peter has often been described as "hobbit-like," and certainly the impish grin coming to his face now supported that notion.

"Sean," he said dryly. "Guess what I saw last night?"

"What?"

"*Icebreaker.*"

Oh, boy . . .

Icebreaker was the rather benign result of one of those "business" decisions I just mentioned. Some two years earlier I had accepted what most people would consider to be a princely sum of money (sixty thousand dollars) for roughly two weeks of work. I had a good time making *Icebreaker*, which was filmed at Killington Ski Resort in Vermont. While there, I dined at a couple of nice restaurants, discovered a lovely antique bookshop, and made a few good friends. Peter Beckwith, the producer, and David Giancola, the director, are genuinely nice men who treated me well. One of my costars was the incomparable Bruce Campbell, regarded as perhaps the king of B-movie stars. If you've seen *The Evil Dead* or any of its sequels, you've seen Bruce. You know his work and his ability to bring a certain campy grace to almost any project. I wasn't really familiar with Bruce's work at the time, but most of the people I worked with were, and they said things like, "Oh, man, you have no idea how cool it is to work with this guy." In truth, Bruce was pretty cool. And a total pro, I might add. I had fun working with him.

Everything about my experience in Vermont was pleasant, if ultimately forgettable. But let's be honest here: the movie is a piece of shit.[1] Sorry, Dave. Sorry, Peter. But you know it's a piece of shit, too. By that, I mean, it isn't socially edifying, and it doesn't aspire to be artistic or even particularly clever. It's just mindless, harmless entertainment. (Check out the movie's promotional poster, featuring yours truly with a pair of ski goggles perched on his forehead, a revolver in his hand, and a look on his face that fairly screams, "Mess with me, and I'll kick your ass!") But we all got along well and had a pleasant enough time, and while we were there we took our work as seriously as possible.

For me—for all of us, really—it was a smart business decision to do *Icebreaker.* These guys figured out a formula: how to package and presell the movie, how to raise the money, how to film the thing, and

---

1. "Piece of shit" is a phrase I use comfortably in everyday conversation. In this context it's meant to be both funny and descriptive, but not mean-spirited. It does, however, reflect a certain point of view, which I can't deny.

how to have fun doing it. So more power to them. And, frankly, I needed the work and the cash that came with it. Little did I know that two years later I'd be on location in New Zealand, working on one of the most ambitious projects in the history of movies, a $270 million version of *The Lord of the Rings* trilogy, and that I'd be standing face-to-face with Peter Jackson, one of the rising stars of the business. Peter, it turns out, is not just a filmmaker, but a fan of films, all films, with a massive private collection that keeps his garage screening room humming day and night, and a penchant for channel surfing in the wee hours that makes it virtually impossible to hide anything from him.

Including *Icebreaker*.

"Very nice," Peter said, and left it at that, because nothing else needed to be said. It wasn't an insult, nor was it meant to embarrass me (well, maybe a little). It was just an acknowledgment of where I'd been and where I was. Most actors (and most directors, too) have such things on their résumés, and part of the obligation of the fraternity is to remind you of that every once in a while. It's healthy for the ego, if you know what I mean. But in this setting no one else had any idea what Peter was talking about. The cast and crew seemed unfamiliar with *Icebreaker*, but they understood that the director was gently busting the balls of one of his actors, and that was sufficient, especially since that actor was a bit of an outsider.

You see, on the set of *The Lord of the Rings* I think I was sometimes perceived as the Hollywood guy (which is not necessarily the same as a movie star). The director and the vast majority of his crew were native Kiwis, and most of the actors were from the United Kingdom, Australia, and New Zealand. Even more so than Elijah Wood, who as Frodo was ostensibly the film's star, I got the sense that I was the *American* actor. I was the kid who had grown up in Hollywood. I had been raised by a pair of pop culture icons, Patty Duke and John Astin. On a production that had been quite vocal and public in its reluctance to hire American actors (not out of any overt jingoism, but merely as a way to demonstrate faithfulness to Tolkien's vision), I was the most visible exception to the rule. I was *Rudy*, for God's sake. You don't get any more American than that. Rudy was the underdog. And I guess, in a way, so was I.

. . .

Let me say something about the purpose of *There and Back Again*. Forests have been felled and more ink spilled about *The Lord of the Rings* than for almost any other film franchise in recent memory. I have talked extensively about how positive my experience in New Zealand was, about the family bonds that were created, and the love and passion and dedication that everyone involved brought to their work. My intent here is absolutely *not* to disavow any of that sentiment; rather, I want to amplify and explore some of the other kinds of emotions and dynamics that I felt. Furthermore, I want to explain how a lot of my early experiences as a professional actor informed my thinking and attitudes during much of the filming. So . . .

To get an idea of how my career has advanced—and sometimes stalled—we should really go back to 1989. Shortly after graduating from high school, I traveled to England to work on a World War II ensemble film called *Memphis Belle*. It was a good role in a major Hollywood movie, starring a handful of talented young actors, among them Eric Stolz and Matthew Modine, and it figured to help me regain some of the momentum I'd achieved a few years earlier, when I'd starred in *The Goonies*. I was serious about my life and career, although admittedly lacking focus and direction. I wanted to go to college, but I also wanted to be a movie star and a filmmaker.

It was an exciting time in my life. I was eighteen years old, had just graduated from high school, and was traveling at my own expense to take part in a Warner Bros. movie. The producer, David Putnam, was one of my heroes. I greatly admired his films and had followed his career as an executive; in short, I wanted to emulate him in some way. I'll never forget the day that he gathered the American actors together at the Atheneum Hotel in London and told us about his belief in the power of cinema. His words confirmed a lifetime of instincts and crystallized my imagination. We were about to embark on a filmmaking experience of real significance. The story dealt with an important moment in American and world history, and we all wanted to get it right. I loved the idea that I was becoming a global citizen and that I was likely to travel all over the world experiencing new cultures and meeting people completely different from myself. I sensed that I was destined to become a star and that my dream of becoming a filmmaker was about to come true. It had been a long time since *The Goonies*, but now it seemed as though my career was ready to take off, and I would be able to accomplish the loftiest of my goals. How? I really had no idea.

One day near the end of principal photography on *Memphis Belle*, I took a walk in the garden at Pinewood Studios with the Academy Award–winning cinematographer David Watkins. This in some way was a rite of passage. David was one of the most revered and gifted cinematographers in the business, having worked on, among other films, *Catch-22* and *Out of Africa* (for which he won an Oscar). He was a legend in the cinematography world, not only because of his artistry, but also because of his personality, which was at once generous and biting. David didn't suffer fools gladly, nor did he fall at the feet of Hollywood's gentry. Warren Beatty told me that David once said to Barbra Streisand, when they first began working together, "We're going to have to do something about *that!*" while pointing rather dramatically at her nose.

Anyway, instead of being rude, David decided to offer me guidance and inspiration. I began telling him about an original idea I had for a short film based on nothing more than a single image I had carried with me since I was fourteen years old. It had popped into my head one day while driving with Mark Marshall, Steven Spielberg's assistant, during the filming of *The Goonies*. Mark was taking me home, and we were on Ventura Boulevard, with the sun setting, listening to Kansas sing "Dust in the Wind" on the radio, when suddenly I had a vision of two soldiers—one Vietnamese, one American—hanging upside down next to each other, with a burning red sun between them. Why? I don't know. My best guess is that it had something to do with my having recently seen Francis Ford Coppola's classic *Apocalypse Now* for the first time. That, combined with the fact that every day when I went to work on *The Goonies*, I was escorted to the set by my guardian, Joseph "Peppy" Passarelli. A big Italian man with a bushy mustache, Peppy had been a corpsman in Vietnam, and during our many hours in the car he often shared tales of his time in Southeast Asia. Anyway, between Peppy and *Apocalypse Now*, and Kansas and the setting sun, I couldn't get this image out of my head.

So here I was years later, walking with David Watkins, trying to figure out what I wanted to do with my life, and sharing with him my idea for a small personal film, not at all sure how he would respond to it, but wanting his feedback nonetheless. The truth is, I was a bit lost. I knew I had missed a window of opportunity for college. I'd applied to Cal State–Northridge right out of high school, mainly because it was one of the few schools that did not require the SAT for admission. This was important to me because I hated the notion of having my intelligence quantified by a single exam. (In the interest of full disclosure, I should reveal that I did once register for the SAT, and even started to drive to the testing site, only to miss the exam after locking my keys in the car at a gas station while battling a bout of performance anxiety.) I was accepted at Cal State–Northridge, but I knew, based on the filming schedule of *Memphis Belle*, that I would almost certainly be in England when the fall semester began. If I'd returned immediately upon the conclusion of principal photography, I might have missed no more than a week or two of classes, and I suppose I could have made up the work, but I opted instead to travel. Some of the other guys had cool trips planned, and I wanted to be like them. I took a cruise through Greece, and I paid top dollar because I didn't know you could do it more cost-effectively than that. To be honest, I didn't really care. I had some money in my pocket and a small degree of notoriety, and so I had a good time. It was a wonderful experience, but I embraced it knowing full well that it would delay my entrance to Cal State–Northridge.

It's fair to say that I was somewhat conflicted about what I wanted to do with my life. Here I was, part of this big World War II movie produced by the estimable David Putnam, who, a decade before *Saving Private Ryan* galvanized public opinion, had captured my imagination and made me understand the importance of movies. One reason David wanted to make *Memphis Belle* was his outrage over the gratuitousness of *Top Gun*, which a few years earlier had trumpeted the machismo and courage of modern-day fighter pilots in what he considered an almost cartoonish manner. David was after something else, something more subtle, more honest. He wanted to celebrate the "greatest generation." He understood how critical and important the images of war could be, and so he believed it was a sacred responsibility to portray such behavior in all its complexity. I believed what he told us with my whole heart. I wanted to be an important filmmaker, just like David Putnam. He had been the president of Columbia Pictures, and now he wanted to try to improve the quality of British film.

The first day I met David, I said, "Mr. Putnam, I'm not going to ask you for anything except, please, let me go to Asia when it's time to promote this movie." He said he'd try, and true to his word, he took me with him to Thailand, Singapore, Japan, and Hong Kong. In no small bit of irony, we wound up promoting the movie on the eve of the Persian Gulf War, and I found myself on a dais with David and Matthew Modine, fielding questions about our positions on the conflict in Iraq. *Memphis Belle* was a celebration of American air supremacy during World War II, and a reflection on the kinds of sacrifices that made Allied victory possible. The Japanese journalists seemed justifiably skeptical about whatever propaganda we were supposedly engaged in. To our credit, David, Matthew, and I took refuge in our roles as artists whose primary mission is to examine and reflect the best and worst of what human nature has to offer. I've always had notions of a political future for myself, probably since my mom told me in the fourth grade that I could be anything I wanted to be, even president of the United States. Well, I believed her, and now at nineteen I found myself "on the record" about serious issues at a serious time. But I remember feeling that my country was at war, and I should be at home with my family.

It was during this trip that I met (via telephone) the woman I would eventually marry. I was sitting in the bathtub of a fancy hotel in Tokyo, watching CNN and listening to Bernie Shaw as he crawled around the floor of the Al Rasheed Hotel, when the phone rang. The voice on the other end sounded as though it belonged to a beautiful young woman, and as it turned out, that was precisely the case. Christine was working for a commercial agent who had set up meetings for me in Japan. It was bizarre to think about "selling" myself as a marketable commodity to advertisers while we were in the first stages of a new war. I couldn't help but wonder about my place in the grand scheme of things. I remember the issue came up of whether the draft might need to be reinstated if the war dragged on. As David Putnam and I were arriving at the airport for our journey home, I said quite emphatically, "I'll go. If they call, I'll go." I knew that I was saying it just because it sounded good, so it was somewhat self-serving. But I meant it, too. Although my political feelings about it were not necessarily the same as my personal feelings, I believed that if the draft had been reinstated, I would have been obligated to serve, and I would have embraced that obligation. Of course, I'll never really know what I would have done.

I guess I was trying to take myself seriously, maybe too seriously, but then there are worse mistakes a young man can make. I was not all that sophisticated and didn't have an extensive vocabulary. Ever since I was a kid I wanted to accept the responsibility of being an adult. I needed help, though. I needed guidance. So as I walked that day through the garden with David Watkins, one of the great artists of the medium, I solicited his opinion and advice. I told him that when I got home, I planned to shoot a 16-millimeter short film about this image in my head, the one of the two soldiers.

"Why do it sixteen?" he asked. "Why not thirty-five-millimeter? You know, it's not that much more expensive."

I felt like I'd been hit over the head with a bat. Until then, I had thought of myself as a student, someone not yet ready to embark on the journey of a grown-up filmmaker. But this simple suggestion from one of the industry's giants changed my life. He wasn't talking to me like a kid or a student. Implicit in his comment was the idea that we were equals. Maybe not in terms of accomplishments, but certainly in terms of potential. I don't think he realized what he did for me in that moment, but I will forever be grateful to him.

Practically speaking, David was right, of course. I'd planned to shoot the film in 16-millimeter partly because it was cheaper, but mainly because it seemed less pretentious. *Real* filmmakers shot in 35-millimeter; *aspiring* filmmakers settled for 16-millimeter. David Watkins understood the difference, and now so did I.

When I got home, I poured tons of energy into my work. Along with two of my friends, I produced and starred in a play. I took an acting class with Stella Adler, and I went to work on my short film. I also began building my own production company, Lava Entertainment.

In late January 1991, I finally met Christine in person, and we were almost instantly inseparable. We became life partners in every way imaginable. We like telling people that we were comfortably codependent. Along the way we moved in together, traveled to Asia, backpacked across Europe, and fell madly in love. I was nineteen when we met; Christine was twenty-two. Not long after we returned from Europe, I went to Indiana to meet her family. I think Christine's father had mixed feelings about me. On one hand, he knew I had at least a shot at the brass ring, and thus might be capable of giving Christine the kind of life he naturally felt she deserved, the life any father wants for his daughter. On the other hand, I'm pretty sure he thought I was a complete Hollywood idiot, because I had no education, no practical experience, and no formal plan for achieving any of my lofty goals. This was a no-nonsense guy who had worked hard his whole life. A career firefighter, he had spent his life's savings and much of his family's emotional equity in a failed attempt to own and run a grocery store. When I met Christine, her family was finally coming out of the aftermath of that experience, so I was viewed by her dad as either the knight in shining armor or a flaky prince. Her family was nervous and scared and hopeful, all at the same time; I just didn't want to let them down.

As I think back, I realize that Christine's dad really wanted me to marry his daughter, which was good, because I never wanted to lose her. The life Christine had known and still does know in Indiana is one of stability, unquestioning love, loyalty, and support from her family and community. I revere that quality in her and them, and I am proud to consider myself a very real part of their family.

I always felt like I was destined for greatness[2] on some level, even if I was afraid to express those feelings out loud, but I didn't mind expressing them to Christine on our first date. It meant the world to me that she didn't laugh. She believed me; she believed *in* me. She took me absolutely seriously, and I found that incredibly romantic. She was

---

2. Please forgive me for being pompous, and grant me a little fun. There's a very thin line between delusions of grandeur and extraordinary human achievement, if only in the early stages of planning. If I succeed—wonderful! If I fail—well, at least you all were gracious enough not to spoil my good time.

the sexiest woman I had ever met, and she was *into* me, which I found inordinately shocking. I remember a couple of rakes who were my friends at the time looking at Christine, and looking at me with utter stupefaction, and saying, "How did you land this girl?"

I had no answer.

Not everyone was happy about my relationship with Christine. Among the skeptics was Milton Justice, a friend and one of my earliest mentors. Milton is a brilliant and creative man, a Yale-educated actor-turned-producer who earned an Academy Award in 1986 for his work on *Down and Out in America*, a documentary feature about the lives of transvestites and transsexuals. Milton was one of the producers of *Staying Together*, a movie in which I had starred in 1987, and he agreed to help me and my friends produce a play in L.A. that we wanted to act in. He would also help by producing my first short film with me, introducing me to Stella Adler, helping me land representation from what was then the biggest agency in town (Creative Arts Agency), and getting me into the Motion Picture Academy of Arts and Sciences. Needless to say, he had a manifest impact both on my career and my thinking at a critical stage in my development.

Our friendship started simply enough. Milton had produced a play that I'd been in, and as I was trying to figure out the Hollywood game of forming meaningful and important relationships, I invited him out to dinner in the hope of picking his brain and perhaps absorbing some of his wisdom. I took him to a nice restaurant, which I think he found rather charming. I was an eighteen-year-old kid, and he couldn't believe I was paying for his dinner, since actors, especially young ones, just didn't do that kind of thing. But there was so much value to knowing him and learning from him. And I liked him a lot, both as a person and a potential business partner.

So we developed what I considered to be more than a friendship; it was a mentorship. Milton supported me; he believed in my ambitions and ability, and wanted to help nurture my talent, and eventually help trade on it, of course.

Milton and I worked well together—until I met Christine. When I told him how much I cared about her, and how I planned to marry her, he was dismissive.

"You say that about every girl."

"I know. But this time it's different."

Not long after that, when I told Milton I didn't want to continue carrying such large overhead expenses—I was spending hundreds if not thousands of dollars a month, with barely anything to show for it—he became incensed. He took it personally and walked out. And I let him go.

We had been working out of a rent-free space, which is a funny story on a couple of levels. First, Milton and I had independently known about a postproduction facility in Hollywood called Matrix Alliance. I knew one of the guys who worked there, having worked with him on several occasions over the years. His name was Barney, and whenever I had a looping session at Matrix, Barney always seemed to be in charge. There was an upper room in the industrial area that nobody was using, and one weekend while Barney was on vacation with his family in Palm Springs, Milton and I literally moved in. We put their boxes into a storage area and turned on phones and furnished the space with rented furniture; I even put some posters up on the walls. On Monday, when Barney returned, I called him in and said, "Hey, Barney, look—Lava Entertainment!" He was, like, "Oh, boy, look what you did."

But I calmed him down by appealing to his genuinely decent nature.

"Please," I said, "I can't afford to pay for office space. Let me use it. You won't even know I'm here. Eventually it'll pay off, and if you need the space, just say the word and we're gone."

The funny, silly, sad lesson for me probably won't ever become the stuff of Hollywood lore that I wish it would. You see, during preparations for *On My Honor*, my first short film, I called virtually everyone I had ever worked with to ask for help. To a person, no one would contribute a cent, but just about everyone offered help in some way, shape, or form. Notably, Steven Spielberg offered to let me use his editing suites at Amblin on the Universal lot. I'll never forget driving into Universal Studios with ten or so reels of film in cans in my hatchback. Those cans represented a thirty-thousand-dollar investment, and I had them cooking in the L.A. sun in my car! Regardless, here I was, a bona fide filmmaker heading for the sacred work space that Spielberg had so generously offered for my use. I found myself alone in the editing room with no idea how to load the 35-millimeter film into the Moviola in order to look at it. I was terrified that Steven would pop his head in, and I would be exposed for the neophyte/fraud/idiot that I had pretended not to be. I opened the first canister of film and picked it up incorrectly. The core of the film fell out, and there I was, sitting in a tangled ball of film. I hightailed it out of there and have only been back once, in a failed audition attempt for *High Incident*, Spielberg's television show about the LAPD. Ironically, Steven told everyone in the room that he'd seen my second short film, *Kangaroo Court*, and that I was an excellent filmmaker.

The point of this story is that I was too embarrassed to ask for help and too impatient to figure out a problem on my own. I believe that mistake cost me the possibility of having Steven check up on me and the untold benefit that might have come from the folks at Amblin seeing me as a familiar face around the shop. While I deeply regret my fallibility in this regard, I am grateful to Milton Justice for stepping into the breach and working with me despite my idiosyncrasies. I think today he still considers me someone he'd be willing to work with, and that thought makes me happy.

As it turned out, Mark Rocco, a young director, was paying for a big suite of offices adjacent to our "storeroom" office, and he was in the process of putting together a movie about homeless drug addicts. Mark, the son of actor Alex Rocco, went on to forge a reasonably successful career, highlighted by a critically acclaimed movie titled *Murder in the First*, which features Kevin Bacon giving perhaps the performance of his life as a prisoner on death row at Alcatraz. At the time, however, Mark was just a hungry young director, eagerly trying to make contacts and assemble projects. Judging from the traffic in and out of his office, it seemed that a key component of his strategy was to form friendships with young Hollywood actors. At first, I thought he seemed like a scurrilous individual, and I didn't have a lot of respect for what he was doing. I knew he was planning to make a movie about street kids, and he just seemed kind of creepy.

Oddly enough, we wound up playing basketball together on a semi-regular basis. I would come out of the little cubicle that I had co-opted and play hoops with the people who were Mark's assistants, friends, partners, and so on, and he ended up offering me a part in this movie about drug addicts and homeless kids called *Where the Day Takes You.* My first response was to turn down the offer, but then I agreed to do a cameo. I was trying to figure out what he was doing, and whether he had a real script, a real budget, and the ability and resources to put together a legitimate project. I had my doubts.

"It's union scale," Mark said. "That's the best I can do."

At this time I knew almost nothing about the fine art of negotiation. I'd had a very complicated relationship with my representatives at CAA, trying to figure out how money was made and eventually coming to the realization (obvious to anyone with a bit less naïveté) that they were more interested in making money for themselves than for me. So I was really grappling with the dynamics of what negotiations were. I was learning on my own the way things work in Hollywood—that multiple sets of books may be kept, and that on virtually every movie a quiet sort of compensation can occur. The studio has contractual obligations with the network or the producers or the distributors, and cash goes under the table, behind doors, and so on. It seems to happen on virtually every project. You just have to decide how much you want, what you think you can get, and what you're willing to not know.

In the grand scheme of things, this is a fairly innocuous little story about a very small, independent film, a director seeming to do whatever was necessary to get his movie made, and a young actor trying to figure out how to make deals and keep his integrity while profiting at the same time.

"I can't give you any more money," Mark said, "but is there anything else you'd like that would make you consider doing this? Can I give you a birthday present?"

My thoughts turned to my younger brother, Mack, also an actor. He'd made quite a good living working on the television show *The Facts of Life*. Unfortunately, he'd spent most of what he'd earned by spending crazily on such things as renting an indoor hockey rink in Los Angeles just so he and his buddies would have a place to play. Mack was always begging me to join them, but there never seemed to be enough time, and anyway, I didn't have any of the proper gear. I'd grown up playing baseball, football, and basketball. Hockey? In Southern California? It didn't make much sense. Now, though, as Mark Rocco asked me if there was something I might need, the thought of Mack and his ice-rink buddies flashed through my mind.

"You know, I could use some hockey equipment."

The next thing I knew, I was in Mark's office, hoisting a huge black hockey bag over my shoulder, filled with top-of-the-line gear: skates, helmet, mask, pads, stick, everything. I remember the weight of that bag felt like the exact weight of compromise; it felt like the weight of having sold out. I wanted the bag and everything in it, and yet I wanted somehow to keep a firm grasp on my own integrity, and it occurred to me then that perhaps it was possible to do both. The very idea of that possibility, that moral ambiguity, confused and bothered me.

Looking at Mark Rocco, I realized that he was a young businessman, maybe even an artist (I wasn't sure yet), who would do whatever was necessary to get his movie made, including extending favors to his actors. Instead of despising him for it, I admired him. I even admired the fact that he'd gotten off cheap with me. That was a conscious decision: I *chose* to admire him, or at least that aspect of him. His determination. His will. His creativity.

"Okay, Mark," I said, "I'll play the lead in your movie."

He smiled.

"What changed your mind?"

My answer was complicated, but it came down to this: Mark had tapped into my own integrity. I had perceived him as something other than what he really was. Originally, I saw him as a guy who was not only trying to figure out how to cash in on actors' success in order to get movies made, but worse, was also trading on the misfortune of homeless kids. I couldn't understand why he was doing that. I questioned his integrity. It seemed like he was profiting from other people's experiences, and he was just a slimy, backroom sort of guy. Mark always seemed to be shrouded in a veil of thick gray cigarette smoke. He had dark unruly hair, he dressed badly, and he seemed to be perpetually sleep-deprived. To my eyes, he could even have had some first-hand experience with the material he was filming. But none of that mattered now, because he had done it. He'd found a way to reach me and get his movie made. I felt like I had compromised my integrity.

There was just one problem.

"We're closing a deal with David Arquette to play your part," Mark said. "But I think we can get him to take the smaller part you had agreed to play, and you can play the bigger part."

Sounded good to me, although there were a few other stipulations. Mark wanted me to visit a juvenile detention center and interview some of the kids there. He wanted me to meet with doctors to discuss the ravages of heroin abuse.

"One other thing . . . ," he said.

"What?"

"You have to lose ten pounds in the next ten days."

"No problem."

Not exactly true, as it turned out. With the help and guidance of a doctor and nutritionist, I shed the weight. I subsisted on four hundred calories a day, mostly raw vegetables and chicken breast, and by the time shooting started I was carrying only 125 pounds on a five-foot-seven frame. (As a point of reference, my ideal walking-around weight these days is about 165; for the role of Samwise Gamgee, I deliberately packed on another thirty to forty pounds, bringing me up to a nearly corpulent two hundred.) The benefits of this transformation were instantly evident on screen: I was gaunt, haggard, sickly. In other words, I looked like either a drug addict or someone who is terminally ill. Not quite Tom Hanks in *Philadelphia*, but definitely moving in that direction. The unwanted fallout of this rapid weight loss was that it wreaked havoc on my metabolism, a problem I still face to this day. But I have no regrets. *Where the Day Takes You* remains one of the greatest creative experiences I've known. It showed me what I could do as an actor, how it was possible to develop my craft through hard work and sacrifice and research. I've done some good movies, and I've done some bad movies. *Where the Day Takes You* is a good one. It belongs in the pantheon of really interesting films about drug abuse, worthy of being mentioned in the same breath as *My Own Private Idaho* and *Drugstore Cowboy*. I'm proud to have it on my résumé. Thank goodness things worked out the way they did, and my initial thoughts about Mark turned out to be wrong. I regret that I underestimated him as an artist.

Oh, by the way. That hockey equipment? It's still in the bag. Never been used.

CHAPTER TWO

While I was working on *Where the Day Takes You*, a friend of mine named T.E. Russell stopped by the set to pay a visit. T.E. and I had gotten to know each other a few years earlier when we worked together on a movie called *Toy Soldiers*. T.E. is an African American with a sturdy presence and a beautiful voice. When Christine and I were married, the ceremony was held in Idaho, and T.E. helped make the event complete by graciously agreeing to sing an a capella version of "You Send Me." His voice poured out majestically through the pine trees, and I like to think that it drifted right up to the front doors of some of our neighbors, most notably an avowed leader of a white supremacist organization.

But I digress.

Shortly before T.E. visited the set, I had received a script for a movie called *Encino Man*. I respect T.E.'s opinion, so I asked him if he'd mind looking at the script with me. It was an almost surreal experience. Here I was, enjoying another day of important work on a thoughtful, considered movie about homeless kids having remarkable, real-world experiences on the streets of Los Angeles, and I was reading a script about a caveman who becomes a high school student! I'd studied with Stella Adler. I'd worked with David Putnam. In my mind, at least, I was finally getting a chance to flex my acting muscles and do the work I'd always been capable of doing. If I hadn't exactly "arrived," at least I was on the right track.

That's how I felt, anyway. But perception is one thing and reality is another, for the script I held in my hand was not really the sort of script that gets sent to an important actor. The biggest, most important issue in *Encino Man* was how a couple of high school students could exploit the caveman to make themselves more popular. Deep stuff. And so T.E., Christine, and I read the script out loud while standing just off Hollywood Boulevard, snorting and laughing and dismissing it as we went along. When we finished it, I can vividly remember looking at T.E. and saying, "This is the biggest piece of shit script I have ever read in my entire life." T.E. just laughed and nodded. That, I thought, would be the end of my association with *Encino Man*. But I was wrong.

I had recently moved from a small, boutique agency to CAA, which at the time was seeming to gobble up all of Hollywood. In one respect, it wasn't a move I enjoyed making. The agent I left was heartbroken, and Marion Dougherty, who had cast me in *Memphis Belle*, was so outraged that she called CAA and chastised them for poaching clients. But I was far from an innocent bystander. I no longer believed that my small agency had the power and influence to take me where I wanted to go. We had made a lot of money together, and I liked them as people, but as I became more knowledgeable, I asked more questions, and they didn't always have answers. It seemed to me that they weren't prosecuting my career interests in the way I knew the people at CAA would. My parents did not really respect my decision, but they didn't attempt to dissuade me.

I sensed that while my new agents were good at representing talent, when I walked into their agency, I didn't feel like it was a power center where information is currency, decisions are made with lightning speed, and careers are built and broken from moment to moment. I don't know if that speaks to the quality of the agency or Mike Ovitz's genius at designing an architectural space (at CAA). My instincts told me that if I wanted a shot at a "big" career, I should try to mix it up with the sharks. I was willing to terminate my professional relationship with people who had genuinely cared about me to go to a place where I thought the agents could capitalize on my success and plug me into the action at the highest levels. I'm not proud of my decision to the extent that I was not necessarily a loyal client, but I understand the mandate of ambition that was burning within me. I would enjoy the fruits of this choice and suffer its consequences. After years of reflection, I can honestly say that the most important characteristic for an actor to look for in an agent is genuine passion. In this regard, my first agents were successful.

One day my new agent, Mike Menchel, asked me to take a call from Jeffrey Katzenberg, one of the most powerful men in Hollywood. This was while Katzenberg was head of production at Disney, before he split with Michael Eisner and founded Dreamworks. The reason for the call, as it turned out, was to secure a commitment from me to appear in Disney's newest project, *Encino Man*. It was being made under the aegis of Hollywood Pictures, a subsidiary of Disney.

"Just take the call, Sean," Mike said. "It's important. See what happens."

He had a point. My father had told me many stories about the way studios worked, the personalities and egos involved, and warned me specifically not to ignore the gift of a personal call from a studio head.

A few minutes later my cell phone rang. It was Jeffrey Katzenberg. I was so nervous that I had to pull over onto Sunset Boulevard, because I knew how important a call it was, that this conversation represented a defining moment in my career. How I handled it—not merely whether I said yes or no—would go a long way toward determining my future in the business.

"Listen, Sean, we really want you to do this movie," he said. The tone in his voice was one of authority, and I admired that. He was selling the project but it didn't seem like he was selling. It felt more like he was trying to make it clear that he had something to offer, and I would be a fool to turn it down. I tried to formulate the proper response, one that would display a proper degree of respect, while allowing for the possibility of walking away.

"I'd love to work with you, Mr. Katzenberg," I began, "but with all due respect"—I swallowed hard—"does it have to be *this* movie?"

There was a pause.

"Yes, Sean, it has to be this movie."

He went on to describe the way they intended to market the picture and said that they knew it would be a successful venture. I'd already been briefed on the specifics of the deal. Disney had offered me roughly $150,000 to play one of the film's three leads, slightly more than I'd earned for *Toy Soldiers*, and infinitely more than I'd been paid on *Where the Day Takes You*. They'd also offered me the potential for an additional $400,000 on the back end, which, of course, I believed I'd never see, because hardly any actor ever sees back-end money. Jeffrey, however, said this movie would be different: there would be a unique definition of "net profit" that would ensure a bonus for everyone involved. Assuming, of course, that the movie performed well at the box office, which, frankly, I thought was a long shot. As Jeffrey talked, I could barely hear his words over the clatter of my own thoughts: *This movie is a piece of crap, and it's never going to make a nickel.*

Since I had some fairly serious career aspirations, I didn't voice that opinion. Rather, I tried to play the few chips I had, in diplomatic fashion.

"Mr. Katzenberg, it seems to me, based on the way you're structuring this deal, that you want me to take a leap of faith with you on this movie."

"That's right."

"Well, if you're willing to sit down and listen to some ideas that I have as a filmmaker, I'd consider making this movie with you."

Again, there was a pause on the other end of the line, this one even longer than the first.

"Sean, please . . . don't blow the deal over twenty grand."

Then I realized what was happening. My agents had been lobbying for more money, when what I really wanted was a chance to express myself as an artist. They had intimated to Disney that if the salary was bumped up twenty thousand dollars, I'd do the movie. Katzenberg naturally thought I was trying to squeeze him in some sort of clever, indirect way, which wasn't the case at all. I didn't want to do *Encino Man*, but if it was possible to leverage my participation into some other type of opportunity, then perhaps it would be worthwhile. But Jeffrey had no interest in me as a filmmaker; he just had a movie to make, and I fit the role.

I called Mench back and told him the conversation hadn't gone well. "Jeffrey thinks it's all about the money," I explained. "He doesn't understand who I am as an artist. I don't think he cares."

"So what do you want to do?" he asked.

Menchel was clearly amused by my chutzpah. He may have realized that I was upset that CAA was managing my reputation, and that I was uncomfortable about trying to tap dance out of the situation in a way that didn't hurt my credibility. I'm sure many an actor would have killed for that offer from Jeffrey Katzenberg, and in subsequent years, I would have, too. But all I could do at the time was follow my gut, believe in myself, and try not to sell out. Funny, huh? Coming from a guy who compromised his sense of egalitarian righteousness to accept a gift while screwing a fellow thesp out of the part he thought was his. But we've been through that. . . . What did I do about *Encino Man* and the extra twenty thousand CAA was gunning for?

"Tell them we'll pass."

"You're sure?"

"Yeah, I'm sure."

The next time I gave any serious thought to *Encino Man* was while I was exploring Europe with Christine. I got a call in Barcelona and was told that Ricardo Mesterez wanted to see my short film. Ricardo was the president of Hollywood Pictures. As such, he reported directly to Jeffrey Katzenberg.

The short film to which he referred was *On My Honor.*

Yep, I had finished it, in 35-millimeter. It was sixteen minutes long, and despite its roughness, it conveyed my sense of morality and had a genuine emotionality to it. And now, Ricardo, another honcho in the biz, wanted to see it. I was apoplectic. Operating behind the scenes during this time, or at least out of my purview, was another person I consider to be one of the giants in Hollywood. Daniel Petrie Jr., who needed a lot of convincing before he agreed to hire me in *Toy Soldiers,* has probably been my most important mentor. Dan spent countless hours on the phone counseling me, guiding me, sharing his wisdom and experience, and trying to protect me from myself. Furthermore, he knew what I wanted to accomplish and offered a considerable amount of his genius to help me achieve it. Why? That's just the kind of human being he is, and my name is one of many on a long list of folks he's helped along the way. Jeffrey and Ricardo knew how close Dan and I were, and they enlisted his help to try to "land" me for *Encino Man.* Dan told them that the way to my heart was through my desire to become a filmmaker.

I want to stop here for a beat. . . .

Picture the scene: It's pouring rain, and Christine and I are standing at a phone booth in Barcelona. All of our worldly possessions are in a storage shed in Van Nuys, California. I have close to eighty thousand dollars in the bank, and Christine and I are madly in love, traveling the world and learning about ourselves. I think at that point we're in escrow on a lovely little two-bedroom house in Sherman Oaks, and we're talking about going to college together. This phone call from Ricardo was like a bolt of lightning from the Hollywood gods. Never mind that I'd been praying to those gods for years, and now in what felt like an unlikely way, my prayers were being answered. But before I tell you what happened during that call, I want to explain a little about my life, my upbringing, and my particular worldview.

The actor Dan Aykroyd once employed an interesting phrase to describe Steven Spielberg: "artist-industrialist." I love that. It acknowledges that some of the most accomplished and visionary men (and women) in cinema are also astute financiers, technicians, and leaders. Spielberg, and others at or near his level, understand the wanton waste that comes with being too self-indulgent an *artiste.* When Spielberg directs a movie, he understands and accepts the extraordinary responsibility that comes with the hiring of a cast and crew, the careful handling of a budget that exceeds the GNP of some Third World nations, and of course, the crushing weight of expectation. Critics, studio executives, and movie fans all expect him to hit a home run on every trip to the plate, to create movies that win awards, earn stellar reviews, and make hundreds of millions of dollars at the box office. It's quite a thing, I believe, for a filmmaker (and Peter Jackson now falls into this category as well) to open his arms to all of this, and to succeed more often than he fails.

I don't mind saying that I've long aspired to join the ranks of the artist-industrialists, and I think that at least partially explains the way I've managed my fiscal life and my career as a business. There are times when I make decisions that I know are going to move toward the pure artist track, and there are times when I make a business-track decision. Sometimes it's just a matter of paying the bills, of being a professional actor—hitting your mark, saying lines, and doing the best work you can, regardless of the circumstances, because you have a responsibility to other people. And then there are times when I make a business decision with the hope that it will in some way facilitate the artist track. *The Lord of the Rings*, rather obviously, is one of those rare and beautiful projects that is symbiotic. You see, the goal is to keep closing the gap: Mel Gibson stars in *Lethal Weapon*, and then he leverages the success of that franchise as a way to direct and star in *Braveheart* (and *Hamlet*, it should be added, not to mention directing *The Passion of the Christ*). That's an extreme example, but I think it illustrates what I'm talking about, and what I've been chasing all these years. It's about power, but it's also about opportunity—using power in pursuit of something more noble. Believe me, I'm not an elitist when it comes to movies. I appreciate a good art-house film—*Where the Day Takes You* or *Cinema Paradiso*, for example—but I don't think there's anything more impressive from a filmmaking standard than creating brilliant technical work that also succeeds on a visceral, emotional level. That's why, as a fan, I love *E.T.* so much, and *Lawrence of Arabia*. And even *Back to the Future*, one of the most thrilling experiences I've ever had in a theater. It's why, as an actor, I'm so proud of *The Lord of the Rings*, and why I understood it was a gamble worth taking.

I grew up wanting to make movies, not just perform in them. Even when I was a kid, it seemed as though I always had a camera in my hand. I remember doing chores around the house so that I'd have enough money to buy film at Bel-Air Camera. Then I'd shoot it and need to get it developed, so I'd say to my parents, "Can I take out the trash? Can I get a paper route?" Anything to get enough money to feed my hobby, which was quickly becoming a habit. My parents were not rich, by the way. (When I refer to my parents, I'm talking about Patty Duke and John Astin. John is actually my adoptive legal father. My biological father is a lovely man named Michael Tell, who was briefly married to my mom in the early 1970s. John adopted me when I was very young and raised me as his own, and I love him dearly; he is, and always has been, my dad.)

My parents' finances are their business, but suffice it to say there was never any huge money laying around, no Hollywood playground. I put myself through private high school with money I made as a child actor. My mother, don't forget, was a classic example of why the famous Jackie Coogan Law protecting child actors became necessary: unscrupulous managers absconded with much of her childhood earnings. To this day she's still not the best with finances. While my parents didn't give my siblings or me a big trust fund, they did something even more important. They raised me with a core set of values. My mom wanted us to be strong, proud individuals. My dad hammered home the importance of a traditional education.

When it came to my aspirations as a filmmaker, my parents were nothing but supportive and they offered practical advice. After I moved out of the house, twice I ran out of cash. My mom loaned me some money, and I promptly paid her back. And of course, it was nice to have an Academy Award–winning actress—my mother—to put in my films. In fact, both of my parents allowed me on one occasion to dress them up in rather eccentric costumes for my film *The Enchanted Dreamer*, which I shot on Super 8. I must have been twelve or thirteen years old, and my father balked a little, saying something like, "You know, Sean, I am a professional actor." But without too much fuss they consented, and their performances were, shall we say, more than adequate.

When I applied to the graduate school of theater, film, and television at UCLA (I was rejected, a fact that left me nearly broken-hearted), I wrote a passionate essay about my love for film. I talked about what it was like when my father would project 16-millimeter footage for us. Images of his work as an actor and director. As a kid I saw almost no difference between what he was doing and what I was attempting to do. Yes, he was John Astin—Gomez Addams!—a classically trained Shakespearean actor and a pop culture icon, but we were both trying to make movies. I was an heir apparent to a tradition. My father was a famous actor. My mother won an Oscar and four Emmys. People used to ask me why I wanted to follow in their footsteps. They worried that it was too much of a burden. No way. I thought an incredible gift had been placed in front of me.

I don't think I ever felt like I couldn't escape from my parents' shadows. They always seemed more like a beacon of light to me than anything approaching darkness. Plus, with my dad's emphasis on education, I've always felt that other careers, livelihoods, and paths are available to me. The only limitations I've ever known are time and space, and perhaps certain physical limits: I don't think I ever felt I could compete at the higher levels of most sports. Most of my life has felt like finding a balance between taking advantage of the opportunities in front of me and trying to play out some sense of personal destiny or mission that must have been ingrained in my DNA. In that regard, I've suffered in trying to overcome the obstacles that have been placed in front of me, but I really do identify with the character of Rudy.

Anyway, as far as my pedigree is concerned, the only time I felt frustrated was when I couldn't figure out how to effectively leverage my lineage and experience. My parents didn't make a habit of introducing me to famous people. In other words, they didn't sit down with us before the big New Year's party, and say, "Here's who's coming to dinner, kids. He's an important director, producer, writer, star..." They didn't do any of that. They just had a party. We'd go down and help direct the parking, and people we engaged in conversation were just the people who were the friendliest. Generally speaking, I had no idea who they were. I knew only that I thought my mother and father had pretty cool jobs, that they were creative, interesting people, and that I wanted to be like them.

What I did not understand until much later was the combination of luck, talent, and dogged determination required to succeed in show business, especially if one aspires to be something more than a mere cog in the system. And I began to understand the meaning of the word "compromise."

Which brings us back to *Encino Man*.

"They've got a revision on the script," I was told. "They want to fax it to you."

"Fine. Go ahead."

"And they've got a guy named Pauly Shore to play the lead. Do you know Pauly?"

"No, I don't know Pauly."

"Well, they want to send you some of his work, too. I think they really want you for the lead in this movie, Sean."

There were admittedly some aspects to the project that were appealing. It was a major studio film, and one of my costars would be Brendan Fraser, who was already generating buzz for his work as a prep-school student battling anti-Semitism in *School Ties* (which was released in 1992, the same year as *Encino Man*). The studio knew that in Brendan they had a young actor who was destined for stardom, and they had him playing against type as a caveman in a completely goofy movie. In Pauly Shore, as I would soon learn, they had a cartoonish surfer dude of a comic who was building a big audience with the MTV crowd. I was exactly who they wanted to play the third lead in the movie: a solid, serious, best-buddy kind of actor. They had liked my work in *Toy Soldiers*, and they thought I'd be perfect for *Encino Man*.

But I didn't want to do it, especially after I got to a hotel in London, opened the FedEx package, and looked at some tapes of Pauly Shore hamming it up on MTV, drawling, "Hey, Buddddddy!" and giggling and staggering around like a stoner. All I could think was, *Oh, it's going to be hard to spend time with that guy*. Then I read the script—again—and of course it was still a piece of shit; they really hadn't done anything to improve it. I fretted for a while, tried to figure out how I could gracefully turn down the project a second time, and then agreed to talk with Ricardo Mesterez. I had no intention of taking the job—until he made his sales pitch.

He began by apologizing and, as he put it, failing to recognize my "value in the marketplace." It occurred to me then that the balance of power, at least as it pertained to this little negotiation, had shifted. But I wasn't really prepared for what came next.

"Number one," he said, "we're gonna double your quote. Number two, we'll give you complete creative control over your character. Number three" (I wasn't sure a number three was necessary, but I wasn't about to interrupt), "we'll offer you a short film to direct. If we like the film, you'll have a three-picture deal with us."

I realized then that it's true that every man has his price, because mine had just been reached. My response, in effect, was, "Sold!"

Well, the devil is in the details, isn't it? It wasn't really a three-picture deal. It was a three-*option* deal. And they had the option. In other words, if I directed the first film, and it won an Academy Award or earned a hundred million dollars, they owned me on the second film, at whatever fee they chose, right down to the minimum established by the Directors Guild of America. When I read the fine print on the contract, I asked my agents, "What are you doing?"

Their response? "That's a high-class problem. Deal with it if and when it happens."

So I did. I cut our trip short and returned to Los Angeles for a meeting with Pauly Shore, for whom *Encino Man* was quickly being designed as a star vehicle. I had a sense that it wasn't really a meeting, but rather an audition, even though my agents had assured me otherwise. It was, they said, simply a casual get-together between actors about to embark on a journey.

Wrong. I walked into Team Disney, right under Dopey's armpit (it's actually kind of cool, architecturally speaking—the dwarves appear to be holding up the entrance), and took a seat in a meeting room, where I was introduced to, among others, Les Mayfield, the director. I sensed right away that Les wasn't particularly happy with me, which was understandable, really. After all, I had passed on his movie, which he probably interpreted as not only a stupid business decision on my part, but a personal affront to him as well. There was personal history, too, some of it based on reasonable assumptions, some of it based on pettiness. Les was a USC graduate, and in my mind USC was where they churned out corporate titans, as opposed to UCLA, where they specialized in the care and feeding of real artists. At the time, I wasn't into being a corporate titan. I wanted to be an artist, and didn't understand that it was possible to blend the two, in that artist-industrialist sort of way. I knew only that when I was approached by aspiring filmmakers from UCLA, they usually wanted to show me their storyboards; aspiring filmmakers from USC usually said something like, "Hey, I've got some investors lined up if you're interested in talking." Then they'd drive away in their Porsches or BMWs.

So there was that between us. Then, too, I was undeniably envious of his success. Les had produced the critically acclaimed documentary *Hearts of Darkness*, the story of the making of *Apocalypse Now*, but his directorial experience was limited to a documentary on the making of *The Goonies*. And yet here he was, directing a Hollywood studio movie. Les had advanced under the tutelage of Spielberg, and while I didn't exactly resent him for that, I did recognize that he had played a smarter game and elbowed his way in and set up shop. In my eyes, he was a rich kid out to have a good time. Not a bad guy, just someone who wanted to do fun things—appropriate enough, since *Encino Man* was supposed to be a funny movie. (Postscript: A couple years later, Les directed a remake of *Miracle on 34th Street*, which has the distinction of being the only movie in Disney history where they offered a refund if you didn't like the movie at all, and people actually took them up on it. More recently, I called Les and practically begged him for a job when I found out he was remaking a movie called *Flying Tigers*. I said, "Les, this is a serious project, and I'd like to be a part of it." He wasn't exactly receptive. In fact, while he was reasonably polite in brushing me off, his tone conveyed the following message: *You shit on me your whole career, and now you want me to help you just because I've found something smart to do? Fuck you!* I had it coming.)

I surmised that it would be easy to work for Les, but it was going to be challenging to live with Pauly Shore, who entered the room on that first day and promptly announced to everyone, "I know comedy!" Just in case we doubted him. Pauly had some serious clout at that time, and would for the next three or four years, and he didn't mind flexing his muscle. I don't blame him for that, and I don't mean to come down too hard on him. He had earned the right to wield a bit of power and deserved some of the success he had, even if his taste in comedy was sort of lowbrow and appealed to the lowest common denominator. Although Pauly is a bit of a dog and loves the idea that he's slept his way through a lot of people's daughters on a lot of college campuses, there is an undeniable sweetness to him, a genuine humanity and pathos that I connected with while we were working together.

But he absolutely hated me. He thought I was just an idiot, perhaps because he sensed that I was not only envious of his success, but dumbfounded by it. Slacker persona notwithstanding, Pauly was a total professional. He worked with a personal trainer to keep himself in good physical shape. He ate right and made sure that he looked good on camera. Most important of all, of course, Pauly was a pretty smart guy who knew his audience and delivered precisely what that audience wanted and expected from him. But I was not part of that audience, and while I kept working hard to find something to appreciate about him, it was a struggle for me. Only in retrospect did I come to understand what he brought to the table. I regret now that I was too young and immature to appreciate the value that he brought to the project; his message was so antithetical to what I was trying to do with my own life that I just couldn't see it—or didn't want to. I was trying to be a "serious" person. I was (and still am) interested in news, literature, global geopolitics, and those sorts of things, and it didn't occur to me that you could have those interests and still be viewed as a formidable man and artist if you worked in movies like *Encino Man* alongside an actor like Pauly Shore.

I was torn about the project. I had read the script, but maybe not thoroughly enough to understand what the movie was supposed to be. If the director had pulled me aside and said, "Let me tell you what we're trying to do here," I might have liked it better. With so many talented people attached, there had to be something I was missing. Instead, I felt like I was struggling along, trying to figure it out on my own, making the transition from "drug addict/serious actor" mode, into "front man on a mainstream, high-concept Disney comedy" mode. I couldn't do it. I just couldn't do it. I was taking myself way too seriously for my own good. I looked at it as a means to an end and nothing more. Rather than feeling excited about the opportunity or proud of the work I was doing, I felt like nothing so much as a sellout.

This was going to be the biggest paycheck of my life ($250,000), coupled with the promise of directing a short film and then a feature (or two or three). I rationalized it, in part, by telling myself that I'd be able to use the money to put both myself and Christine through college, which I did. (This is no knock against my parents. My father made it clear that he would have been happy to pay for my education—if I had pursued it in a more traditional manner by going to college directly from high school and focusing exclusively on academics. And I'm sure that my mother would have helped.) The movie would open doors. And yet, my attitude just sucked. When I walked out of the meeting, the first thing I did was call my agent.

"How did it go?" he asked.

"Oh, great. It was an audition for Pauly Shore, just like I figured."

"Well, you can always walk away from it."

"I can?"

"Absolutely."

The studio had planned a promotional photo shoot the next day at the famous Pink Car Wash on Ventura Boulevard. The plan was for Pauly and me to ham it up, act like the best buddies we were supposed to portray in *Encino Man*. He was into it, of course, because he understood the value of what he was doing, and because that's the kind of person he is, but I felt like a complete fool. For one thing, physiologically, I was a mess. I had shocked my system by losing so much weight so quickly, and then I had stopped working out while Christine and I traveled around Europe, so my weight had ballooned to 175 pounds. I didn't like the way I looked or felt. But mostly I just resented the fact that Pauly was being goofy, and I didn't know what to do. It was like I'd run off to join the circus without having an act to put on display. I was embarrassed. I didn't understand the character or the movie; I was totally out of my element but wasn't smart enough to ask anyone for guidance or help, because I was so focused on the business element of things. I wasn't thinking the way I should have been thinking: as an actor. *Be natural, concentrate on each scene . . . do the job!* I was completely lost, and yet here I was, before filming even began, before a single rehearsal, having my picture taken so that my image could be made into a poster with Pauly fucking Shore! Meanwhile, I was thinking, *Oh God, what have I gotten myself into?*

A couple of days later, after I had challenged my agent and accused him of withholding information about potential jobs, I was called into the offices of CAA to be publicly rebuked. My anger stemmed in part from a conversation with a friend. Will Wheaton—a contemporary who had played one of the lead characters in *Stand by Me* and who would later become a regular on *Star Trek: The Next Generation*—had called to ask me why I wasn't interested in a particular project to which he had been attached. I told him I wasn't even aware of it.

"Oh," Will said, "well, your agency got the call."

I blew up and accused my representation of lying to me and, worse, of trying to make me feel bad about accusing them of lying. (In fact, they had lied, but they hadn't thought anything of it, because lying is considered by many people to be acceptable behavior in Hollywood.) I was venting some of my frustrations and trying to figure out exactly where I was going with my career, and whether my management team had any specific plan for getting me there. I didn't understand then that it was all up to me, that I had to be in control of my own destiny. So I had to make a decision. I could say, *The hell with you people. I don't want to be here, in your agency, because you lied to me and you're treating me badly.* But that wasn't me. I put my head down, stuck my tail between my legs, apologized for my behavior, and that was that. Then, as I walked out of the office, I ran into Josh Lieberman in the hallway. Josh was a young cub who wanted to represent me, so we drove together, along with my manager, to the Palm Restaurant on Santa Monica Boulevard, one of those great movie-industry places where deals are made and broken, and where the famous and the almost famous routinely stop by for lunch or dinner.

This was one of those big Hollywood moments, the kind you see depicted in movies or books, and think, *What a cliché.* But the fact that the stories are rooted in truth is what makes them clichés. As we ate lunch and discussed my situation, I tried desperately to prove to them how sophisticated I was about the machinations of Hollywood, the art of filmmaking, and the evolution of an actor. They listened and nodded a lot, but in the end I pretty much left them in the position of saying, *We wish you had more power than you do, Sean. But we can't get that for you right now. So your only option is to do this movie or not do it. It's your call.*

That wasn't quite true. CAA was the five-hundred-pound gorilla of the entertainment world, and if they had chosen to fight for me and my interests with a little more vigor, it might have made a difference. Looking back on it, however, I understand their reluctance. There is a pecking order in Hollywood, and I hadn't yet reached the level of influence that warranted the agency's devotion. That comes only with success on a grand scale. It has nothing to do with honor or integrity; it's simply business, and the business can be ugly.

After lunch, on the drive back to CAA, I thought hard about what I was going to do. I was angry, but trying not to let my emotions rule my intellect, because I knew that if I chose poorly, my career (and my family) would suffer. I remembered my father's stories about how he once got everything he could get out of a deal on a television show. He pissed off the head of a studio because the network wanted him and he had them over a barrel. So my dad, lovable Gomez Addams, beat them up and left them bloody. The result was a predictable degree of satisfaction for having gotten what he could, followed by the inevitable professional backlash. In the end, my father realized he had overplayed his hand. And it hurt him. So his admonition to me was, "Be careful." Those words echoed in my ear as we pulled into the lot at CAA. Before the doors opened, I said, "Guys, I'll do it." They asked me if I was sure, I assured them that I was, and I walked away figuring that at the very least I had bought myself a few more months at the power station.

There was just one problem. I had already arranged a meeting with Ricardo Mesterez, the head of Hollywood Pictures, the man who had figured out that the best way to get to me was to appeal to me as an artist and a filmmaker. Everything about my experience with *Encino Man*, thus far, had led me to question my involvement in the project, so I figured who better to help me through the crisis than the man who had secured my services. Ricardo graciously agreed to see me, but I realized almost instantly that there was nothing to be gained from the meeting. He asked me what was wrong, and I began stumbling over my words. Here was this well-educated corporate success story, and I couldn't articulate my problem for him. I told him I felt lost in the project, and that I wasn't happy. Calmly, pleasantly, Ricardo asked, "Well, what do you want to do about it?"

I'm impulsive and emotional by nature, but I realized then that the best thing to do was to give the matter some serious thought before saying another word. I had given my word to my manager and agent that I would perform in this movie without complaint, and yet here I was, getting ready to complain again. I asked myself, *Who am I, and how do I want to be perceived?* By whining to the studio every time something bothered me, I risked getting a reputation for being "difficult." So I leaned forward in my chair and said, "You know what, Ricardo? I'm sorry I called this meeting. I'll go back to work now. I'll figure everything out on my own."

"Are you sure?"

"Yeah. I think I just needed to see you and be reminded of my responsibilities. Thank you."

"No problem."

The first day I showed up on the set, Pauly was barking out orders, almost running the show, and the director was responding to him the way directors respond to a star. My situation was a little different. The idea that I had complete creative control over my character, as I'd been promised, was a joke. Not that I really wanted or expected that. I was trained to believe that the director is in charge. As a journeyman, working actor, I believe that you give the director what he or she wants. And you gauge your success by how happy the director is. That's how I was operating on the set of *Encino Man.* I didn't want to think about what I wanted for the character; it was too hard and required too much emotional investment on my part. I didn't view it as an important enough movie to warrant that kind of investment, so even if I had a chance to employ creative control over my character, I wasn't especially interested. Sometimes I'd express an idea, and Pauly would sort of run over me; then I'd apply a little emotional balm by calling my accountant and saying, "Did a check clear today?"

"Yeah."

"How much was it for?"

"Twenty thousand dollars."

I'd hang up the phone, walk up to the service truck, and say, "Can I have another burrito, please? Thanks. And can I get some chocolate bars, too?" Then I'd sit there and stuff my face.

I'd use food to anesthetize myself. I didn't want to be there. I had sold out, and I felt bad about it. I felt bad about myself. I remember my agents visiting the set at a warehouse where we were filming out in Valencia one day, and we sat down for lunch, and I had a big plate of food in front of me, but I couldn't eat. Not a bite.

"Sean, you're not eating anything, man. What's the problem?" somebody said.

"I'm not hungry."

Well, that made no sense, since eating was what I did best. Day and night. Eat, eat, eat. At that moment though, I couldn't eat, because these were the guys who got me to sell out. I blamed them, not myself, so when I was with them, I lost my appetite. At least when I'd sold out to Marc Rocco on *Where the Day Takes You*, I could say, *Okay, this is the price of compromise and screwing with my integrity. I'm going to recognize the righteousness of the decision that guy made and create value because it's a damn good movie.* But not now. Now I was in a movie I didn't respect, making obscene amounts of money (five times what a teacher makes, and teachers do infinitely more important work)—and it just felt wrong. Please don't misunderstand me. I'm as greedy as the next guy. I want to be compensated for my work, and generally I feel as though I'm entitled to whatever I can earn. However, the degree to which I feel entitled to that earning power ebbs and flows with the quality of the work being done. In other words, it's a lot easier to feel like you've earned the money when you're proud of the work, and I wasn't proud of this. I also resented that the power brokers on the other side of the table had played better chess than I had. In that sense, I was merely a poor loser.

Nevertheless, I remained committed to the work and tried to do the best job I could do. I actually got injured while filming a scene that called for my character to run and jump on a wheelbarrow, and then catch a bowl over his shoulder while diving headfirst. I was still a young kid and I'd been pretty fit my whole life, so I didn't think the stunt would be a problem. But this was the first time I'd let myself get out of shape, and even become borderline fat, so it wasn't as easy as I had imagined. We shot five or six takes, and on what would prove to be the last one, I fell and cut my head open, just above my eye. But it was nothing too serious, and the next day I was back at work, where a crash helmet was waiting with my name on it. A little joke from the studio.

So I was "earning" my salary. And yet I was just out of my depth. Pauly had his thing going, and that's what excited the studio the most. That and the presence of Brendan Fraser, an Adonis—he looked like Marlon Brando on his best day—who had quickly established that he could be effective as a comedic or dramatic actor. Just as, even now, he can bounce between Oscar-caliber fare like *Gods and Monsters* and harmless trifle like *George of the Jungle* or *The Mummy*, Brendan could shift gears from important work to disposable work, and he could do it with an elegance that I found admirable. He could do a thoughtful movie like *School Ties*—and then do this thing. All without missing a beat or wallowing in self-doubt. I could see that Brendan was different. This was a guy who was creating power at the studio, and to some extent I was awed by his ability to do so. I thought I was supposed to be doing that, too, but instead I felt trapped in this role, between these two other actors who clearly were the focus of the movie and the studio's attention. The thing that made me right for the role—a certain quiet intensity, an everyman quality—was precisely what made me dissatisfied with it. I looked at Brendan and thought, *I'm not going to be that guy, the leading man.* And I looked at Pauly and thought, *I'm not gonna be that guy, either, the . . . well, whatever Pauly is.*

I was just an honest kind of actor. Not long ago, my father told me, "Try not to use your authenticity in service of a subpar script." That was the first time he ever articulated it to me. In hindsight, I think that was the source of my discontent, the reason I was fat and unhappy.

Try not to use your authenticity in service of a subpar script.

A simple little gem of advice. Unfortunately, like so many actors, I've not always had the wisdom to heed it.

CHAPTER THREE

During one of my first visits to Indiana, while spending time with Christine's family, her Grandma Schroeder offered a thoughtful notion: "You know, Sean, you really ought to make a movie around here. Sam Elliott did *Prancer* in the next town over! We'd get to see you kids more often."

I couldn't help but smile.

"That would be wonderful, Grandma. But it doesn't really work that way. You sort of have to go where the jobs are."

She nodded. "Okay—but I still think you should make one here."

I love Christine's family. It may sound trite, but there is a peacefulness to the rural Midwest that I find very calming, soothing. Celebrity doesn't seem to mean as much; certainly it isn't the coin of the realm the way it is in Hollywood. Still, I never expected to spend time in Indiana for reasons that were anything other than personal. So imagine my surprise when less than two months after Christine and I were married, I was asked to read a script for a movie titled *Rudy*, set at the University of Notre Dame in South Bend, Indiana.

Now, I was a West Coast kid, so I didn't know a whole heck of a lot about Notre Dame, aside from its fight song "Cheer, cheer, cheer for Old Notre Dame..." and the fact that Johnny O'Keefe, who lived down the street from me when I was growing up, used to watch college football every Saturday and liked Notre Dame a lot. But to me, college football was UCLA, not because I went to many Bruins games (I didn't), but mainly because from my house I could always hear the school's marching band practicing. We lived that close to the campus. (Not only that, but my aunt and uncle were professors at UCLA in the department of education, and every year we'd get Christmas presents from the college bookstore.)

Reading the script, however, was a revelation. It was like I was reading my own life.

Everything about Rudy's mentality matched the way I looked at the world. Of course, Rudy's story and my story were vastly different, but in terms of his ethos, it felt like I was reading about an alternate version of myself. In Little League, for example, I spent a lot of time on the bench, waiting, begging to get in the game. Even though my parents were famous and made very good money, their attitudes and values created in me a sense of connection to working-class people. That may sound condescending or convenient, but if you think that, well, you don't know me. When my mom got remarried, it was to a soldier. Sure, he was a sergeant, first class, but he was "real people." When my dad remarried, he was fortunate to find a woman who exuded a kind of nobility and an understanding of all people. I've always admired the working people I've met; everyone's work—from the garbageman to the rocket scientist—seems valid and honorable to me. So my mind and spirit were primed to read Angelo Pizzo's brilliant screenplay about Daniel "Rudy" Reuttiger.

Rudy was a working-class kid who talked his way into Notre Dame, an elite private college, and eventually onto the school's storied football team, even though he was neither a great student nor a great athlete. Rudy was an underdog, and I found it easy to identify with him.

The movie would be directed by David Anspaugh. He and Angelo Pizzo were the same writing/directing team that had done such an impressive job of capturing small-town life in Indiana in the 1950s with the beautiful basketball film, *Hoosiers*. Like *Hoosiers*, *Rudy* was a fact-based, almost achingly earnest story; in lesser hands, both stories might have fallen victim to hackneyed clichés and stereotypes. But *Hoosiers* remains one of the best sports movies ever made, a nearly perfect tale of David rising up to defeat Goliath, told on a simple, heartfelt, human scale. Reading the script for *Rudy*, I knew it had the potential to be every inch the movie that *Hoosiers* is, not least because it was being made by Angelo and David. With every page I liked it more and more—it was just screamingly obvious that this would be a really good movie—and I became so excited that my fingers kept slipping off the pages. *Rudy*, I knew, was exactly the right prescription for the malaise that had set in while I was making *Encino Man*. I would be the star, the lead, the hero. And I knew I could do it.

I was so relieved that this wasn't an ensemble film. Rudy was the title character, the role a tour de force for any actor lucky enough to land the job. I was determined to be that actor, to not let anything, including petty squabbles over compensation, stand in the way. After meeting with the director, I got the sense that he liked me and that the creative people behind the project—as well as the titular character himself, Daniel Reuttiger—thought I was perfect for the part. The head of production, on the other hand, wanted Chris O'Donnell. This was no small obstacle. Like me, Chris, who I've come to know pretty well and admire a lot, was a young actor (we were both in our early twenties) whose stock in trade was an earnest, boy-next-door quality. And like me, Chris was on the smallish side—physically correct for the part of Rudy. Unlike me, Chris had just seen his career take flight. In the previous year Chris had costarred alongside Brendan Fraser in *School Ties* and Al Pacino in *Scent of a Woman*. The latter performance had earned him a Golden Globe nomination. It's fair to say that Chris was the hotter actor by far. Knowing that I was the preferred candidate of the writers and director, and that the role was mine to lose, I waded carefully into the waters of negotiation.

I had just made $250,000 on *Encino Man*, so I was surprised when they offered me roughly half that amount to play Rudy. After all, I'd be carrying the movie. Now, I realize that while it had major studio backing, *Rudy* was designed as a small, personal film, one that would tug at the audience's heart rather than grab it by the jugular. Those types of movies don't necessarily become blockbusters. But the budget for *Rudy* was at least double the budget for *Encino Man*. *Hoosiers* grossed $60 million domestically, while *Encino Man* grossed nearly $40 million. So it wasn't a stretch to believe that *Rudy* could perform just as well. At the least, small movies can be successful; otherwise the studios wouldn't produce them. They can win awards, satisfy audiences, and make money, too. Although probably not as much money. Personally, I didn't really care. I was told the offer was what it was, and it wouldn't go any higher. The job was almost mine to accept or reject. If I played hardball, they'd make a deal with Chris O'Donnell.

Now, I'm not sure how much most people care about the art of the deal in these situations, but I'm happy to share a level of detail about my experiences because I think folks can learn from it. Obviously, we're not talking about chicken feed here—$125,000 is a lot of dough. Never mind that we pay half our salary to the government and ten percent to an agent, ten percent to a manager, and a little more to a publicist, business manager/accountant, physical trainer, etc. It's still a lot of money. But that's not how you think in these situations. Showbiz is one of the only fields I can think of where what you've made previously can prove to be only a minor factor in determining what you might/maybe/should/ought to/probably will get paid this time. How much they want you relative to how much they want someone else, while factoring in everyone's availability and the risk of possibly losing you or your competition, means much more to the bottom line than does past salary.

Christine and I were fresh back from our honeymoon, in love and feeling great. I was in excellent physical condition, running four miles a day and thinking pretty clearly all of the time. It was summer, so I could usually be found in our pool pondering business and creative issues. The head of production at Tri-Star then was Marc Platt, an extremely intelligent and proud family man. He was also a shrewd executive. I knew, or at least believed, that Kevin Mischer, the junior executive who was "covering" or championing *Rudy*, was in my corner. Kevin was a good friend of my agent, Josh Lieberman (I probably would not have played Rudy if I had stayed at the smaller agency at that point in my career). Kevin was an executive I had worked with on *Toy Soldiers*, and he would go on to have a very bright career—despite having worked with me twice!

I'm half kidding, but I'm pretty sure that's how folks think: *These movies grossed X number of dollars; therefore, nobody wants to see Sean carrying a picture.* Of course, everything can change with a hit. All things being equal, I'd rather feel that a studio executive sees me as a good-luck charm for his career, rather than a two-strike stink bomb that.

To the best of my recollection, the way it was presented to me was this: *Everyone wants you but Marc Platt. He insists that you "test," and he swears he's not budging off the $125,000.*

I was in no mood to risk a game of poker, so I settled for it. Actually, that's not quite accurate, for I didn't consider it to be "settling." I wanted the part. I *needed* it. Some jobs you take for your wallet; others you take for your soul. *Rudy* fell into the second category. And as Dominic Monaghan would admonish me years later during the making of *The Lord of the Rings,* sometimes you have to have a little perspective. Dom, who played the part of Merry, wears his hardscrabble Manchester (England) roots on his sleeve, and more than once he rather wisely pointed out to me, "You know what people earn in the real world, man? We are so fucking lucky!"

Absolutely right. We are lucky. But as with any line of work, it's not what you earn that counts; it's what you keep. I figure if I'm going to take the time to write a book, I might as well be honest about aspects of the movie industry that aren't ordinarily discussed candidly, such as compensation and representation. The numbers I've mentioned are not insignificant; to most people, $125,000 sounds like a lot of money—and it is. But playing Rudy was now clearly not a decision about money. It was about my destiny. Thoughts flickered through my mind about old Hollywood screen tests and the building of stars from within the studio system. I envisioned my house in an earlier time, surrounded by orange groves, with crop dusters or biplanes flying overhead rather than private jets. I calculated that Marc Platt could rest comfortably knowing that if he didn't get his first choice, Chris, he would at least have saved the studio a pretty penny. I felt emboldened by knowing the creative auspices supported me, and so, the gauntlet having been thrown down, I accepted the challenge.

At a certain point, of course, it really doesn't matter. It all becomes Monopoly money. But at that stage of my career, I hadn't accomplished anything remotely close to this. I'd never had this kind of opportunity. I was constantly trying to make enough money to carry me through the next six months—to bankroll a film I wanted to direct, or to put myself through college. And to simply pay the mortgage. In this case, though, there was no debating about whether to fight for the role, or to hold out for more money. This was a defining moment in my career. I felt like the universe was conspiring to make it happen. I was meant to play Rudy—it was as simple as that.

Accepting the financial terms of the deal was only part of the process. I also had to agree again to change my body for the part. I was simultaneously nervous and emboldened by this stipulation, since by my estimation I was pretty fit. Christine and I had gotten married, and I'd run off all the weight I'd gained during *Encino Man* so that I'd look reasonably attractive while standing next to my beautiful wife in the wedding photos. When I did my screen test for *Rudy*, I weighed 135 pounds, and the studio executives were less than thrilled with my newly svelte appearance. They offered me the role on the condition that I gain ten to fifteen pounds of muscle before the start of principal photography. In their opinion I was too skinny, too waiflike, to ever be believable as a football player at Notre Dame—even a famously small football player who made the team as a walk-on.

It seemed to me an ironic turn of events, since I'd been so fat in *Encino Man* that Disney didn't even want to put me on the promotional poster. Talk about embarrassing! That movie cost six or seven million dollars to make and grossed forty million. But my focus wasn't on using the forty-million-dollar success story of *Encino Man* to get the next acting job. Instead, I had turned my focus to directing the short film I'd been promised, and on building my own production company. Cashing in on the success of *Encino Man*, with all of the emotional baggage I carried from that movie, failed to appeal to me. So instead of hiring a personal trainer and trying to sculpt my body in the way that Hollywood demands, I was satisfied with just getting skinny in time for the wedding.

Now, though, I was ready and willing to do whatever was asked of me. I agreed to put on the weight, and pretty soon I was working out daily at the Sony gym, pounding weights, pushing myself harder than ever. Interestingly, I was there at the same time that Tom Hanks was losing the weight he'd gained to play a paunchy baseball coach in *A League of Their Own*, in preparation for his Oscar-winning role in

Philadelphia. I'd make jokes as I passed him on my way out of the gym to my third or fourth high-protein meal of the day: "Hey, Tom, want me to pick up a burger for you?"

His response? Something along these lines: "Screw you!"

In so many ways, acting is an intensely weird, narcissistic endeavor. It requires immense self-involvement, the belief that people want to watch you perform, *play.* It's like athletics without the competition. And as in sports, there is an assumption, a pact between performer and spectator, that the actor not only will give his best, but also, in most cases, will *look* his best. It seems part of the contract. While it may sound silly and shallow to suggest that most folks don't go to the movies to watch unattractive people, it's also probably true. At five-foot-seven with a body that does not naturally lend itself to wash-board abs, and a face that is more cherubic than chiseled, I know I am not the classic Hollywood leading man. But there is a certain level of fitness and attractiveness that I can attain, and that I suppose a studio has a right to expect its stars to have. (For me, *The Lord of the Rings* is the rare exception to the rule. In those films Peter Jackson's expectation, based on Tolkien's writing, was that I look *less* like a leading man, not more; thus, Samwise Gamgee's portly appearance.)

Obviously, I haven't always lived up to Hollywood's expectations, *Encino Man* being just one example. I remember Dan Petrie Jr., my friend, my mentor, my trusted ally, coming up to me at my wedding and saying, "Sean, you look good; don't ever get fat like that again."

I laughed, shook his hand, and didn't really say anything other than, "I understand."

"No, man, I'm serious," he added, his eyes almost pleading with me. "For your career. Don't let it happen."

I knew he meant it. I'd heard it before. In fact, when I showed up on the set of *Toy Soldiers* a couple years earlier, Mark Berg, the film's producer, fairly blanched at my softness in the midsection: "Come on, Sean. Get to the gym!"

I sort of resented it, because I thought I looked sufficiently heroic the way I was. But I was wrong. I wasn't disciplined enough to take care of my body, which should be among an actor's most important responsibilities. That's not to say that an actor should be excessively concerned with superficiality. Of course not. Actors come in all shapes and sizes. But an actor's instrument is in part his physical body. Sure, the mind, the spirit, general knowledge, and technical training are critical factors in being a solid, well-rounded actor, but the body is the vessel through which you communicate the ideas of the script. And I didn't want to play tuba parts at that point in my life. I wanted to be able to do a drum solo or be the first violin. On *Toy Soldiers* I knew the genre. It was an action picture, a smart pubescent thriller—and I was the mini Bruce Willis. I can see Dan cringing while reading this, because he wrote a very sensitive character and I'm reducing poor Billy Tepper to a Slim-Fast cautionary tale. But I'm making a different point.

I needed to be told what to do, which is sad. I'd had no trouble working out when I played organized sports as a kid, or when I was training to run 10K races or even marathons, but I hadn't yet reached the point where I was willing to accept it as part of my job. I felt I needed a reason. The obvious logic—it's good to be fit—just wasn't enough motivation. For better or worse, my life has been one of extremes, and that extends to my commitment, or lack thereof, to physical conditioning. Make it part of my daily regimen? Nah. I'm not a granola guy. Although I admire granola guys, I happen to love greasy food. Always have, probably always will.

The other obvious logic is that I needed to be fit and attractive for my career, but that didn't resonate with me as being righteous. To be good-looking for the sake of being good-looking, well, that just bothered me. I wasn't ever "turn-heads-on-the-street" good-looking, and never would be. Once, many years ago, I had a great photo session when I was in the best shape of my life. I was waterskiing a lot, running, and lifting weights, and my metabolism was still roaring in the way that it does when you're almost out of your teens. By twisting and turning my body, and lighting the set just right, the photographer managed to transform me into someone I barely recognized. Someone with a solid, square jaw, and if not a six-pack, at least a two-pack. I look at those photos now and almost laugh about how good I look. But sustaining that? No chance. I was more concerned with the entrepreneurial part of my career, even if I understood on some level the importance of just simply looking good. It makes sense from a business standpoint to focus on the basics of being a movie star, and part of that is being in great shape. It just didn't interest me to focus on it consistently.

For *Rudy*, however, I was willing to accept almost anything the role required, and that meant not only getting fit, but staying fit during filming. We began shooting in the fall, just as the leaves were changing in South Bend. Only months earlier I had married a Hoosier whose family lived a scant twenty miles down the road, so everything about the project felt right. On the first day of filming, the mayor of South Bend showed up on the set and welcomed everyone to the city.

He had a special message for me: "I don't know what your political aspirations are, but there's a little history here, you know? The last person who starred in a movie filmed at Notre Dame went on to become president of the United States."

He was referring, of course, to Ronald Reagan, who had portrayed the heroic but doomed Notre Dame running back George Gipp in *The Knute Rockne Story*. (Yes, I know, Reagan wasn't really the star. It was Pat O'Brien who played the titular character.) It was a nice thing for the mayor to say, and I kind of chuckled and tried to be appropriately gracious. This was a nonpartisan event, so I didn't make a big deal out of the fact that Reagan was famously Republican and I was a Democrat. And while I wasn't yet famous, I did (and still do) have political aspirations of my own. Never mind that the press conference was being held during our lunch hour and I hadn't had time to change out of the football uniform I had been wearing. I felt at best unworthy, and at worst a little fraudulent sitting there pretending to be a bona fide, hard-core Domer! The appropriate thing to do was to keep my mouth shut, focus on the work, and try to honor the integrity of the movie.

The real-life Rudy, who has become a Notre Dame icon almost as recognizable (in name, at least) as the Golden Dome or Touchdown Jesus, had arranged for me to have access to all of the school's athletic facilities, including the football team's locker room and weight room. I had a personal trainer. I lifted weights and ran every day. When the weather was bad, I worked out on a stationary bike that I had begged for, and that Rudy had arranged to have sent to our house. It occurred to me that I was being treated like the star of a movie, and while there was a certain pressure associated with that position on every level, I enjoyed it.

Christine, too, was happy. We had our "boy" with us, a Siberian husky named Byron. She could visit her family every day, and on weekends we'd have dinner on the farm where she'd grown up. It was wonderful, practically the perfect moviemaking experience. Every so often, we'd be featured on the cover of the local newspaper, which was kind of quaint and cute, and in the eyes of my in-laws, such local recognition was a unique and important sort of validation. On some level I believed I had arrived at what I was destined to do, which was to carry a movie, to be a movie star. I'd already been the star of *The Goonies* and *Toy Soldiers*, and even though I had done a bunch of ensemble films, I wanted to carry a studio picture; I wanted to be ... well, I wanted to be Kevin Costner. That's who I wanted to be.

I remember going to the premiere of *Dances with Wolves* in 1991, shaking hands with Costner, and thinking, *Wow! He's accomplishing so much.* Costner was still in his thirties, and yet somehow he had the talent, the drive, and the intelligence—not to mention the balls—to put together this incredible project, one that no one initially wanted to support. It was too smart a movie, too ambitious, too political. Worst of all, Costner himself was a first-time director. A neophyte trying to make a historical epic? A western, no less? Everything about the project must have seemed misguided. But there was Kevin Costner at the premiere, smiling proudly, working the room like a pro, confident that he'd not only survived the process, but triumphed. You could just tell: he knew.

Dances with Wolves made a ton of money and won the Academy Award for best picture, and Kevin Costner became one of the most influential artists in Hollywood. I couldn't help wondering if that was my destiny, too. Pretentious? Well, it was pretentious for Kevin Costner to think he could make *Dances with Wolves*. But he did. What really struck me was the fact that he was the director; he was a filmmaker. If it had been Robert DeNiro or Robert Duvall that I'd met at the premiere, I might have felt some distance from them, but this was what I wanted to be: a guy who could carry a movie and make a movie, all at the same time. I looked at Kevin as a likable, accessible film star who also produced and directed a brilliant film. He was the living embodiment of what I wanted to achieve.

What I lacked was the overt self-confidence that Costner obviously possessed. To a degree, all actors are neurotic and insecure, and how they manage those feelings, how they keep the demons of doubt at bay, goes a long way toward determining their success or failure. I can vividly recall being at the Omni Ambassador in Chicago toward the end of filming *Rudy,* and having a terrible crisis of confidence: *What if this is it? What if this is the best thing I ever do?* Christine still loves to tease me about our "pinnacle" conversations. I'll have a moment of self-doubt, and she'll just roll her eyes. For this particular pinnacle conversation, there was snow on the ground and we were filming the earlier scenes in the picture, interiors that did not require an autumn landscape and a packed stadium. Because the football scenes had been shot and I was no longer required to look quite as much like an athlete, I had stopped training feverishly and was letting myself slip out of shape again—in part because it fit the character, who begins the film as a factory worker, and in part because I really didn't feel like working out. There seems to be a direct correlation between my percentage of body fat and how I feel about myself, and as the percentage began to climb, I was gripped somewhat irrationally by a nagging sense of doom.

What if I just peaked?

A similar feeling would permeate *The Lord of the Rings* nearly a decade later. It happens on good movies. The exhilaration and pride in having accomplished something worthwhile are inevitably replaced by feelings of sadness and regret. After all, how can you top *The Lord of the Rings?* And how could I, as an actor, top *Rudy?* I had played a drug addict in *Where the Day Takes You,* which was so far from who I was, and I had done *Encino Man,* which was a major hit for the studio, regardless of how I felt about it. Now with *Rudy* I had done . . . well, me. And I didn't know what else I had to offer. I had played myself, or at least some idealized, amplified version of myself, and I had no idea where to go next. Christine witnessed my anxiety and was sympathetic if not bemused.

"What is wrong with you?" she asked. "You should be proud and happy."

The waiting really is the hardest part—the six months or the year that passes between the time a film is wrapped and the time it comes out is agony for an actor. If the film is bad and you know it's bad, there is dread at the prospect of having to promote it, which you are duty bound and contractually obligated to do. If it's good or you think it's going to be good, the experience can be different, complicated, with a daily shifting of emotions, ranging from genuine excitement over seeing the work put on display, to crippling fear that you might be wrong. And if in fact the movie is bad, there will be proof that you have not only bad judgment, but also no taste.

I didn't think that was the case with *Rudy*. I knew in my heart that it was a very good film, and that my work in it was strong. I was reasonably confident that people who get paid to recognize and comment on such things—namely, film critics—would have no trouble discerning the merits of *Rudy*. What I did not know, and could not know, was whether any of that would translate into the type of box-office success that can, when combined with an artistic and critical success, transform a career. To be honest, I wasn't convinced that *Rudy* was going to be a hit. *Hoosiers* had done great, but that movie was about a championship high-school basketball team. The climactic sequence is a lengthy game featuring a buzzer-beating basket and a wild celebration on the court. Tears of sadness on one side, tears of joy on the other. As General George Patton once said, "America loves a winner." *Hoosiers* was about a winner. *Rudy* was a different kind of winner. He was the last guy on the bench, the last guy to get in the game. His achievement was no less meaningful, but it was smaller, quieter.

Christine and I went back to California and enrolled in community college, which had the not unpleasant effect of allowing me to pursue my longtime goal of getting a degree, while distracting me from the postproduction phase of *Rudy*. In retrospect, I realize that distraction, while in some sense soothing, was not a sound career strategy. I remember trusting in the back of my mind that everything would work out all right, that Hollywood was built on a system predicated upon the assumption that agents and managers wanted to make money, and to do that they had to find work for their clients. That's the business they were in, and they'd figure out how to do that for me. They'd make the necessary phone calls, hold the necessary meetings, and devise a way to capitalize on the work I'd done, most notably *Rudy*. Even though the film hadn't been released, there was, as they say, a little "buzz."

I was waiting for the world to knock at my door. To my agents, I said, in effect, "I was in the title role of a major studio's picture, so do your job, and I'll be focusing on developing myself the way I want to while waiting for the next opportunity you people present me." That's the way it was supposed to work, or so I thought; nevertheless, it wasn't happening. I got the distinct impression that my agents were hedging their bets, not wanting to pick up the phone and call people, or that people were just waiting to see what would happen with *Rudy*. Meanwhile, I wasn't paying sufficient attention to the business of my own career. Basically, I had this complex psychological issue, related to my own feelings of intellectual inadequacy, that made it imperative for me to get a formal education. I wanted that degree—and I needed it. It was one of the most important things in my life, and the fact that I was able to put myself through junior college, transfer to UCLA, and graduate with honors remains one of my proudest accomplishments.

Of course, I probably never would have realized that dream if it wasn't for having Christine in my life. She is my life partner, my wife, my study buddy, mentor, disciplinarian, and taskmaster. Our college transcripts are virtually identical. For example, when I'd pop off for a week to work for Ed Zwick on *Courage Under Fire*, she would audiotape the lectures, FedEx them to me, and be the "face" of our team to the professors or the study groups we were in. I'd fax my homework to her, and she'd hand it in for me. We worked together brilliantly. Probably our favorite part of college was that I read just about all of our assigned books out loud to Christine. That exercise satisfied the performer in me and focused my mind on what I was doing, and she simply loved being read to. People either admired us for the way we worked together or thought we were crazy, but we didn't care. It worked for us and we loved it.

I can't deny that I doggedly pursued the goal of earning my degree. And yet, doing so contributed to my career stalling out. I was concentrating on school, exercising my mind rather than my body (and getting fat again), and at the same time feeling at least a modicum of resentment that film offers were not tumbling in. I wanted everything all at once. Hollywood doesn't work that way. Life doesn't work that way. Essentially, I had just miscalculated. I trusted that my income and the potential for my income were so enormous and so obvious to my agents that they would be working hard outside my purview to help bring about a successful ascent for me.

At a certain point I realized that not only was my career stalling, so was CAA's perceived power—the ambient sense in the air that they were *it*. And perhaps a change was in order. My mother had been a client of William Morris for years, and had repeatedly tried to convince me to join her as a client of the agency. As time passed and my frustration with CAA and its handling of my career continued to grow, I warmed to her overtures. I remember on several occasions trying to get information from my agents that I felt was important to my career and personal situation, and essentially being dismissed. I knew the door that had opened when I'd made *Rudy* was now closing. The movie had been warmly received by critics, and my work had been politely applauded, but the film itself, while not a box-office failure, was hardly a hit. The time to capitalize on my work in *Rudy* was shrinking, and I no longer felt as though my agents were committed to me or my career. So, even though I liked them all as individuals—I could have a pleasant dinner with any of them right now—I decided to leave. It wasn't personal. CAA, in my opinion, simply didn't recognize my value and didn't find a way to take advantage of the work I'd done.

Concurrently, it's also true that I was failing to live up to my responsibilities to present a marketable package to studio executives and audiences. I wasn't doing my part. I kept waiting, thinking, *If I get offered what I made before, then I'll jump in. Now, excuse me, I have a class to attend.* I had told my agents many times that if there was a great job or a great part available, or a brilliant filmmaker to work with, I'd stop college in a heartbeat, knowing that it would always be there when I was finished. I trusted that the agents' self-interest would keep them focused on that mission. Had I stayed at a smaller agency or been with agents who really cared about me or knew my heart and mind, I could have rested assured that my interests were being looked after with sensitivity. My miscalculation!

The "power center" that I wanted to be part of by definition feeds on success. It is a mistake to think that money made even within a given year is an indicator of money to come for an actor in Holly-wood. It's not like being a rising executive at a company who makes fifty thousand dollars one year, seventy-five the next, and one hundred the year after that. There's no logic. You could be offered scale for a movie you really want to do this week, and turn down five hundred thousand for a movie that shoots for six weeks but will stop you from making the one you really want to do. It's random and arbitrary, and each individual actor has to make the right decisions in order to develop a relationship with an audience and sustain credibility. Some performers deliver exactly what their audience wants, time after time, and their pay increases accordingly. Others try to develop themselves and hope the audience grows with them. While I was struggling to sort out these dynamics in my own mind, I sensed the time was right to make a move—that's industry shorthand for changing agents. Christine agreed, and so we held a rather clandestine meeting with some folks at William Morris, including the head of its film division, and pretty soon I had a new agency.

The reaction at CAA was mixed. I'm sure some people couldn't have cared less, because I was not exactly the biggest stallion in the stable. One of my agents, however, was hurt and angry.

"You're firing me?" he asked incredulously.

"No, I wouldn't put it that way," I replied.

He seemed to think this was coming out of the blue. Months earlier he had said, "You know, movies like *Rudy* don't come around every day."

Now, I took a deep breath. I'd be the first to admit that I have a bit of a temper, and I knew the potential was there for me to say something I'd regret, so I bit my tongue. Here's what I was thinking: *Nothing is coming around for me! I'm watching the things you're doing, and some of it doesn't make sense. You guys call me to ask if I mind whether you bring in Chris O'Donnell? Come on! I compete with him! Not only that, but I know the studios like him better than me. Remember when I had to cut my rate in order to beat him out for the job on* Rudy? *You promised me the part of Robin in* Batman, *and now I read in the trades that it's Chris O'Donnell's job? What do I do, sit around forever?* That's what I was thinking, not what I said. What I said was, "Look, I like you; I respect you; I will never forget that you made *Rudy* happen for me, but this is something I have to do."

And that was that. I left CAA and, like a grown-up taking control of his own life and career, went to the esteemed William Morris Agency where, well, where nothing really changed. The joke was on me.

Actually, that's not entirely true. My mom's agent, Marc Schwartz, did a lot for me. He essentially helped put me through college by negotiating three different deals for television pilots, each involving less than two weeks of work but enough money to get my wife and me through several semesters of school, and to allow us to pay the mortgage on our house. If the shows went over (which they didn't), I'd become a millionaire. So the television division of the William Morris Agency at least saw my potential and tried to do something with it. The film division, however, did not.

Again, I have to acknowledge some culpability in the sputtering of my career. I was concentrating on my studies and thus allowed the professional side of my life to slip, to the point where, the week that I graduated from UCLA, I was nearly broke. Not because we'd been irresponsible or lazy. We had reinvested all the money I'd earned from *Encino Man, Rudy,* and other smaller projects into our education and my production company.

By the way, around this time I made Christine a partner in Lava Entertainment. To this day she remains the vice president and chief financial officer. Oh, and treasurer, too. Technically, she can vote me off the board, I think. The point is, she's also my business partner in Lava Entertainment ventures. I'm proud that her name is next to mine on the Academy Award nomination certificates we received for producing *Kangaroo Court* together. But the fact remains that around the time we graduated, we were just about broke. We weren't living lavishly, but neither were we too careful about money. We traveled a lot to visit Christine's family in Indiana or my mother in Idaho during breaks, and the result was a bank account that was dangerously, frighteningly close to depletion, with no obvious work on the horizon.

I don't mind admitting that I was scared. Although I was realizing my lifelong dream of graduating from UCLA, I felt like my acting career was running on vapors. I was engaged in playing what seemed to me like a suicidal game of chicken with my William Morris agents (if you tell them exactly how desperate you are, they may undersell you or slot you into a subpar situation). The delicate poker game with potential employers requires all of your (and your agents') acumen. Luckily for me, the education and Hollywood gods conspired to rescue us. I had started thinking about turning off the fax line, cancelling the subscription to the newspaper, those kinds of things. Then, out of the blue came a substantial offer to star in a film called *Harrison Bergeron*, based on Kurt Vonnegut's collection of short stories, *Welcome to the Monkey House*, and suddenly everything was okay. Another actor had fallen out at the last moment, and big-agency politics suddenly worked to my advantage the way I had always hoped it would.

Such is the Hollywood roller coaster.

Throughout the mid-1990s, I worked steadily if unspectacularly. Admittedly, I was not on the radar of most studio executives, and my name rarely, if ever, came up at news meetings of major entertainment publications. But it would be wrong to say that I had failed. My short film, *Kangaroo Court*, the story of a Los Angeles police officer who is captured and "tried" by members of a violent street gang (the late Gregory Hines starred as an attorney who defends the officer), was nominated for an Oscar in 1994. Not that anyone cared. I remember at the Academy Awards luncheon, the press didn't want to talk to me. They seemed kind of bored when I stood at the podium to discuss *Kangaroo Court*, as if they were just killing time between appearances by the real stars. Finally, out of politeness, someone asked a question.

"What are you going to do next?"

"Finish college," I said, pointing out that I had enrolled at UCLA. They all started chuckling. Later, Dan Petrie Jr. explained their reaction: "Sean, this is not how the big successful directors got their careers going. You don't get nominated for an Oscar, then go to college."

Ed Zwick, Dan pointed out, did a short film for the American Film Institute; he then created the television show *Thirtysomething;* and then made *Glory* as his first full-length theatrical release. If there's a map for building a filmmaking career, that's it. But as much as I admired Ed Zwick, I didn't have his kind of confidence, his mastery of the language. Every time I met a college graduate in Hollywood, I was stung by a feeling of insecurity and inferiority, as if they had something on me, something that prevented me from competing with them. For that reason alone, I needed to get a degree. A dispassionate observer might find that hard to fathom, for there are in Hollywood today any number of people who eschewed college for one reason or another. Experience is perhaps the most important form of education to them. But not to me. Keith Addis, one of my former managers, once said to me, "I'm leery of working with you because I don't like working with anyone who hasn't been to college." It seemed at the time to be a rather arrogant, condescending remark, but I have to say, as soon as I got my degree, I called Keith and thanked him. For a while, whenever I got distracted, Keith and my father (another vigorous proponent of higher education) were like twin demons in the back of my mind, reminding me of the importance of what I was trying to do.

And it wasn't as if I retired from the movie business while I went to school. I finally started directing professionally. I got the opportunity to do some episodic television and took smaller parts in a number of movies, some of them memorable, some not so memorable. Among the former was Ed Zwick's *Courage Under Fire,* during the filming of which, as I've mentioned, I devoted considerable time to studying for my classes. As usual in my life, I was trying to get sixty seconds out of every minute, as Rudyard Kipling writes in his classic poem "If."

I've worked with a number of world-class filmmakers (Steven Spielberg, Richard Donner, Peter Jackson, among them), and Ed Zwick is up there with the best visionaries. If Kevin Costner was an emblem of everything I wanted to achieve when I met him at the premiere of *Dances with Wolves,* then Ed Zwick became my model both as a pure director and a director/producer, and in some ways I felt like I was following in his substantial footsteps. For example, in college, he had studied English and history, just as I had. He did his short film at

AFI; I did my own short film and got nominated for an Oscar. I looked at Ed and thought, *There's the template. There's my path.* Granted, he's probably a little bit smarter than I am, a little bit sharper (okay, maybe a lot smarter—he went to Harvard), and probably more honestly passionate about drama than I am. If you cut our minds open and laid them out on a table, his would look better than mine; but I wanted to do as much with mine as I possibly could. The point is, Ed was a beacon to me, and I wanted to bask in the glow of his talent.

The word "prescient" comes to mind when I reflect on Ed's choice of material. For example, *The Siege* is a picture that looked at issues related to domestic terrorism years before September 11. He is unafraid to use his talent and considerable skill to explore serious issues facing even the most sacred institutions in our society. Unwittingly, Ed Zwick's influence in my life taught me a very important lesson.

A little background . . . I auditioned for the part that Zwick eventually offered to Matt Damon in *Courage Under Fire*. While I was extremely disappointed that he chose Matt over me, I could certainly understand his choice. Once I saw the finished film, I really understood. I remember when I lost a part in Rob Reiner's movie *Stand by Me* to River Phoenix, how crushed I was initially, and then how utterly inspired I was by River's stunning performance in the picture. It became clear to me that River was ready to perform with a vastly more intense emotionality and basic level of toughness and sophistication than I had at that point in my life; I would only have been pretending. Similarly, Matt Damon was more capable of capturing the nuances required by the role he played. I could have made a good stab at it, but Matt just nailed it. I remember at the premiere that I was worried for him that after so dramatically altering his weight for the part, he might fall victim to the same problems I had endured. While he appreciated my gentle warning, he was totally unconcerned and has proven over the years that his commitment and discipline are unimpeachable. For all this and more, Matt has my admiration.

So, I'd like for it to be clear that as an actor—for example, in a picture such as *Memphis Belle*—I am proud to perform in movies that depict the United States and possibly other armed services honestly and in a way that feels historically accurate (one of my favorite films is the German classic *Das Boot*). *Courage Under Fire* promised something even more interesting than simply honoring the valiant service of brave men and women. In choosing to make *Courage Under Fire*, Ed raised the uncomfortable issue that the proffering of medals is, by its very nature, a political process. The director leveraged his power in Hollywood to make a film that did not initially receive approval from the United States Army. I had a unique vantage point from which to gain insight into the process, because I was then serving—and continue to serve—faithfully, proudly, and honorably as a civilian aide to the secretary of the army. During preproduction, I was waiting and trying to help work through the necessary bureaucracy in the eager hope that the army would agree to be involved in the making of the picture. Absolutely nothing can replace the realism and power of an MIAI tank, to say nothing of a brigade-level array of them.

But the army had certain stipulations, and Ed would not adjust the script. I was in an interesting position, because Ed offered me a small part in the picture. I was going to play the part of a tank gunner who accidentally commits the atrocity of killing a "friendly"—someone on his own side. Despite my frustration at not getting the part I wanted, I was grateful that Ed saw a way to use me. I thought the part had merit because it showed the reality of the horror that a brave, heroic patriot can suffer during the heat of battle, as well as afterward. I remember being in an odd position at the National Training Center in the California desert. One week I was the guest of General William Wallace, the commanding general on the base, and the following week I was the guest of Colonel Terry Tucker, who commanded the opposition force against the troops who went to the desert to train. On one trip I was a distinguished guest with a protocol ranking; on the next trip I was an actor in the entourage of Denzel Washington getting critical time to prepare for my role.

During the National Conference of the Civilian Aides that year, I approached the head of the public affairs office to inquire about the status of the film company's request for the army's support. I distinctly recall feeling that I might be forced to make a choice between acting in the picture and continuing to serve as a civilian aide. At the time, if forced, I would have chosen the movie. In my heart, I believed a few things: First, I am an actor, and acting is my craft, my profession, and my passion. Second, I thought, whatever the army's objections might be, the movie ultimately showed the army in an extremely positive if not perfect light. As it turned out, the army chose not to support the film, and the director was forced to go elsewhere for realistic props. He eventually got Australian Sheridan tanks and dressed them up to look like American and Russian/Iraqi equipment. The lesson I learned is that the military's primary objective is to fight and win wars when called on to do so, and that artists have a separate charge: to tell stories they can believe in regardless of how those in power may feel about them.

This next little story deals with the politics of celebrity, and I want to tread cautiously and sensitively. We filmed *Courage Under Fire* in the late fall or early winter around the time that American forces had been deployed to Kosovo. A friend and colleague of mine was running the Armed Forces Radio Network in Europe. He asked me to record some holiday greetings that could be played for the soldiers, many of whom would have absolutely no form of entertainment during the holidays far from home. I wanted to honor the request that had been made of me and, in so doing, I asked others to help. Of course, my mom was the first to volunteer, and her greeting was heartbreakingly sincere and beautiful.

Knowing that the army had turned Ed down, I probably should have wondered how well the director would treat my request. To Ed Zwick's absolute credit, he allowed me to approach his stars. I think it was unfair for me to even ask him or them for this kind of permission. Life is a lot about timing, and I made my request impulsively, which was wrong. Unfortunately and unintentionally, I put Ed in an awkward position. He would either have to disappoint me by turning me down or run the risk of having Meg Ryan, his leading lady, upset by being distracted from her work with a political request. I sensed Ed's displeasure, but he didn't try to stop me, and I never felt an iota of reprisal from him. To the contrary, he has always been gracious and supportive any time I have seen him since.

As I've thought about it over the years, I've realized that it may have been a little inappropriate for me to inquire spontaneously in the way that I did. At the very least, I was being opportunistic.

As far as Meg Ryan goes, well, to say that I have anything more than a passing connection with Meg is just not true. Sure, my mom played her mom in a movie, and she and I acted, if not together, at least in the same film. She has been polite to me when we've met each other at parties—maybe even something a little more than courteous. But we've never had a fully realized exchange about anything, and that makes me a little sad. I wouldn't mention it except that this is a feeling I've had many times before, mostly in "Hollywood" settings.

Denzel Washington was a prince. We recorded his greeting in the morning right after the sun came up, with Denzel waving a big cigar around, smiling and turning on the charm. Meg, interestingly, was a different story. She initially agreed to my proposal while seated in the makeup chair, and then she got up to do her scene—but when I approached her afterward, she apparently had changed her mind.

"Do you want to do this now?" I asked.

Meg sort of hemmed and hawed, then drifted away, saying, "I think I'm going to do something else for that."

Maybe she did; maybe she didn't. I don't know. In fairness, I'm not sure she even realized who I was (we had no scenes together) or what I was talking about, but I was disappointed nonetheless. There is a certain shallowness to Hollywood relationships that sometimes leads to disappointment, at least on my part. I like to think that I'm open with people and that I can find a common ground with almost anyone, so when what appears to be a friendship instead turns out to be nothing more than a short-term working relationship with no real foundation, it bothers me. The truth is, people in show business, probably more so than in other walks of life, are accustomed to feigning interest or protecting reputations, for whatever reason.

CHAPTER FOUR

In the summer of 1995, when I first was drawn into the strange and surreal world of Warren Beatty, my plate was already full. To be specific, three important things were happening in my life: I was in summer school at UCLA studying the Bible as literature and taking a class on Scandinavian cinema; I was editing an episode of a television anthology series called *Perversions of Science* that I had just directed; and most important of all, Christine was pregnant with our first child. While I was always open to new creative and business opportunities, I didn't need any more anxiety or responsibility. I knew I'd have to find a practical way to support my growing family and my various interests, so whenever the phone rang and a reasonably dignified acting offer was presented, I listened.

A call from Warren Beatty, of course, holds the promise for much more than a paycheck. We're talking about a man who is larger than life, a true Hollywood icon whose body of work is so substantial that it demands to be taken seriously. No amount of tawdry tabloid gossip or even the occasional *Ishtar* (which I actually liked) can diminish or overshadow his accomplishments. Warren is an artist, actor, businessman, director, producer, writer. He is a filmmaker in the most complete sense of the word. His acting credits alone are enough to merit a lifetime achievement award: *Bonnie and Clyde, Shampoo, Reds, Heaven Can Wait, Bugsy,* just to name a few. But he's often the driving creative and entrepreneurial force behind these films as well, which places him in a very different category. As with Woody Allen, Steven Spielberg, and a handful of other filmmakers, Warren's is a meeting you show up for, regardless of the circumstances in your own life. The opportunity to work with him or for him is something no actor (no smart actor, anyway) would summarily dismiss. To her credit, my then William Morris agent, Samantha Crisp, recognized that fact, and so she set it up.

That's how I came to find myself in a big suite at Warren's Beverly Glenn offices, sitting on a sofa, hands folded, calmly but eagerly waiting to meet the man and discuss his latest project, a movie about an offbeat politician called *Bulworth*. I knew almost nothing about the project; as is typical with Warren's films, it was shrouded in secrecy. I'd been told that he was interested in having me play the part of a character named Gary C-Span, who was some sort of roving journalist assigned to document the travels of Warren's titular character. I hadn't seen a word of the script, didn't even know if there was a script. I knew only that Warren had supposedly expressed an interest in having me sign on. Why? I wasn't sure. Because of my work in *Encino Man?* Unlikely. *Rudy?* A better guess was that he was at least marginally impressed that my short film had been nominated for an Academy Award. I'm sure that represented a type of validation in the eyes of someone like Warren; at the very least, it might have momentarily prodded him into looking in my direction with a sense of curiosity.

In just about every way imaginable, Warren met my expectations, which is not to say that working on *Bulworth* was a wholly positive experience. It was, however, an experience I'm proud to have endured, one that meets the standard for Hollywood extremism. Our first meeting was, in my mind, one of those classic Hollywood introductions. Warren entered the room wearing sweatpants and a fanny pack, and despite the casual look, the disheveled hair, the stubble on his chin, he carried himself with a decidedly regal air, like a princely pauperish genius—like a man who knows he's a megalomaniac and sees nothing wrong with that description. In other words, exactly what you'd expect of Warren Beatty.

My goal was to harness whatever nervousness I felt and project an image of an honest, earnest, open-faced ideologue, which wasn't hard to do since that's pretty much the way I am. And he loved it; he just soaked me in, told me right away that he could use that persona in his movie, which I found genuinely exciting. Toward the end of the meeting, though, he really piqued my interest.

"I'm going to want you to do some writing," Warren said.

"What kind of writing?"

He smiled. "You know . . . things."

Cryptic as that was, I was intrigued. Would I be contributing to the script? Working on future projects? No matter. I wanted in. But there was one thing that concerned me.

"I'll do whatever you want," I said, "but I have to be honest. I can't sign on without reading the script."

Warren shrugged. "Fine. You can go in the other room there and read the script, but you should know that there's really no part for you yet. And you should do the movie anyway."

He paused, waited for a reaction. I offered none. Then Warren smiled, in the way that only a person who is supremely confident can smile. "Just come along . . . see what happens. It'll be worth it."

I should have been wary, but I remember feeling something akin to awe. I loved this guy, and I loved the fact that he was, in some small way, courting me. I sat there knowing full well that I was going to be able to add my name to the long and illustrious list of people who got seduced by Warren Beatty, and instead of being conflicted by that recognition, I was excited by it. Even now, nearly a decade later, I remain curiously ambivalent about the experience. My name is proudly on that list somewhere (near the bottom, no doubt), but instead of feeling resentment, I'm grateful that Warren was able to get creatively aroused over me for a minute or two, that he recognized who I was and thus invited me into his inner circle, if only for a brief time, on the simple premise that something interesting could happen. The reason that something interesting ultimately did not happen was my limitation, not his.

"Okay," I said, "I'll look at the script."

"Good."

I got up, left Warren to his business, and went off to read the script. Indeed, just as he had promised, there was no role for me, no Gary C-Span to be found anywhere. Nevertheless, I shook Warren's hand and agreed to be part of his movie. I rationalized the decision on any number of levels. We were running out of money, the baby was coming, we had the fall semester of college to look forward to, and I was trying to figure out how to balance it all—how to pay for the house, be a new father, and keep Christine happy while we ran our production company together. I looked at the script, thought to myself, *The part is not on the page; this could be trouble,* and accepted the job anyway. I figured that I'd have only ten or twelve days of work during a four-month shoot, I'd learn something from working with one of the masters of cinema, and the rest of the time I'd be free to concentrate on school and family and entrepreneurial ventures.

That proved to be an enormous miscalculation.

"Great," Warren said as his hand enveloped mine. "Now remember, Sean, I want to hear your ideas. I want you to be writing. All the time."

I looked him in the eye and, with only a trace of irony, said, "Thank you, Warren. I look forward to writing and handing you pages and having you turn them down."

It was almost like something buried deep in my consciousness was saying it, the thing that I knew I needed to say in order to get the job. Not to be irreverent, not to be disrespectful or funny, but to let him know that I understood my place in his world, a world in which it is perfectly acceptable for the director and star to torture and humiliate his writers on a daily basis. That's what it was like on *Bulworth*. Amiri Baraka, a poet and scholar and sometime actor who played the part of a character known as Rastaman, had been given the same instructions and encouragement that I'd received, and he took them to heart. Amiri showed up almost nightly on the movie with reams of paper, detailed notes on his character and how it fit into the story, only to have them dismissed out of hand. And he kept coming back for more!

No one experienced more anguish than Jeremy Pikser, the credited cowriter (along with Warren) of the screenplay. (Little known fact: Aaron Sorkin, the creator of *The West Wing*, is one uncredited writer on *Bulworth*. Exactly what that means, I'm not sure. Did Aaron write the original draft? Did he rewrite Jeremy's work? Who knows? I'd be the last person to try to explain how Warren Beatty concocted the idea for this strange and brilliant movie, or how he captured the imagination of somebody like Aaron Sorkin—a genius in his own right—the contract that was written between them, or why Aaron had his name taken off the film. I'm going to understand or explain that? No way.) I watched Jeremy suffer, day in and day out, at the hands of Warren Beatty. Jeremy tried to help Warren create a counterculture figure in the character of Bulworth, while trying to create a career for himself, and toward the end the poor guy seemed like an emotional wreck.

I think of all of this now as I remember that first conversation with Warren at his office, when I stood in the doorway and told him I'd be honored to experience his firm editorial hand, to have him reject every idea, every written word and thought, that I threw his way.

And his response was a single simple word, spoken with a smile: "Good."

The next day I visited the set of *Bulworth*, primarily to soak up some atmosphere and meet a few of my coworkers, including Oliver Platt. Oliver is a big hulking behemoth of a brilliant actor, and a man who has, shall we say, a *presence*. He entered the stage like a summer thunderstorm and thrust out a meaty hand.

"Sean, nice to meet you! Man, I loved you in *Rudy*. What a great movie!"

"Uh, thanks, Oliver. Nice to meet you, too."

"Yeah, this is going to be special. Gary C-Span is so cool, the way he doesn't do anything the whole movie, and then he gives a speech at the end? That's brilliant, man. Fucking brilliant!"

Whoaaaaa . . .

I didn't agree with him, but I didn't want to disagree either, because the truth was I didn't know what the hell he was talking about. Oliver had more information about my character than I did, and it occurred to me that somehow he'd gotten deep inside Warren's head (in much the same way that Ian McKellen would burrow into Peter Jackson's head during the filming of *The Lord of the Rings*). He was so far inside Warren's head, in fact, that there was almost no way to separate them. Oliver, I suspected—and later this was demonstrated to be true—had suggested to Warren that the character of Gary be mute throughout the film, and then spring eloquently to life at the climax; Warren had liked the idea, and so they had moved forward believing it. My heart began to race. A day earlier I had met with Warren, had heard him say, "Come along with me, and we'll see what evolves." And now I was standing on the set, having my hair blown back by Oliver Platt as he dissected the character I had been assigned the task of not merely playing, but interpreting—even, to a degree, creating—a dissection I found baffling, but that apparently made sense dramatically to the director. I hadn't even signed a contract yet, and already I felt trapped. The only way to get out of the trap was by advocating for myself, quickly and aggressively. Why I didn't want to do that is . . . well, it's the imp of the perverse, isn't it? That little node of self-destruction that people allow in themselves, and that always leads to trouble.

Bulworth proved to be an unbelievable four-month apprenticeship that I wouldn't trade for anything in the world, because I learned so much not only about the art of filmmaking and cinema culture, but also about what it means to use and abuse power. It was in some ways the most important four months of my professional life, although I'm not sure I'd want to live through it again. Before accepting the job, I had sought the advice of a friend and mentor, and his response was thoroughly negative.

"Don't do it. You'll hate it."

He was right—and he was wrong. I accepted the job not only because it would allow me to be in the Los Angeles area when my daughter was born (in November 1996), and because it was, I thought, a small amount of work for reasonable remuneration, but also because I wanted to test myself, to see if I could acquit myself admirably while working alongside one of the most inspired and notorious taskmasters in Hollywood. Whatever else might transpire, I figured I'd at least learn a lot from Warren so I made the decision to do it. I don't blame Warren for anything that happened. I think he was exactly as I thought he would be, but I did suffer on that production. And the suffering was mostly of my own doing.

If you watch *Bulworth*, you'll notice that I'm barely in the movie, which doesn't really bother me; I understand the reason. I don't think Warren respected my capacity as an actor or an artist, and the fact that he didn't, coupled with my own hurt feelings, created a kind of sour mixture on the set. The responsibility for inspiration was on both of us; the implied understanding when I agreed to do the picture was that we would both be inspired. So it was disappointing in terms of output. In a sense, merely by watching him, I was inspired every day, but what I was writing and what he was capturing on screen were all overshadowed by Warren and his megalomania.

Of course, it was his movie. He was the writer, director, producer, and star; I was contractually merely a piece of casting. It was Warren's prerogative to use my acting talents as much or as little as he saw fit. The contribution of any writing on my part was a private understanding between Warren and me. This dynamic exists a lot and shouldn't be condemned by the Writer's Guild or its arbitrators. It goes to the notion that a healthy creative environment should allow for inspiration from all quarters to the betterment of the film. Credit and remuneration can impede creativity, and the balance is rightfully left to the development of trust between artists. To that end, I went willingly into Warren's world to see what the sky looked like.

There was one particular day when I watched with what can only be termed immense fascination as Warren staged a close-up of himself. Vittorio Storaro, one of the most brilliant and accomplished cinematographers ever to light a scene (his credits include *Last Tango in Paris, Apocalypse Now,* and *Reds*), was shooting it, and I remember being fascinated with Warren's capacity for introspection in the middle of this huge multimillion-dollar movie. Afterward, I quizzed him about it. I had seen *Dick Tracy* and loved it, and so I asked him about how he had put that movie together and how it had led to *Bulworth.* Everything on *Dick Tracy*, he explained, was planned to the inch—it was the exact opposite of *Bulworth. Dick Tracy* was an artistic endeavor, to be sure, but it was intended to be a big-budget, mainstream popular success. *Bulworth* was different, almost experimental in nature. Here Warren was using his stardom in service of the promotion of certain liberal ideas; to be perfectly honest, I'm not sure how he even got the studio (Fox) to pay for it. I believe it had something to do with Warren forgoing bonus money on an earlier film in exchange for the right to make a smaller, more personal film. Or agreeing not to sue the studio and forcing it to incur big legal costs. Only Warren and the studio really know. Either way, the movie was smart and in some ways coura-geous, and it spoke volumes about Warren's commitment to his craft and to his personal ideology. He is a formidable man and artist.

As far as my acting and writing and how I was perceived by Warren, however . . . well, that was a different story. For example, when it came to the letter of the contract, Warren was utterly unforgiving. The pro-duction owned me; *Warren* owned me, and he wanted me in close proximity—on the set, in the green room, or in my dressing room—all day, every day, no matter what. I was one of the colors on his palette; he wanted to have the freedom to go to that color whenever the mood struck him, and frankly I resented it. On a purely human and interpersonal level, I thought it was rude and inconsiderate, mainly because I didn't think he had any intention of using whatever talent I could supposedly bring to bear. Warren abused the privilege of having me at his disposal. I had signed a contract giving him power over where my physical body would be, on the premise that he would be respectful of it, and he was not respectful.

Over time, as it became apparent that I would play no major part in the construction of *Bulworth*, my frustration grew. As did my body. Warren had a very small dressing room by movie-star standards, but it was substantial compared to the tiny cubicles assigned to some of the actors, myself included. These were painfully small, private changing stations in which you couldn't spend more than a few seconds without suffering bouts of embarrassment. Whether this was by design (to dis-courage performers from hiding out in their dressing rooms) or sim-ply a prudent cost-saving measure, I don't know; I do know that I, like most of the actors, tended to gravitate toward the motor home that served as the cast's green room.

The green room was a fairly lavish setup, with satellite television, gourmet food prepared by a cadre of chefs, and an assortment of newspapers and magazines. The green room was where Warren spent most of his off-set time, too, and it was indeed a place where interest-ing things happened. He invited all kinds of movers and shakers and people of cultural, artistic, and political influence. I saw them come and go, because I basically sat my widening ass in a chair not far from him, and said to myself, *If Warren is going to have me here, he's going to have to see me every time he walks in and out of this room.* I was determined not to be out of his sight. He'd developed a pattern of telling his assistant directors to find particular actors and bring them to the set, and I didn't want to make it convenient for him not to need me. (One of the assistant directors, by the way, was Frank Capra III, grandson of the idealistic director of countless Hollywood classics, including *It's a Wonderful Life* and *Mr. Smith Goes to Washington.* It would be absolutely awesome when Warren would shout, "Frank Capra!" People would stop in their tracks, and you'd find yourself thinking, *I'm a part of Hollywood history—this is so cool!*)

But those were small and fleeting moments of joy, of legitimate creative wonder. By and large, for me *Bulworth* was a bizarre and discouraging experience, a marathon of boredom punctuated by strange and humbling interactions with the director and star.

"You should be writing your speech," Warren would admonish me from time to time, when he'd see me sitting in the green room, reading a book for some class I was taking at UCLA. "Remember, what's in here" (he'd tap me on the chest, over my heart) "is more important than what's in here" (then he'd tap me on the forehead).

"I know, I know. I'm working on it."

But I wasn't. Not really. I remember thinking, *You know, Warren, if I had even an iota of faith that you would honor my thoughts or contributions, I'd allow myself to go there. I'd plumb the depths of my soul. But you basically just want me to clean up a mess so you don't have to look at it.* That's how frustrated and angry I'd become. One day, though, for reasons I still don't quite understand (perhaps out of some pathetic need for approval, or maybe just to prove I was right), I surrendered to Warren's will and went off with my laptop. And I wrote. And wrote. And wrote. In a single, frantic, cathartic session I produced a seven-page, single-spaced treatise on the character of Gary C-Span, his importance to the film *Bulworth,* and what I believed Warren Beatty was trying to accomplish. These weren't pages from a script, but more of an intellectual diatribe—an attempt to demonstrate my passion for art and ideas.

Did it work? Of course not.

On the day I presented the pages to Warren, we were sitting together in the makeup room. Warren had just finished eating lunch and was expressing an interest in returning to the buffet table for a refill. With a wry smile he turned to me, held up his plate, and said comedically, for he isn't really a tyrant or a bully, "Sean, do you suppose there is a minion about?"

Now, I believe this was Warren's way of jokingly pointing out that on movie sets there are always people milling about, people whose job descriptions can never quite be pinned down. He wasn't really asking for a minion because he felt he was entitled to it—in fact, he wasn't asking for a minion at all—but he was enjoying the kind of self-awareness that comes from knowing that he is a man who does indeed have minions. When push comes to shove, I believe Warren Beatty is as in touch with the common man as any multimillionaire actor/director/mogul could be. And yet, he did say, "Is there a minion about?" Which I find rather amusing.

"I'll tell you what, Warren," I said, taking the plate from his hands. "I'll go get you some more food, on the condition that you let me read my pages to you when I get back."

"No, no, you don't have to get me food, Sean," he said at first. But I interrupted him.

"That's all right. I want to."

He nodded. "Okay."

So I retrieved a heaping plate of food and placed it in front of Warren, and began performing my rambling diatribe. I was nervous, so I stumbled and stammered a bit, but I got through it quickly enough, and I was pleased that he actually seemed to be paying attention, maybe even taking me and my words seriously. In all candor, I thought it was not only pretty well written, but also reasonably astute; it was a celebration of Warren and his idiosyncrasies, as well as an indictment of some of those things. I thought I'd found a way to make my point and comment on the character and the story, even though I hadn't found a way to integrate it seamlessly into the story. Never mind that none of us had been issued a script! Basically, this was performance art, a weird combination of improvisation and detailed speech reading, which was precisely the way Warren seemed to like to work. By the time I finished, I was sweating and breathing hard; my heart was racing. I looked at him and waited for some type of reaction.

"Well?"

He paused, poked at his food, and said nonchalantly, "Not bad. Why don't you try another version where you focus more on the girls?"

The "girls" were two African American women who, like Gary C-Span, were part of Bulworth's ever-expanding entourage. The point, I later discovered as the movie came into focus, was that Warren was thinking about trading on a kind of hippie sexuality, something reminiscent of the spirit of the sixties. You could see him looking for it, looking for *something*, but apparently I'd missed the mark in my presentation.

As I've reflected on it over the years, I've come to think Warren might have had in mind a sort of comedic trio. Perhaps if there had been more of a spark between my personality and the personality of the "girls," Warren might have seen some value in cutting to us as a kind of miscegenation or menàge comic-relief element. But I didn't allow myself to go there, and I don't think my personality had evolved enough to "play" in an improvisational way with them. One of the highlights of the shoot for me was making friends with some of the other actors. Notably, Josh Malina did just the kind of sketch or character comedy that Warren was looking for, and his stuff is rightfully all over the movie.

But let's get back to me standing in front of Warren, having presented him with my outpouring of creative writing. I was demonstrably hurt by his reaction, almost as though I expected him to jump out of his chair and offer to relinquish his credit to me.

"Try another version?" I asked incredulously.

I didn't bother. Instead, I just sat there all day long, every day, feeling undervalued and underappreciated, eating myself into a stupor, getting fat and angry and depressed, much as I had during the filming of *Encino Man*. The funny thing was, eventually I came to understand my character. There wasn't much written for him, but that was typical of Warren. He wanted his actors to be totally naturalistic and comfortable, to allow performances and stories to grow organically. The weird thing about my situation, though, is that Gary C-Span is a pivotal, if largely observant character; he's there, hanging around, the entire movie. He's following, videotaping, watching. But in terms of interpreting what's going on, he does nothing; so I ended up in this odd position where I was there and present on the set, but not really focused on the movie. The result was a kind of amused reconciliation: while trying to be ready for the possibility that Warren might want to shoot a close-up with me, I had to accept the notion that my role would be reduced to a cameo.

It was a unique Hollywood experience, trying to not just endure, but to also honor, the opportunity that had been presented to me. I fully accept responsibility for the way it turned out. I know that if I had been working out every day, if I had factored into the equation some cardiovascular exercise and had been disciplined about how I ate and transformed myself into the good-looking guy that's (sometimes) within me, not only would my attitude have been better, and not only would I have felt more creative, but Warren might have used that energy in a way that would have yielded something more valuable in terms of the final product. So, to a certain extent, I'm culpable for my own frustration, as well as the fact that Gary is little more than a shadow in the movie *Bulworth*.

Power, I've discovered, is an interesting thing, and sometimes the biggest challenge is knowing whether you have any control over a situation. Warren Beatty is like a Hollywood supernova: you can get burned right out of existence being anywhere near him. If you don't know how to protect yourself from guys like him, or how to work with guys like him, or how to survive despite guys like him, you'll have a short, forgettable career.

Bulworth was not an experience I'd want to relive, but I'm proud to have it on my résumé. Simply by showing up for work each day, by being in Warren's proximity, I heard stories I couldn't have heard anywhere else. That was worth it to me, and Warren knew it was worth it to me.

One could argue that I got exactly what I wanted, and just what I deserved.

CHAPTER FIVE

L et me take you back to the spring of 1999, when Christine and I decided to buy a $650,000 house in Encino, a suburb of L.A. Forget for a moment the utter insanity of the Southern California real estate market, and the fact that six hundred grand doesn't buy you all that much in L.A. (God knows, when my friends from Texas came to visit, they were shocked to discover that we didn't live in anything remotely resembling a mansion.) This was to be our home, the place where we would raise our children and continue to fight the Hollywood wars. I was thrilled about it.

And I was scared to death.

Here's the truth: I was worried about looking after my family, and not being able to keep our brand new house because I wouldn't be able to pay the mortgage. I'd made the decision to purchase the house based on an interesting psychological conceit. Inside my head, I was bothered by the fact that because Christine needed to spend tons of time with Alexandra, our gorgeous daughter, and that because I was failing to live up to my commitment to coparent all the time, there was a little tension between us. I knew she rightfully resented my feelings in this regard, but I was wracking my brain trying to figure out the best direction for my professional life. I believed that I had the primary responsibility to be the breadwinner for our family. Never mind that Christine had already successfully run a 4½-star restaurant and worked a dozen different jobs in her lifetime. I was addicted to the old-fashioned chauvinist notion that the *man* should make the money.

That we are still together is a testament to how forgiving Christine is, and to how I've managed to care for her at least enough to keep her from changing the locks or inviting someone less self-centered than me into our bed! A gift every husband should know not to take for granted.

I still cringe when I recall how I managed to convince Christine—and justify to myself—that the $650,000 purchase made sense. I calculated—well, spitballed is more like it—what I'd been earning in recent years as a lead actor in independent films who also picked up the occasional small part in big films. On average, my income was about $250,000 per year. Now, you might think that someone who has made more than forty films and starred in a few substantial ones would have no problem meeting this standard, but as I've indicated earlier, that's one of the curious things about the entertainment business. When it comes to financial reward, there is a disparity between truth and perception. Sure, some actors are ridiculously wealthy and lead lives that would make a pharaoh blush. But there are plenty of working actors, successful by any reasonable definition or objective standard, who lose sleep when they buy a new house or hear that they're about to become a parent.

I'd had an unusual life and career. I'd grown up in the business and made a little bit of money, but I'd also tackled some of the responsibilities of adulthood when I was barely out of my teens. I'd married, put myself and my wife through college, and invested tidy sums of my own money in my work as an aspiring director and screenwriter. Yet, while it was all rewarding in an intellectual and spiritual way, we weren't seeing much of a return on our time or financial investment. By the time we bought our house, we were fairly racing through our savings account, to the point where it became critical that I hit that quarter-million mark yearly in order to keep the house. There was little margin for error.

How had I allowed my life to reach this level of anxiety? Well, that's a complicated question with complicated answers. At the time, I had a relationship with a personal manager who knew how to cash in on what my success would yield, and I was willing to settle for the small independent films that paid reasonably well but required little of my time. Then I could concentrate on other things, rather than focus my energy on acting and competing for the roles that would have resulted in an escalation of my stock as a Hollywood commodity—that is, roles as leading man. As I've explained, part of the reason for that was the convoluted relationship I had with my body. I knew that in any given week I was capable of treating my body like a high-performance race car—or a dump truck. There are periods of my life that reflect this battle, and when I look at the photos, well, sometimes it's not a pretty sight. Alternately, I see a relatively good-looking guy or a fat slob who is so unappealing that no director in his right mind would hire him for even a secondary role, let alone ask him to play a heroic or romantic lead.

There are, no doubt, complex reasons for this fluctuation, and if you put me through psychoanalysis you'd probably discover all sorts of issues related to loneliness and self-confidence and, yes, entitlement. My feeling of, *Gee, my mom's made all this money (even if she pissed most of it away). She was a famous actress; the least she could do is set me up with a little annuity. I mean, really, why should I have to follow a more rigorous, traditional path? I'm not just anyone, you know?*

I never said that, of course. I never voiced those thoughts—until now—because I know it's wrong to have those feelings, which represent nothing but the whining of a self-centered, spoiled Hollywood brat. But I had them anyway. It's funny, too, because I used to scold my mother when she exhibited similar tendencies. Why should Patty Duke—Oscar winner, Emmy winner, important actor—have to audition for parts? Wasn't she above that?

"Mom, the young directors out there now didn't grow up with you. They don't really know who you are. Of course you should audition for them."

"But why?"

"Because even though he's young, he's spent his whole life preparing for this project, and it's his prerogative to do it any way he pleases."

My mother spent a lot of time frustrated with her career because she didn't want to do the work necessary to land the best jobs. She didn't like the fact that she had pulled herself up by her bootstraps, carved out a meaningful career, and now, even as an adult, faced the uncertainty of unemployment, or underemployment. She had trouble developing the self-confidence required to say, *I know I'll be in this busi-*

ness a long time; I'll always work; now what kinds of things do I want to work on? It was more about, I've made X number of dollars; I'm entitled to this type of lifestyle. Bad business and bad economics. When I finally read books like *The Richest Man in Babylon, The Millionaire Next Door*, and *Rich Dad, Poor Dad*, I realized there are certain laws of money. Like, if you spend it, it's gone. As was the case with my mother, my inability to manage my own finances and to invest intelligently has caused me a bit of heartache. I've tried to turn it into a spiritual life lesson, into understanding who I am as an animal on the planet who needs to eat and forage, but it's been painful, and it was particularly challenging around the time that I purchased our house.

I had a young daughter, and it had been eight months since I'd made any money in acting. I'd been killing myself working eighteen-hour days, trying to figure out how Hollywood functioned—how to get screenplays sold and movies set up. I had written a screenplay, developed deals, and tried to improve as an artist, all while earnestly trying not to be just another child actor who couldn't make the transition to adult performer. It was like there was a voice in the back of my head that kept saying, "Okay, you're out of college, you're married, you've got a kid, and you want to be the CEO of a multimillion-dollar production company? What steps are you going to take? How do you make it happen?" But the truth was, it wasn't happening. We were almost out of money. I was floundering. So it was an emotionally exhausting and scary time, and there was this thought that kept me up at night, the nagging sense that I might not make it.

Ever.

And then, at precisely that moment, a project that carried with it the promise of greatness fell from the sky.

It's interesting the way things work, how sometimes there seems to be a greater force at play in the universe. No sooner had we made a decision to buy the house than I got a phone call from my agent at William Morris, Nikki Mirisch. It was a call that would change my life. I was in my car at the time (the cliché that a lot of Hollywood business gets conducted behind the wheel happens to be true), driving on Burbank Boulevard in the San Fernando Valley, not far from my home.

"Honey, it's Nikki."

This was a good sign, for the simple reason that she had initiated the contact. The truth was, I hadn't gotten many calls from my agent in recent months; it always seemed as though I was the one reaching out. But not now. Best of all, there was more than a hint of excitement in her voice.

"Listen, Peter Jackson is doing *The Lord of the Rings* trilogy for New Line. You'll need a flawless British accent by Thursday."

That's what she said, but for some reason—the traffic? the noise? the fact that the tone of her voice indicated this was important?—well, for some reason, that's not exactly the way it registered in my mind. I heard three things: *Peter Jackson, New Line, trilogy*. But the most important part of the message—the words "Lord of the Rings"—sailed cleanly from one ear to the other, without pausing to introduce themselves to my brain. So that's how I came to hear of this project, which in fact had been in one stage of development or another for several years—not through *Daily Variety* or any of the other trade publications covering the movie industry, not through any of the hundreds of Web sites devoted to J. R. R. Tolkien. No, the first time I had any inkling that *The Lord of the Rings* was being made into a movie was at this very moment. And it meant nothing to me. The most important thing I had heard was the name of Peter Jackson.

I knew Peter not as the mad scientist behind such cult splatter flicks as *Dead Alive* or even as the genius behind *Heavenly Creatures*, the critically acclaimed 1994 film starring Kate Winslet as a young woman involved in one of New Zealand's most painful and famous murder trials. I knew Peter as the man who had directed my father, along with Michael J. Fox, in *The Frighteners*, a weird and morbidly comic film released in 1996. In fact, I had met Peter at the movie's premiere, and had spoken on the phone both to him and to Fran Walsh, his wife and creative partner, while Dad was making that movie. So there was a bit of personal history, including the vivid memory of my father showing me footage from a documentary Peter had produced and directed. It happened one day when I visited his condo in L.A. Dad popped in a videocassette, stood back, and said, "Watch this. It's incredible."

Indeed it was. On the television screen was Peter Jackson, with his rumpled hair and cherubic face poking through an unruly beard. "I've found the most amazing thing," he said to the camera. "My neighbor next door had a chest of drawers downstairs in her basement, and I went in one day because she needed help moving stuff. I noticed some old film canisters, so I asked if I could look at them." Here Peter paused for dramatic effect. "And what I discovered was an absolute treasure."

Then, in perfect documentary fashion, Peter invited the viewer into the house—and it was clearly the neighbor's house, exactly the one my father had shown me in pictures. With camera in tow, he guided the viewer downstairs, explained again precisely where he found the film, and how it was old and brittle and had to be painstakingly restored. But, oh my, was it worth the cost and effort! For what Peter Jackson had discovered, right here in his neighbor's house, was something so remarkable, so shocking, that it would change the course of cinematic history.

With that, a sample of the footage was played, in all its fragile, ancient glory—shimmering black-and-white images of a rickety airplane wobbling down a makeshift runway before climbing into the sky. The narrator explained that this was, in fact, the first footage ever shot of an airplane, and that the flight took place in 1903, approximately two months before the Wright Brothers' historic accomplishment at Kitty Hawk. Hard to believe? Not to me. I had been to New Zealand once before, when I was sixteen years old and working on a movie called *White Water Summer*. While there I got to know a few guys who made homemade planes and helicopters, and I came to think of it as something of a pastime in New Zealand. I can remember sitting outdoors at lunchtime and hearing something that sounded like a loud lawn mower, and looking up to see a man flying a . . . well, I'm not quite sure what it was. It was less than a plane but more than an ultralight. He was doing all kinds of wild aerial maneuvers, climbing high into the sky and then diving straight back down, pulling out of a death spiral at the last second. I thought of that pilot as I sat in my father's living room, watching this amazing documentary film and thinking, almost incredulously, *Well, why not? There's a tradition of adventure and exploration in New Zealand, and a tradition of aviation as well. It's a land of pioneers, so . . .*

I bit.

"Dad, this is amazing! Did Peter give this to you?"

Poker-faced, my father simply nodded.

"And the world news media hasn't picked up on it yet? They don't know that Americans weren't the first to fly?"

"That's right."

I could barely contain my excitement. "Oh, man, we have to call CNN. *The New York Times!*"

At that moment my admiration for Peter Jackson was immeasurable. No wonder this guy was able to get Universal Studios to give him forty million dollars to make *The Frighteners*. He had discovered a moment of human history that had been captured on cinema, and he'd restored it. My God! He belonged in the pantheon of the cinematic greats: Steven Spielberg, David Lean, Martin Scorcese, Francis Ford Coppola. Suddenly, in my mind, these titans had nothing on Peter Jackson.

I noticed my father chuckling.

"What?"

"I'm sorry, Sean."

"Sorry about what?"

My father has always had a healthy sense of humor, and this was a practical joke he couldn't resist.

"The footage isn't real," he said. "It's a hoax."

You gotta be kidding me!

What I had seen, in fact, was a clip from *Forgotten Silver*. Ostensibly a short-form documentary made for New Zealand public television, the film's subject was a man named Colin McKenzie, a Kiwi filmmaker who, unbeknownst to the rest of the world, supposedly pioneered synchronized sound in 1908 and color film in 1911. According to the documentary, McKenzie was denied fame on any grand scale not only because he was working in New Zealand, an artistic outpost, but also because he committed a few, shall we say, tactical errors. His sound film featured Chinese dialogue (understood by no one who saw it), and the groundbreaking color film included scenes of topless natives on the island of Tahiti, and thus was deemed "obscene" and quickly pulled from circulation.

The story of Colin McKenzie and his work would be tragic as well as fascinating, if only it were true. In fact, Colin McKenzie is the product of Peter Jackson's wildly inventive imagination and devilish sense of humor. Codirected by Jackson and noted documentarian Costa Botes, *Forgotten Silver* has more in common with *This Is Spinal Tap* than *Hearts of Darkness*. It is a "mockumentary" rather than a documentary, a playful yet awesomely well-executed send-up of the genre, predicated on the simple yet stunning notion that Jackson has stumbled across a cache of cinematic classics. McKenzie is credited with any number of ground-breaking cinematic achievements, including the first tracking shot and the invention of the first trick camera, as well as the aforementioned footage of the first airplane flight, which, seen out of context, as it was presented to me, looked like one of the greatest discoveries in history.

Seen in its entirety, *Forgotten Silver* is easily identifiable as a parody, and a marvelous one at that. Or maybe not. When the film was broad-cast on television in New Zealand, it was greeted not with the sort of gleeful approval that met *Spinal Tap*, but with something akin to the shock that resulted from the Halloween radio broadcast of Orson Welles's *War of the Worlds*. Which is to say, viewers took the bait—hook, line, and sinker. There was no disclaimer, no warning. Just a serious presentation of a decidedly unserious film. In the days and weeks that followed, New Zealanders embraced Colin McKenzie as a new national hero, and Peter Jackson was applauded for bringing his achievements to the public eye. All of which was a little more than the filmmakers had intended, and in the end Peter apologized to just about everyone who had been offended, including the prime minister. I felt incredibly stupid for falling so completely for the ruse, but I also felt tremendous admiration for Peter. The making of *Forgotten Silver* required creativity and ingenuity, but it also took guts.

So when the call came from my agent, it was Peter's name that got my attention.

Oh, my, it's the Peter Jackson my dad described to me; it's the Peter who had called me from his screening room to say how much he loved me in Rudy. *It's Peter of "Peter and Fran"—Fran, who once told me that my work in* Where the Day Takes You *was what they were watching on video in their hospital room when she was giving birth to their son, Billy. That Peter.*

Instantly, what was triggered in me when I heard his name was a heightened sensitivity, a feeling that something important was about to happen. An opportunity of the sort that didn't come along every day. "Trilogy" obviously meant three, as in three movies, as in three jobs, or one very long job, which was good news, and obviously I knew New Line was in the business of making movies, so right away I knew this was one of the more important phone calls I'd ever received. I knew Peter's career was growing, moving in a particular direction; even though *The Frighteners* hadn't been as successful as it could have been, it was still a big-budget Hollywood movie, and I knew that Peter was not going to be doing anything smaller than that. "Trilogy" sounded good. It sounded right.

Let me explain. I know I would not have been cast in *The Lord of the Rings* if not for my work in *Where the Day Takes You* and *Rudy*. Those two movies ingratiated me, demonstrated the caliber of my talent to Fran and Peter, two incredible artists who were open-minded and forward leaning when it came time to hear my name on the list, and so they invited me to audition. *Encino Man* didn't help me get the job, but neither did it hurt me—not in this case. Peter understands the arc of a career, the choices and compromises that are made, and he was willing to give me a chance based on the fact that at times I had done some pretty damn good work. I'm grateful for the way things have turned out, but I don't see it as mere serendipity. Tolkien's brilliance, the incredible mythology, the spectacular business success of those books, the quantum readership that's there, and the generational following the author has—well, I feel like there's a balance between me seeing that ship flying by and desperately throwing a lasso around it and sailing with it, and me kind of running alongside, keeping apace, so that I was able to step on board at just the right moment. It wasn't like I was watching opportunities go by, flailing helplessly away, and I finally grabbed that one, the *big one!* That makes me sound helpless. While I would be the first to acknowledge my great fortune in being a part of this project, I also think I deserve some credit for my own involvement.

Ignorance of the subject matter notwithstanding, I knew this was a big deal. I knew it from the names of some of the people involved, and from the excitement in Nikki's voice. The fact that it was New Line, which didn't throw money around casually, implied that there would be a relatively tight fist on the wallet, but that was all right. If Peter Jackson had signed on, then it had to be worthwhile. And I

trusted Nikki. She was always very sweet with me. I liked her personality a lot, even though in some ways she was a stereotypical agent. She
spoke in a lilting, reassuring way, yet didn't hesitate to let you know
when you simply weren't going to get what you wanted. I got along
well with Nikki and was happy to entrust my career to her straight-
forward, honest approach. The truth is, all agencies work in a conflict
of interest, even smaller ones, because they have a roster of clients
who often compete for the same jobs. The best you can hope for as an
actor is that, when they're pitching you to the casting director or to the
director or the producers, they're up to speed on your latest accomplishments. But as soon as they get an indication that it won't work,
that you aren't first in line for the job, they switch gears.

"*Hey, have you thought about Sean Astin for this?*"

"*No, not really.*"

"*Well, you know, he's gotten some great reviews lately.*"

"*Uh-huh . . . Who else you got?*"

Boom! That's it. The agent immediately transitions to another
client, because all he or she cares about—naturally—is keeping the
commission in house.

I'd been through that sort of thing a lot. I didn't want it to happen
again now. The stakes were too high. I was worried about my family and
career. I knew that I was in a rut. Despite becoming better educated, better read, and more equipped to navigate the shark-infested waters of
Hollywood, I hadn't made the progress I wanted to make. A lot of the
movies I was doing went right under the radar—nobody saw them or
would remember them—so I felt like I hadn't reached critical mass yet
on having done schlock. But I was getting dangerously close, and that
was the source of much of my anxiety: among the kind of smart, interesting, creative people who drive the movie business, I was afraid I wasn't
perceived as someone who was really dedicated to his craft. Instead, I was
perceived as the guy who was going to school and raising a family and
struggling a bit after *Rudy.* And that's an accurate reading on it.

All of that contributed to my intensely acute reaction to Nikki's
call. I tried to absorb everything while simultaneously asking the right
questions and looking for a place to pull off the road and park the car.

"*The Lord of the Rings?*" I asked, repeating the one piece of information that meant almost nothing to me.

"Yes, yes," she said. "You know, Tolkien. *The Lord of the Rings.*"

"No, I don't know."

"*The Lord of the Rings!*" she shouted. "They're the sequels to *The Hobbit.* You do know *The Hobbit?*

I took a deep breath. *The Hobbit.* Okay, that I knew. Somewhere deep in the dark recesses of my memory, I thought I recognized *The Hobbit* as a book my mother had read to me when I was a kid. Upon further review, however, I must admit that I'm pretty sure I was confusing *The Hobbit* with *The Phantom Tollbooth.* Either way, it's fair to say that I was basically a blank slate on the subject of Tolkien. But there was no point in admitting that to Nikki. I wanted the job. I *needed* the job.

"A flawless British accent by Thursday, huh?" It was Tuesday afternoon. I laughed nervously. "Can't it be Friday?"

"No! They're faxing the pages to you right now, and Victoria Burrows will meet with you on Thursday. Take it or leave it."

There was no leaving it, of course, and not merely because it was such an awesome opportunity. Victoria Burrows was an important person in my life and career. As the casting director on *The Frighteners,* she was responsible for bringing my father in to meet with Peter and Fran. I had met Victoria at a gathering at Universal Studios following the premiere of *The Frighteners,* and had found her to be enormously engaging and interesting. She knew about *Kangaroo Court* and the fact that it had been nominated for an Academy Award, and she seemed to genuinely admire my work. Whether she actually did, I'm not quite sure, but I do know that she was a smart, beautiful woman, with no small amount of power, and I was completely taken aback that she had any idea who I was. It was immensely flattering.

Victoria asked me if I was interested in any more directorial work, and I said that indeed I was. She then told me that Richard Donner was in the process of lining up directors for the television series *Perversions of Science,* which had been adapted from *Tales from the Crypt.* Well, that was a critical piece of information, for the next morning I went straight to my publicist's office and said, "You know what? Get me Dick Donner on the phone." A few minutes later I had Dick cornered.

"Remember when you promised me an episode of *Tales from the Crypt* in the first season or, worst-case scenario, the second season?"

"Look, Sean . . ."

"And it went five seasons and I never got a shot? Well, now I hear you've got this new show, and you're looking for directors. I'm on the list, right?"

"It's not my money, kid."

"Come on, Dick. I was nominated for an Academy Award."

"I know."

"It isn't rocket science. I'm overqualified to do this thing. So let's go! What are we waiting for?"

Eventually he got tired of my badgering him, and I got him to promise that if my name came up, he wouldn't reject me. So I hung up and started calling around to see what I could make happen. I worked closely with the rest of his team and landed the job. But the point is this: without Victoria Burrows, I wouldn't even have known the job existed. So she's on my list of angels who have helped me and given me insight at critical moments in my life and career.

Now, while on the phone with my agent, I learned that not only was I being considered for a role in what sounded like an important project, but the person charged with the task of casting the film was none other than Victoria Burrows. I couldn't help but smile.

"Nikki, was it your idea to put me up for this part—or Victoria's?"

The line went quiet for a moment.

"Honey . . . it was both of us."

Which meant, of course, that it was Victoria's idea. But what the hell. This was no time to argue over loyalty. This was a time to argue over *time*. I needed more. Lots more. There was research to conduct, material to read, a dialect coach to be hired. How could I possibly develop a flawless British accent in two days, and still have time left over to figure out who the hell Tolkien was? It just wasn't possible.

I tried to make this case to Nikki as I steered the car back into traffic and began looking for the nearest bookstore. In desperation, I played what I thought was a trump card.

"Look, Peter Jackson is a friend of my dad's. I'm sure if he knows that I'm preparing an audition tape, he'll wait a couple more days." (My dad later told me he had promoted me to Victoria before I got the call. Frankly, I'm grateful to all who played a hand in my future!)

Dead silence on the other end of the line.

"Nikki?"

"Thursday, Sean. Be ready."

I hung up the phone and immediately called Christine, who somehow interpreted my breathless ranting and understood the importance of what was about to happen. She was familiar with Peter's work, but she also admired him for his ability to forge a seemingly perfect creative alliance with Fran. Christine, too, had met Peter at the premiere of *The Frighteners,* and she'd seen my father's scrapbook documenting the making of that film, with hundreds of pictures of the magnificent prosthetic work of Richard Taylor (which would also be a vital component in the making of *The Lord of the Rings*). In sum, she knew Peter was a master craftsman. Of equal importance to Christine, though, was the memory of one evening at our home in Sherman Oaks, sharing dinner with my father and his wife, Val (Valerie Sandobal), during which they waxed eloquent on the subject of marriage and work, and how, under the right circumstances, the two can be combined to form an almost perfect union. Fran Walsh and Peter Jackson had done precisely that, according to my father. They were a team in the purest sense of the word, utterly committed to a common goal in their professional lives, as well as to each other. They believed in making work part of their family, and family part of their work. And they did it beautifully. Christine and I came away from that evening longing for a similarly powerful creative relationship, so when she heard that I had a chance to work with Peter and Fran, she was almost as excited as I was.

"I'll be home in a little while," I told her. "Gotta make a quick stop."

"Where?"

"The bookstore."

I pulled into the Barnes & Noble parking lot, jumped out of the car, and practically sprinted to the front counter. Then I made a fool out of myself.

"Excuse me, do you have anything by Tolkien?"

The clerk stared at me with a furrowed brow.

"It's J. R. Tolkien . . . or J. R. R. . . . something like that? Does it ring a bell?" I always get crazy in bookstores, kind of excited and lost, and sometimes I end up looking pathetic and pleading for help. This, however, was an unusually sad display.

The clerk rolled his eyes. "Yes, sir. It's J. R. R. Tolkien, and it's right over there. Section seven. I'll show you."

I'd spent a lot of time in bookstores in recent years, but I can honestly say I'd never been in the area devoted to fantasy, science fiction, and mythology. I had been living in Biography and History and Film Criticism. That's what interested me; that's what I knew. Imagine my surprise when the clerk guided me to section seven, pointed in the general direction of the middle shelf, and said, "Here it is." I looked up to see not one, not two, not three, but four books by Tolkien. Then my eyes kept moving up, and I realized there was a second shelf, and a third shelf, a fourth, a fifth . . . There were dozens of books. Maybe scores.

"Anything else?" the clerk asked, giving me a self-important smirk.

"Uh . . . no. Thanks. I can take it from here."

Rarely have I felt like such a total moron. How, I wondered, did I get to this point? Here I was, twenty-eight years old, with a degree in history and literature from a major institution of higher learning. I had graduated with honors, for Pete's sake. I considered myself a pretty well-read person. So how did I miss this entire *thing*? This movement in publishing? This cultural phenomenon? I was flabbergasted, and the embarrassment washing over me felt like someone had poured hot water on my shoulders. Like all the floodlights were on me, and everyone was watching, and all I could do was scratch my head and wonder, *What else am I missing?*

I'm extremely proud of my academic accomplishments. I'm never too shy to boast that Christine and I successfully completed what I consider to be one of the tougher liberal arts double majors—history and English. But unfortunately, there was a gaping hole in my knowledge. Should I blame my parents for never reading me *The Hobbit,* or UCLA for failing to assign it? Not to mention the ten other schools I'd attended? I guess it doesn't matter. At least I was prepared to hit the ground running!

CHAPTER SIX

It took me a while to figure out which of the books would best serve as my introduction to Tolkien. I dismissed the biographies and quasi-academic analyses—there simply wasn't time to digest them, and even if there had been time, what purpose would they have served without proper context? Nope. I had to go straight to the source: the three-volume set of *The Lord of the Rings*.

But even that wasn't such a simple matter, since there are countless editions of the books, in myriad forms, all of them thick and meaty and utterly imposing to someone unfamiliar with the story. My eyes went first to a version illustrated by John Howe, whose sketches were vivid and visceral, which I guess is why they've long appealed to pubescent boys. A lot of kids get hooked on Tolkien and his mythology around that age, but not me. I think unless my mother had read the books aloud to me, that never would have happened. In fact, that's how I "read" numerous classics. John Steinbeck's *The Pearl* and *Of Mice and Men*, and countless others—all of them were practically performed to me by my mother. I had neither the patience nor the inclination to read alone. I couldn't sit still long enough. But I did have the patience to sit with Mom and spend that special time with her, to hang on her every word. That felt more like theater and less like work. Not surprisingly, I always did better on school essays when my mother helped by reading the material to me; I could write endlessly about something I'd heard. But words on a page? That was a problem.

Early in my school career I suffered because of this inability to focus, to simply sit down and do the work uninterrupted and without accompaniment. I know what you're thinking: *Sounds like a kid with attention deficit disorder.* Well, the truth is, there was a period of time when I think that diagnosis would have been made so hard and so quick and been so totally accurate that it's not even funny; then again, they probably could have gotten me for a bunch of things.[3] There was a time when my parents were worried that I was depressed because I was so much shorter than everyone else, so they had me meet with a psychiatrist. We chatted for about a half hour, after which he shrugged his shoulders and said, "This kid is fine." Not entirely true, but pretty close. I had goals in mind. I wanted to write and direct movies. I wanted to act. Hell, I wanted to be president of the United States. There was no way I was going to allow myself to be assigned a label. Somehow I'd fight through all the ideas in my head and find a way to harness the motor that never stopped running.

And boy was it humming now, as I stood in the bookstore, shifting my weight nervously from one foot to the other, thinking about how I had to have a perfect British accent so that I could portray this famous character, known and apparently loved by millions of readers, yet completely foreign to me. I'd already called Christine and asked her to line up a dialect coach— fast!

And oh by the way, honey, make sure the fax machine has paper in it, because we're going to be getting an important correspondence from New Zealand, and another from the casting director, and I have to buy this book, and I don't know which one to get, and, and, and . . .

There was an urgency to it—not quite a sense of panic, but a real determined urgency, accompanied by an implied ticking clock and the feeling that I had to get a handle on what this whole thing was about. All of which provoked some uncomfortable yet familiar emotions. When we were kids, my little brother would wear certain clothes to school, and I would look at him in wonder and say, "What are you wearing *that* for?"

He'd just laugh. "Oh, you don't understand."

---

3. Please take the paranoia reference in the spirit it's intended: Funny, people, funny . . .

Sure enough, the next day, or the next week, everyone would be wearing what Mack wore. He was smart that way, savvy and cool about trends and fashion and style. Not me. I was the guy who was happy during my three years at Catholic school because we all wore uniforms and I didn't have to worry about what to wear; I was the guy who on "free dress day" would have a panic attack because he had no cool clothes and wouldn't have known they were cool even if he did have them. That was the feeling pouring over me as I looked at this cool, hip thing—the Tolkien section of Barnes & Noble—that I knew nothing about.

I flipped through the Howe book first. For some reason it just didn't trigger anything that normally draws me in. I felt bad about that years later, when I was in Paris and attended the opening of one of John's art shows, and saw firsthand the original artwork he'd created for those books. It was absolutely stunning. On that day in the bookstore, though, in my frenetic state, I didn't give John's illustrations the time and consideration they deserved, and so they didn't grab me.

But Alan Lee's did.

Alan, as most Tolkien fanatics know, is one of the most prolific and revered book illustrators in the world. Inspired by Tolkien, his fellow countryman, to devote the lion's share of his considerable talent to the realm of fantasy, Alan has become forever linked with the characters who inhabit Middle-earth. He also was awarded the Carnegie Medal for his illustrated edition of Homer's epic *The Iliad*, which implies a different sort of sensibility, one that is rooted in mythology as well as fantasy. Perhaps that's what struck me that day, when I picked up Alan's illustrated edition of *The Lord of the Rings*. It looked like mythic history, rather than fantasy—a book that had more in common with the Arthurian legend than it did with *Harry Potter*. I ran my fingers over the cover, leafed through the pages, pausing not to read but merely to admire the artwork, and I couldn't help but think, *Wow, these drawings are unbelievable. It looks and feels like real history.*

So I bought *The Lord of the Rings* illustrated by Alan Lee. Unfortunately, I didn't buy *The Hobbit*, which, in retrospect, was a mistake. If I'd been listening more closely to Nikki, I might have absorbed her reference to *The Hobbit* and understood the value of reading that as well. Reading it first, actually. But I didn't. Instead, I went home with Alan's three-volume set and read aloud with Christine the first 150 pages in about three hours, reading very quickly, not really understanding the story, but soaking up descriptions of the land and characters, and stopping to reread, or at least read more carefully, any time I saw the words "Sam" or "Samwise Gamgee," the character I hoped to portray. My goal was to absorb as much as I could, as fast as I could, to figure out how important Sam was to the larger story and the world in which he lived. And it seemed to me that he was indeed a pivotal character.

A few things resonated. For example, I liked that Sam was a gardener, and I liked the way he spoke. There was, it seemed, a rural, almost agrarian, pastoral sound to his speech. I thought that the simplicity of it, the idea that Sam was at peace with himself and the land he tilled, was so cool. Not that I understood what it meant. I had no idea yet that Sam's heroism and courage were rooted in his simple, noble approach to life. I knew only that Nikki and Victoria were excited about this project and this story, and I figured I'd better try to find out what it was that piqued their interest. So I didn't come to the character organically; I didn't really appreciate the value of Samwise from the beginning. I just knew that he was an important character, and that if I was playing him I had to present myself as an important actor, someone whose credibility and credentials—from starring in *Rudy* (whose titular character displays a courage that, in a way, mirrors Sam's) to putting myself through college, where presumably I had done a fair amount of reading (though obviously not quite enough). No problem there, really, since I considered myself to be a serious actor, recent setbacks notwithstanding. I was a legend in my own mind, if not in the minds of studio executives, and I knew that if *The Lord of the Rings* was an important project (and what trilogy isn't important, at least from a financial standpoint?), then I had to approach it with the proper combination of reverence and confidence.

What I understood from the moment I began reading the trilogy was its level of artistic achievement. It was clear from the first three paragraphs that the language employed by Tolkien was exceptional.

He was brilliant. The book was brilliant. This was not a dressed-up, fleshed-out comic book,[4] which is the way I had viewed most books in the fantasy realm or genre. It was literature, and I felt humbled and embarrassed that I had never read it and knew nothing about it. It was important, serious, world-class art, and the moment was now upon me to demonstrate that I was equal to the task of engaging the material in a serious way and bringing my talents to bear on a cinematic interpretation of Tolkien's work.

Understand, please, that this is not the response typical of an actor being introduced to a project. What usually happens if you're offered a role in a movie is this: you sit down with the script, or with the book or magazine article on which the script is based, and with sweaty palms sticking to the paper, you begin to read. In those first few paragraphs or pages, the thought running through your mind is: *Oh, God, please don't let it suck. Let it be something I can sink my teeth into.* You want more than anything to be working, to be earning a living, but you also want to have an opportunity to work on something you feel really good about, because that makes the process enjoyable, fulfilling. Acting is hard. Not hard in the way that firefighting or law enforcement is hard. But it is hard. Even on the best of days it's emotionally exhausting. There's a stunning openness to it, a vulnerability that comes with stripping your soul bare in front of a group of strangers (and that's what actors are in the first days of a movie production) in the hope that your combined efforts will result in work that will be sufficiently interesting to another, much larger group of strangers—the moviegoing public—a few months down the road. But it all begins with the written word. If the source material fails to hold your interest, well, you know it'll be a long, uphill climb. Therefore, *Please don't suck* becomes the mantra in your head.

Sadly, the undeniable truth is that much of what gets produced does, in fact, suck; there are so few scripts of quality, and so many that are merely retreads. In the years leading up to *The Lord of the Rings* I reached a point in the auditioning cycle where I lost faith, where it

---

4. Not that I have anything against comic books. In fact, one of my goals now is to work on a film actually based on a comic book.

simply wasn't fun anymore. I had starred in enough movies, and had done enough television pilots that didn't go. I hated the feeling of auditioning cold for parts that I really didn't want, in projects of modest to little merit. And yet, like my mother before me, I wasn't at a place where I felt particularly confident about being selective, saying to my agents, "No, I don't want to do that." Like anyone else, I had to earn a living. Moreover, I wanted to have the freedom to flex my entrepreneurial muscles on occasion, and that was an exercise regimen requiring substantial capital. As a result, when it came time to audition for a given director, especially first-time filmmakers or people who hadn't done well in their previous endeavors (and that happened a lot), I had difficulty mustering the requisite enthusiasm. I preferred going to meetings, pitching projects, because I do those things pretty well. In general, my auditioning skills had dulled considerably, although my level of self-confidence and interest ebbed and flowed according to a variety of factors: whether I was physically fit, working out, eating right, and feeling good about the project at hand. If I was in shape and excited about a particular project, I'd get a little of the swagger back and be happy to go into a room and put on a show, just as I had so many times when I was younger.

As a kid, I loved auditioning. The idea of competing was exciting. I was cocky and confident and enjoyed the process. I wanted to go in and prove to myself, and anyone else who happened to be around, exactly what I could do. A long time ago I did a Disney TV movie called *Brat Patrol*, about a bunch of rabble-rousing kids who live on military bases and have a lot of fun by riding around on their skateboards, crashing the officers club, having water-balloon fights, and generally driving the stiff-shirted adults crazy. Formulaic stuff. The character I played was described in the teleplay as a tan, brash, skatepunk kind of kid, about fourteen or fifteen years old. Before auditioning I made a decision that the way to get the part was to *become* that kid, so I put on the appropriate clothes, adopted the appropriate attitude. I walked into a room filled with studio executives, sat down, threw my feet up on the desk, and acted real cocky. As soon as I walked out after the audition, I had a nervous feeling in my stomach, like when you almost get into a fight, but you avoid it at the last second. My knees were shaking, and my body was bathed in sweat.

Oh, boy, if they didn't buy that act, I'm in big trouble. They might really think I'm a jerk.

It wasn't the most professional approach, and it wasn't something I ever tried again. But I wanted to blur the line for them; I wanted them to wonder whether they were hiring the actor or the character. Not that they didn't know who I was. I had already starred in *The Goonies*, which had made $100 million, when I was twelve, so in that world, the Disney Sunday-night world, I was a reasonably well-known commodity; I had some cache, and while I didn't understand it completely, I was unquestionably emboldened by that knowledge.

The Method approach of auditioning (in which the actor disappears into the character) is not the sole province of desperate, unknown actors. There are A-list performers today who are more than willing to act the part in order to get the part. And there always have been. A few years ago Dan Petrie Jr. shared with me an interesting story that illustrates this point. Dan's father, Dan Petrie Sr., was a very successful director whose credits included *A Raisin in the Sun*. According to Dan Jr., Mr. Petrie told the story of a visit to the home of Gregory Peck, at a time when Peck was one of Hollywood's greatest and more bankable actors. The director was casting a movie that featured a character who was a rather rustic, gardener type, a man who liked to have his hands in the soil. Petrie was interested in hiring Peck, but wasn't sure whether the actor was serious about getting involved—until he went to Peck's mansion. A butler answered the door and invited Petrie into the foyer, where he waited for several minutes. Finally, Gregory Peck walked into the room, sunburned and wiping sweat from his brow. He removed a glove and extended his hand.

"Sorry," he said. "I was out in the garden."

Interpret that any way you like, but to me it's fairly obvious. I mean, we're talking about one of the biggest stars in the history of Hollywood, a man revered not only as a performer, but as a consummate professional. He knew he had an appointment with Dan Petrie Sr. He knew the subject of that meeting and the time it was supposed to begin. His intent, subtle as it may have been, was to make an impression, to demonstrate that he was right for the part. And perhaps to provoke a reaction from the director.

It had been a while since I'd been willing to take a chance like that. Truth be told, it had been a while since I'd felt even a ripple of enthusiasm over an audition. Nausea was a more common response. *The Lord of the Rings* was different. In this case, I felt nothing but excitement. The fact that there was so much history with my father and Peter and Fran, and with Victoria Burrows—well, it just felt safe. I had no problem with the process of preparation, of diving into the book and hiring a dialect coach, and working on Sam's Cockney accent. I must admit, however, that I did not read the entire book at that time. I stopped when the fax arrived: it consisted of four or five pages about the language of Tolkien, and a handful of speeches by and about Sam, including one from the first movie in which Gandalf yanks an eavesdropping Sam through a window, and another from the third film in which Sam laments the apparent death of Frodo after his epic battle with Shelob, the giant spider. ("Please don't leave me here alone. Don't go where I cannot follow.") As I read that language my heart swelled with hope, and I fell in love with the character.

This is poetry. This is . . . beautiful.

The dialect coach came to our house that night, and we put in a good long session together. I wanted to play Sam, not only because it was a substantial part in a substantial movie, but also because I thought there was strength and dignity in the role. Rather than being too daring or experimental, we settled on a rather standard Cockney accent, a reasonable choice given the character's rural heritage. I wanted the accent to be real, more like a working-class Michael Caine than a broad style like that of Mary Poppins, so I dialed it back just a bit, curled the vowels a little less obviously, and tried to soften the pitch of my voice. The effect was my own personal brand of Cockney, and within a few hours I felt reasonably confident that I had begun the process of inhabiting the role. Like Rudy, Samwise Gamgee is indeed a working-class hero, a distinction that holds tremendous appeal to me. You may think this sounds odd, coming from someone perceived as having been raised in the bubble of celebrity, but I always felt as though our family had its collective heart in the right place in matters of class and social justice. We weren't blue-collar people, but we were progressive and liberal, and our sympathies and sensibilities rested earnestly with those who knew what it was like to really work for a living. I like to think that my father was basically a hippie. My mother was president of the Screen Actors Guild; matters of business were routinely presented to us with a particular slant: us versus them. "Us" was the rank and file, and "them" the suits in the front office. As much as I wanted to be a Hollywood mogul, maybe even the head of a studio, in my family you couldn't help but absorb into the fabric of your skin a kind of passion for working-class people. I married a girl whose father was a firefighter and operated a crane. Normal, good-hearted, hard-working people. I relished that kind of normalcy, and I recognized it at once in the character of Sam.

At the same time, because I'd been reading so much, I admired the quality of Tolkien's writing, and felt it was an elegant, emblematic vision of working people. One of my favorite books in college was *Candide,* the last line of which, when translated roughly to English, is, "Cultivate your own garden." There's something sacred about having your hands in the soil, planting seeds and growing food that can sustain you. So what the hobbits represented, what Samwise represented within the context of the hobbit world, just felt right. It was to me a no-brainer. I was meant for the role. It helped, too, that right from the beginning I enjoyed the process of preparing for it. I'd lived in London for a while, so I had no problem popping into a British accent. By the end of the night, I found myself not just excited about the audition, but ready, too. And I hadn't felt that way in a long, long time.

The next day I talked by phone with a friend named Dan Lyons, who had been a technical adviser on *Kimberly,* starring Gabrielle Anwar. We'd filmed for six weeks in Philadelphia, and had a wonderful time living in a great apartment and shooting on Boathouse Row. Dan and I developed a strong connection. A graduate of the U.S. Naval Academy, he had rowed for one of the best crews in the school's history, a team that won the equivalent of the national championship by beating Harvard, Yale, and all those other traditional powerhouses. Dan is a smart, successful man who moves easily among the East

Coast cultural and social elite, yet somehow remains eminently approachable and pleasant in virtually all interactions. In short, he's a good and decent man, and we've maintained the friendship forged while working on *Kimberly*. When I called Dan from my office and told him I was auditioning for the part of Sam in *The Lord of the Rings* trilogy, he practically flipped out.

"Oh, man, I've read that book every year since high school!" he shouted. "I cry in the same spots every time. You're perfect for that role."

This to me was not a hollow endorsement. Dan probably has a couple of postgraduate degrees and is married to a woman who is some kind of rocket scientist for the navy. He's one of the smartest people I know. And here he was freaking out, yelling into the phone.

"This was meant to be, Sean! It's perfect."

The fact that this man, whom I had placed on a pedestal and tried to emulate, a guy full of integrity and good feelings—well, for him to react in this way really increased my appreciation for the power of the franchise. I knew *The Lord of the Rings* was a big project, but suddenly it seemed even bigger. Dan was more excited than I was. Oh, I was diligently doing what I needed to do, but his reaction was just frenzied. I was focusing on getting the job; he was thrilled with the whole concept. He understood the magnitude of it in a way that I did not and could not.

What I also got from Dan was a kind of profound confidence that I was right for the part. I was having trouble with the notion that Frodo and Sam, in the book, are fifty-five years old. Granted, they live to be more than a hundred, so they're still somewhat youthful, but the fact remains that I was, physically, not quite what the role called for. I was only twenty-eight at the time. None of this bothered Dan in the least. That he knew me so well and knew the book so well, and felt we made a good match, helped erase any doubt that lingered in my mind. His endorsement, combined with Victoria Burrows's involvement, my father's history with Peter Jackson, and my own connection with the character made it feel as though the stars were lining up.

I dressed casually for the audition, just jeans and a T-shirt. No costume, no makeup. I worked "off-book" (without a script) because,

helped as usual by my wife, I had memorized the scene completely—
not a difficult task when the material is compelling and you really
want the job. The only people in the room were myself, Victoria, and
an assistant whose chief function was to videotape the audition for
Peter. Ideally, an audition involves a second performer, someone with
whom you can share the task of bringing a scene to life. Often, as in
this case, you simply work with the casting director, which is more
difficult simply because you're not getting as much as you're giving.
Acting, even when it's just an audition, is a collaborative endeavor. It's
much easier to sink into a character when you're acting on the set, with
cameras rolling—or better yet, onstage, in front of an audience—
when you're with other people who are similarly invested. On this
occasion, though, it didn't seem to matter, for I absolutely nailed the
audition. Victoria deserves a good bit of the credit for that. She handled the process extraordinarily well, making me feel like I wasn't just
another guy on the long list of actors hoping to portray Samwise
Gamgee, even though I knew that Peter was indeed looking at a lot of
different candidates, from all over the world.

Even before the audition, I got the distinct impression that I had
a legitimate shot, and that they—specifically Victoria—wanted me
to do my best. How can I say that? Well, it's an intuitive thing; if
you've been through the audition meat grinder enough times, you
begin to sense whether you're being taken seriously or not. Often
the atmosphere that permeates an audition is one of exhaustion and
annoyance: *We've been through hell to get this movie off the ground; now we'll sit
back and wait for the perfect guy to walk in. Then we'll get excited.* You don't
usually get the feeling that the casting director really wants you to
do your best.

With some casting directors, it's such a callous kind of transaction;
they're trafficking in human flesh. They have filing cabinets filled with
résumés and perfectly airbrushed photographs, but they develop a
rapport with certain actors, and those are the ones who get the jobs.
The good casting directors genuinely care about the people they're
calling in. They get offended when you're late or don't take the audition seriously. There's always a Cinderella element to it: *Here he (or she)
is—the perfect fit!* To a degree, my motivation was no different. I had to

audition, I had to prove I was right for the part, I had to work for it and want it bad. But within that context, it was a safe, nurturing environment, one that discouraged the little voice that sometimes pulls an actor out of focus. That voice, the voice of doubt and fear and insecurity, did not win the day; instead, I sailed through the audition. I knew I had met the challenge. It's like when a singer has the opportunity to interpret great material, or when a race-car driver gets behind the wheel of a perfectly tuned automobile. Something happens when you are resonating correctly with good drama. You feel it in your stomach, in your heart, and it's visible to everyone in the room.

Moreover, Victoria projected an attitude that reflected a certain kinship or camaraderie. I felt as though she wanted me to have this job. Now, the truth is, I'll bet she made a lot of actors feel that way, because that's her job; that's how she gets the best possible audition out of every candidate. But she was so good at it that I really believed she wanted me. I think she was doing her job to make sure the director had a good selection from which to choose, but I also felt like she had a special something inside of her that wanted me to have the job. She was simply too nice to me the night of *The Frighteners* premiere, and I knew from my agent that much of the excitement about my potential involvement stemmed from Victoria. As an actor, you get that feeling sometimes, that someone is really pulling for you. There's so much negative energy in the world, so many people who don't treat you that way, that when you do experience it, it's identifiable and palpable and genuinely inspiring. I could tell when I walked into the room that Victoria was happy to see me and wanted me to do well. Whether that means she wanted me to get the role, I don't really know. But she was a very positive, nurturing woman, and I don't doubt for a second that her attitude and outlook played a role in what turned out to be the best audition of my life.

"I'll send everything to Peter right away," Victoria said afterward. "Good luck. You did great."

I thanked her, gave her a hug, and walked out. Before I hit the parking lot, I was on the phone, calling everyone—Christine, my father, my manager, and my agent—to tell them I hadn't screwed the proverbial pooch. The audition had exceeded my wildest expectations. I had a legitimate chance to get this part.

And then I waited. And waited.

And waited.

Feedback, direct and indirect, came sporadically. I tried to put it out of my mind, because to fixate on it was to court madness. And yet, how could I think of anything else? This was not just another little independent film that would go straight to the art-house circuit or, worse, straight to video. This was *The Lord of the Rings*. This was a movie—three movies!—that would dramatically impact the career of anyone and everyone involved. It often takes time for a project to come together, especially one of this magnitude, but that knowledge was only moderately reassuring. I couldn't tell if the studio was simply taking its time or posturing so it could get me cheaper; after all, *The Lord of the Rings* was such a big epic adventure that you just knew the studio was trying to get everybody to work for less money so it could afford to make the damn movie.

At one point Nikki heard through the grapevine that Peter Jackson was seriously interested in someone else for the role of Sam—a British actor who tended to be more naturally stout than I was. In an attempt to refute the wrongheaded notion that I wasn't capable of "playing fat," my father and I spliced together some footage from a few of my earlier movies, including numerous scenes that, under different circumstances, might have caused me considerable embarrassment, so obvious was it that I'd let the health-club membership lapse. Accompanying this montage was a deeply sincere letter to Peter, thanking him for the opportunity of a lifetime. I closed the letter by saying, "I know this is going to be a great adventure. Whether I'm along for the ride or not, I wish the best for you." That probably sounds a bit desperate, if not downright unctuous, but I was willing to do or say almost anything to get the job. Besides, I meant it. It *was* going to be a great adventure, and I *did* wish Peter nothing but the best. But I also knew how I would feel when the movie came out if I wasn't part of it. At different times Peter has said that he remembers that note, and that it was meaningful to him. At other times he's said,

"You wrote me a letter, Sean?" Where the truth lies, I really don't know. I don't even know if he ever saw the tape, either. I only know that I sent it, and that I hoped it would have meaning.

After the audition I went back to what would, for most of our time in New Zealand, affectionately be called the "bible," the three-volume set of *The Lord of the Rings*. I remember picking up the book one night to read to Christine, starting where I'd left off at page 150, and continuing to page 166. And then stopping. Cold. A week later I picked it up again. And stopped again. Three or four times I did that, started reading with the best of intentions, only to give up after ten or twenty pages. Why? I couldn't concentrate on the story, couldn't enjoy it, and the reason was simple: I was afraid I wasn't going to get the part, and that possibility was paralyzing. To read the trilogy and fall in love with it and then not get the part—that would have been too painful. So, time after time, I respectfully closed the book and placed it on the nightstand next to my bed.

Don't worry, I'll be back. Soon as I get the part.

A second audition followed a couple of months later. Same office, higher stakes, for this time I was auditioning for Peter Jackson himself. Fran Walsh was there, too, and I have to say that they seemed almost as supportive and nurturing as Victoria had been. It was amazing, seeing these people who had been so nice to me years earlier, and who seemed so familiar because of all the stories I'd heard from my dad. After I walked into the room, we embraced, shared a few stories about my father, and then we went to work. But the wall—that barrier between actor and director, between employer and prospective employee—never really went up. It was like we were already part of the same team.

That day Peter talked about Tolkien's service in World War I, and how important it had been to him. It was clear that Peter was a student of the war, and that he understood how Tolkien's wartime experiences shaped both his artistic sensibilities and his worldview. Peter also told me that he considered the relationship between the characters of Frodo and Sam to be the central relationship in the books, and that making the relationship believable and viable on film was crucial to achieving his vision for the movie. It was, he said, a specifically English relationship, not just a mythological thing that happened in the space of your mind. It was based on a kind of history. That was exactly what I wanted to hear, supporting as it did everything I believed and suspected about the character of Sam: his inherent nobility and loyalty and courage.

Hearing it wasn't enough, though. The point of the talk, and the subsequent exercise, was to give me a chance to demonstrate to Peter and Fran that I truly understood the character. To that end, I fought my natural tendency to claim at least fifty percent of the words in any given conversation. I'm a chatterbox by nature. Always have been. Here, though, protocol and common sense dictated that I take a different approach: *Shut up, listen, absorb, and give back what he wants.* I was given an opportunity to offer my take on the subject: *Who is Sam?* As I rambled on, though, I noticed Peter nodding, and it became apparent that he was constructing something in his head, quietly multitasking, as it were, and I took that as a cue to wrap up my biographical synopsis. But he was doing his best not to let me know that he was starting to drift away.

Later I would learn that Peter is an unusually adept and versatile leader: he has a quiet, intellectual mode, but he can turn up the volume when the situation calls for it. He is most assuredly not a screamer or tyrant; in fact, he is a perfect example of how a director can accomplish great things and motivate a veritable army of foot soldiers without resorting to hysterical, petulant behavior. Neither is he naturally a showman, except to the extent that he has to be one to accomplish whatever task it is that needs to be accomplished. For example, one of the untold stories, one of the great achievements of *The Lord of the Rings*, is that Peter actually directed six or seven other directors. Because we were all over the place, with different units in different locales, he was compelled to cede control to others. He'd essentially have to say to John Mahaffey, the second unit director, "You need to film the sequence; I trust you." Then Peter would watch the dailies and make comments. The hard part for those directors was to try to capture Peter's vision. One of the most memorable sequences in the trilogy, the battle of Helm's Deep in *The Two Towers*, involved ten or eleven weeks of night shooting. (I don't mean evening; I mean *night*, as in, "Show up when it gets dark; go home when the sun comes up.") Peter wasn't there for most of the Helm's Deep shooting. He was with us, the hobbits, during the day, doing myriad other things. That was the nature of his job, to serve as general manager of the project. He directed, to be sure, day in and day out, scene after scene. But he also *directed*, in a macro sense, taking complete charge of a project that required him to be all things to all people, and to never show the strain of the effort. Not often, anyway.

Peter's capability as a director, as someone who can inspire actors as well as martial every technological device at his disposal, is easily illustrated. Take, for example a sleepy Saturday morning in New Zealand, when we all showed up to rehearse what would become one of the most memorable scenes in the trilogy: the nine members of the Fellowship battling against a giant cave troll. On film, the scene is a wonder, a visceral thrill ride that demonstrates the power of computer-generated imagery and world-class sound design—when applied by the right hands. In rehearsal, though, it was a tour de force for Peter Jackson, who endeavored to ensure that everyone in attendance—actors, stunt doubles, cinematographers, assistant directors, and the second unit directors—understood what he wanted to see on the screen. Peter had an idea of how the scene would be played out, and the best way to convey that idea was to perform the scene himself. Every word, every movement, every role. Every thrust of a sword, every grunt and growl and howl. The way he assumed the visage of each character—in front of an awestruck crowd of roughly sixty people—was nothing short of remarkable. Aragorn, the hobbits, the cave troll—he played them all. Flawlessly. He choreographed the fight sequence, and by watching him, we all got it. Then, for the next week, we filmed the scene, each of us giving Peter what he wanted; interpreting it in our own way, too, of course, but essentially following his lead.

If we had merely looked at the storyboards or discussed the choreography over dinner, it wouldn't have been the same. By acting it out, by throwing himself completely into the process, Peter got us to understand what he needed, and the tone that he had in his performance was exactly what was captured in the final film: that feeling of adventure reminiscent of *Raiders of the Lost Ark*, a feeling and scene that were central to the movie, capturing as it does the bonding of the Fellowship. It is one of the most thrilling sequences in the movies, and it wouldn't have happened if Peter hadn't been willing to risk embarrassment and let his imagination run wild.

Not that I knew any of this when I auditioned. I had no context at the time, only a proper degree of reverence based on my limited personal experience and the tales my father had shared. For some reason, though, I wasn't terribly anxious. Just as Victoria had done, Peter and Fran created an atmosphere practically devoid of tension. They seemed to me almost like long-lost relatives, and I was filled with a sense of wanting to please them, a sense of excitement and anticipation, rather than the feeling of dread that is generally common during an audition. Not that I wasn't nervous; I was. But once again, I thought I performed well—really well. Afterward, Peter and Fran paid me nice compliments and said they'd be in touch. We shook hands and I left. Then Christine and I drove right around the corner to a coffee shop, where my father and my stepmother, Val, were waiting for us.

Dad took one look at me and smiled.

"You did it, didn't you? You got the job."

I took a deep breath. "I don't know. I mean, I think I nailed it, and they were really nice to me. But . . ."

"What?"

"I'm just not sure. Peter is so hard to read."

That was the truth. I would come to discover through my long months in New Zealand that being hard to read is a trademark of Peter Jackson's, a signature of his unflappable managerial style. It's not that he's joyless. He just never gets too high or too low. Or at least that is the image he projects and cultivates, never letting anyone see him as anything other than a rather rumpled, bearded, unkempt fellow in baggy shorts and sandals (or bare feet) seemingly floating through life—despite carrying an enormous weight on his shoulders. I remember being exhilarated as I walked out of the audition, but not quite sure what to think. I knew that an answer would not come right away, so I had to keep busy with the business of life: spending time with my family, trying to be a good husband and father, and working.

Among the job opportunities I explored was a relationship with Four Square Productions, a San Diego communications and production company. Four Square had been responsible for, among other things, the 1978 sci-fi/horror parody, kitsch classic, and cult hit *Attack of the Killer Tomatoes*, as well as its 1990s-era sequels (*Return of the Killer Tomatoes*, *Killer Tomatoes Strike Back*, and *Killer Tomatoes Eat France*). My father played the mad scientist Dr. Gangreen in the sequels, and for some time he'd been promoting the company to me. It was, he said, populated by good, smart people who knew how to get movies made and distributed, and make money in the process. That summer, with time to kill and nothing heavy on my plate, I decided to take Dad's advice and drive down to San Diego with my family. A tour of the production facility revealed a company that seemed to be every bit as viable as my father had indicated, and I wondered if there might be some way to form a strategic alliance that would benefit Lava Entertainment. But I wasn't really as focused as I might have been, for even as I engaged in meetings with the company's executives, I kept thinking about *The Lord of the Rings*.

Oddly enough, the good news arrived while I was sitting in the office of Michael Bayer, Four Square's vice president. It was my agent, Nikki, on the cell phone, saying the producers at New Line had called. They wanted quotes.

This was important. "Quotes" refers to an actor's salary history. A studio asks for quotes only when it's serious about making an offer. Nikki said she'd get back to me when she had more information.

When I hung up the phone, I turned to face Michael and Christine. "What's up?" he asked.

"I think I'm about to get offered an amazing job," I replied. "I'm gonna get to play Sam in *The Lord of the Rings*."

Unfazed by the unraveling of yet another potential Hollywood marriage, Michael merely laughed. "I'll remember you were here when it happened," he said, reaching out to pat me on the back.

"It hasn't happened," I corrected him. "Not yet."

Two weeks later, just as I was leaving my office late in the afternoon, Christine and Jeff Owens, my assistant, told me my agents were on the phone.

My mind had not been on work that day. Christine and I had gone forward with plans to purchase our dream house, and we had closed escrow that very morning. Scrawling my signature on the contract, I felt a maelstrom of conflicting emotions brewing in my stomach, everything from joy to dread. Like anyone who buys a new home, I was thinking about it a lot. Of course, Christine is an amazing work-horse, so she shouldered much of the burden. For her, every day was filled with the minutiae of real estate transactions: phone calls to lawyers, brokers, and bankers; estimates from moving companies; packing, unpacking, shedding the detritus of a life in transition. As the closing date grew near, fretting about whether I'd be able to earn enough money to support our new home and lifestyle became not just an occasional emotional indulgence, but a perpetual state of being. I was constantly trying to figure out which deals were about to close, and which ones were likely to fall through; whether it made more sense to try to build our company or just take the first acting gig that came along. What I felt, more than anything else, was pressure. Intense pressure.

And now, here was a phone call that held the promise of something great. Christine stood next to me as we waited for the news.

Remember I said earlier that it's always nice when an agent calls? Well, when two agents call, it's never bad news. Two agents call because they want to celebrate with you. Nikki Mirisch was my feature-film agent, the point person in my movie career. Mark Schwartz had handled my television work. Now they were on the line together, scream-ing, each trying to outshout the other.

"You got it, Sean! You got the job."

That was the good news—the *great* news, actually. But there was at least a small piece of bad news, although it wasn't presented to me as such. You see, while New Line understood the necessity of spending great gobs of money on what would prove to be groundbreaking visual effects and a landmark cinematic achievement, they did not necessarily see the logic in splurging on actors' salaries. My fee, I was told, would be $250,000.

All right, I can live with that. Three movies . . . that's $750,000. I'm covered for the next three years.

"Uh, Sean?"

"Yeah."

"The offer is $250,000—total."

I was shocked. A total of $250,000 for three films and up to two years of uninterrupted work, during which time I'd be unable to accept any other offers. And it would be several months before I'd receive a penny.

Oh, no, I just bought a new house, and now I'm going to take a cut in salary?

I didn't whine for long, in part because Mark and Nikki wouldn't allow it. We all agreed that compensation notwithstanding, this was the opportunity of a lifetime. When I got off the phone, I literally fell to my knees and cried, and began to say a prayer of thanks. Then I looked at Christine and Jeff, who were smiling and obviously happy for me. I thought, *Life is going to change, man. These offices aren't going to be here, and Jeff . . . you're not going to be working for me. Everything will be different.*

I remember once seeing videotape of a woman collapsing to the ground as she approached the end of a marathon and then, flopping and flailing like a wounded animal, crawling across the finish line as the crowd stood and cheered. She was at once an object of pity and admiration, a profile in desperation and courage. That's the way I felt. As a man, as a father, as someone who was trying to survive in a career, and as someone who was trying to pretend that he had more influence than he really did. I had begun to question my own strength and determination and talent. I wondered if failure was suddenly an option.

But no more. With a single call, everything had changed. There was no question that *The Lord of the Rings* was going to be one of the greatest experiences of my life. I don't think, however, that I really understood what that meant; how could I? Sure, I knew it would be an epic adventure in New Zealand, with Peter Jackson and an incredible franchise, with its millions of fans; because of those things, I knew it was going to be big. Whatever else it might be, it was certainly going to be big. There was, however, no frame of reference, no way to anticipate what the experience was going to be like. For me, it was more about thinking, *Thank God, I'm going to be able to feed my wife and daughter; they'll be proud of me.*

They'd also get to share in the adventure, which was a bonus. One of the things Peter had sought to ascertain during the audition was my attitude toward what could euphemistically be termed "location work."

"You know, we're filming this whole thing in New Zealand," he had said. "And it's going to take some time. Probably a year and a half. Is that a problem?"

Peter and the producers were very clever about doling out information and getting information. They wanted to know how each participant felt about working on such an unusual project. For Peter, a part of the selection process boiled down to a simple question: *Are we going to be able to live with this person? Is he going to be able to come into our family and survive and not make everybody miserable?* It was an important consideration, and one that was obviously addressed with great care, because there was so much cohesion on the set. Not that there weren't problems. As in any "family," tempers occasionally flared and personalities bumped up against each other and created friction. In the end, though, respect and love (for each other and the film) triumphed over greed and egotism, and that's a rare accomplishment in any movie, let alone the most ambitious movie in history. When Peter revealed the timetable, I didn't blink.

"You won't have to ask twice," I said. "It's not an issue for me."

That would prove to be a naive response, but it seemed reasonable at the time. I'd been to New Zealand and had worked on *White Water Summer* with some of the people Peter knew. In fact, on the day I arrived in New Zealand for *The Lord of the Rings*, I ran into a guy at Peter's house who looked somewhat familiar. I couldn't place him at first, but he ambled right up to me, gave me a pat on the back, and said, "Hey, Sean, how you doin'?" After talking for a few minutes, I realized who he was: a buddy of Peter's—a fellow Kiwi, of course—named Dan Hannah. Dan was a member of the set crew on *White Water Summer.* He'd built a suspension bridge from which I was supposed to take a fall. I hadn't seen him in a dozen years, and now here he was, at Peter's house, returning a pile of videos he'd borrowed. So before I even landed the role, I felt comfortable with the notion of working and living in New Zealand for eighteen months. In a sense, I felt like I'd already been to Rivendell and Hobbiton.

I reviewed the offer with Christine. Predictably, since she's one who appreciates a good adventure, she just smiled and said, "Let's do it. It'll be a great experience for the whole family."

In some ways, Christine was more excited than I was about the prospect of moving to New Zealand. We'd experienced some serious losses in the previous few years. Christine's father, who suffered from manic depression, had taken his own life; a friend had been murdered. But my wife is sort of a Ramblin' Rose: when things happen in her life, she allows herself to adjust and to move on. She grieves and she cries, but she retains her faith and her belief in the inherent goodness of people. I'm a compulsive worrier; Christine is an unbridled optimist. She's a pretty amazing woman in that way. She saw going to New Zealand as an incredible opportunity and instinctively knew that it would be something wonderful for all of us.

There wasn't even that much discussion about it. I think Christine felt that this job offer represented a logical progression in my career. During the low moments of my life, I've often looked to Christine for confirmation of my pessimism, for support of the notion that *this is bad and it's going to get worse and why don't I just get the hell out of this business?* But it never happens. In marriage, I think, the unspoken can be as powerful as the spoken. I felt strength and approval from Christine. I had explained to her what I wanted to accomplish with my life and career, and she had believed in me. Now, with the offer to play Sam on the table, she would have to do an even better job of convincing me that she still believed in me. And she didn't have to work that hard. Christine's worries tend to lean more toward the philosophical and spiritual: *Am I appreciating it?* That's a sentiment she uses a lot.

"It's going to be over so fast, Sean," she'll say. "Try to enjoy it."

Christine sees time racing by and wants to absorb it, to slow it down and figure it out, and make sure she isn't missing anything. So when I run around like a chicken with my head cut off, she just sits there quietly, smiling, saying, "You know, hon, we're going to be in rocking chairs before we know it." She knew before I did that this job and this adventure would be one of those life-altering experiences, and on the other side of it we'd both end up better. During the deal, as I fretted about money and time and commitment, Christine was bemused.

"Do you have any concept of what you're talking about?" she asked. "Do you have any idea of the magnitude of this project, as compared to the stuff you're bickering over?"

"Uhhhhh . . ."

"Well, do you? You moron."

I did, of course, somewhere deep in my bones. But I needed to be reminded. I needed Christine as a barometer.

That said, it wasn't until three or four months down under that I realized what I had committed to. There was no possible way to know just how demanding and consuming a job it would be. I was also looking at it like this: *My daughter is two, and she'll be four or five when this is all through, and seven when the last movie comes out.* I didn't understand the sheer, groundbreaking enormity of it, and how that would affect all of us on a day-to-day basis. Even the way my agents explained the negotiations—"You'll be paid for each film, but it's all one job"— provoked a certain blind response. I was looking at it as one film. I said, "What's the total compensation?" I didn't understand the signif-icance of the individual films. In my mind, I just blocked off a chunk of time—a year and a half—without giving too much consideration to the layers of nuance involved with the nature of time as it was going to relate to my experience on the pictures.

My attorney, Dave Feldman, was working hard to get me a favor-able deal, but I sensed that the "times" on the contract would bear lit-tle resemblance to what we actually did. I think it's fair to say that the project was like a supernova blighting many of the finer points in the deal as it pertained to actual time worked. The assumption was, "Lis-ten, they're not gonna kill you; they need you!" Still, a contract was necessary, and very smart people worked hard to make the legal lan-guage match the reality we were going to experience. What I'm talking about here is the way the contract was structured to allow for the pro-duction's *ownership* of my time. On some level I expected to go down to New Zealand and give myself over to Peter. One of my more endearing qualities (I make people crazy!) is that somehow I used to believe that I could give myself *completely* over to a project, while retaining an inordinate amount of faith that I could do fifty other things simultaneously. When most people would relax or take up a hobby or rededicate themselves to a given assignment, I'm usually just getting warmed up. My mom used to tell me, "Sean, you can't do it all. You can't have everything all at once!" I love my mom and she may be right, but I've yet to be totally convinced.

Anyway, at the time I was in negotiations with New Line to play Sam, the agents and lawyers were working hard to interpret the contract, especially as it related to time commitments, because essentially we were making a deal ahead of time, and nothing like this had ever been done before. *The Lord of the Rings* was conceived as a trilogy from a marketing standpoint, but it's really one movie sliced into three movies. New Line figured out how to make it beneficial to them all the way through, and thank God they did, because if they hadn't, we couldn't have gotten the movie made. The studio deserves credit, and so do the actors and the directors and the writers and the crew and . . . everyone.

It's my guess that virtually everyone accepted less money upfront than they had earned before, or less than they could have if they had chosen to work on something else. In some way, we all understood that this was an opportunity to do something special. There was a feeling of frustration and exhaustion that permeated the entire project, and yet no one would admit to it, in part because of job security and in part because we realized the sacrifices were worth it. In low moments, when I was worried or frustrated about money, because of the house or other factors beyond my control, because my body was bloated and I was tired and homesick or just plain sick—in those moments, the money issue was a problem for me. Yes, I had entered into the contract with my eyes open. Nevertheless, I was at times bothered by what I considered to be an unfair deal. The work was exhausting and endless, and the financial reward insufficient. I didn't blame this on the studio or on Peter Jackson. I blamed it on the circumstances, and sometimes I blamed it on myself.

I like to think that I'm a professional, that I'm on time, that I give my bosses what they want. I can do foot soldier as well as anyone. I am not a prima donna. But I do remember a couple of times this feeling washing over me, a kind of panic or claustrophobia, and thinking, *What if my body won't do this?* My consciousness hadn't approached thinking about calling in sick or asking for more sleep. That's the purview of rock stars, not actors. And certainly not actors at my level. In the beginning I had made a promise: *I'm going to give myself over to this process and trust that these are good, decent people and that their artistry is so worthy of sacrifice that I'll come out of it on the other end saying, "Look what I've accomplished!"*

But there were times along the way when doubt seeped in and I thought, *If I don't set some limits here, I'm going to die.*

That *The Lord of the Rings* was going to be a nonunion production was one of my primary concerns. Not so much from a physical standpoint, but definitely from a philosophical standpoint. My mother, president of the Screen Actors Guild, was obviously a staunch union supporter, and I held close to my heart aspirations of one day following in her footsteps. I tried to imagine how I'd be able to look at my fellow union members and have any credibility if I had a reputation for cutting and running whenever there was a better opportunity. While I wouldn't call myself a socialist, I think it's fair to say that in matters of politics, I'm left of center. But what I developed throughout this experience was a vantage point from which to view all the different perspectives. I could understand from the studio executives' perspective how they put their deals together, and what was important to them, and why this movie could only be made in this way at this time. I could understand exactly how they were taking advantage of people, and when and why. I mean that in both a positive and negative way: they took advantage of resources available to them to create the best possible work of art, but they also "took advantage" in the more cynical sense, by taking advantage of people who were unsuspecting and unwary and grateful to have a job. The cold hard truth, however, is that Hollywood couldn't have made this movie. Working within the traditional system, *The Lord of the Rings* would have taken ten years and cost a billion dollars. It just wouldn't have worked. Most of the time in Hollywood, everyone looks out for themselves. On this project, just about everyone, to some extent, sublimated their own immediate self-interests to be part of the process and to get the work done.

Ultimately, I made a personal decision that involved a certain degree of compromise. This was a world-class opportunity, and the evaluation—okay, the rationalization—I made was, *If I hold the line here and say I won't work unless it's a project certified and endorsed by the Screen Actors Guild, they will absolutely hire the fat guy in England. Do I want to make a principled stand and be a martyr for a union that doesn't give a rat's ass about me and my career, or do I want to embrace this opportunity and endure whatever it means to work under a nonunion contract?*

I knew on a gut-check level that playing the role of Sam would be the hardest work of my life. I'd done some thirty movies, had grown up on sets, and had worked with a lot of terrific directors, some of them quite demanding. Even as a child and teenage actor I had understood the fundamental dynamics of the employer-employee relationship, so the unpleasant and sad reality that people will sometimes try to take advantage of you was not foreign to me. But I went along for the ride whenever it was necessary, which was most of the time. Brendan Fraser went off and did a ton of great work after *Encino Man*, and I remember playing video games with him at my house in the wake of that success. It seemed to me that he had a real callous attitude toward the production he was working on at the time, and I was trying to figure out why.

"Listen," I said, "even though there are rules about turnaround and set time, if you're there because you want to be there, what's the problem? Do you like the movie?"

He shrugged. "Sure, it's fine."

"Then what's the problem? Why not just give the director what he needs?"

But Brendan's attitude seemed pretty sour, and I remember thinking that the pendulum had swung to the other side, that he seemed a bit harsh and cocky. "They've got me for ten hours a day; that's enough."

I was honestly concerned for him, but I have to admit that my concern wasn't entirely benevolent. A part of me worried that Brendan was changing, not necessarily for the better. But another part of me was envious that I wasn't in the same situation. Studios weren't backing up to my front door with truckloads of cash; I didn't have the luxury of taking such an aggressive position on the set. Not that I would have, because it's inconsistent with who I am as an artist and a man. I think

I'm at my best when I'm working with a director who is passionate and driven. In that atmosphere, the hours slip away, and it doesn't really matter, because you're both trying to create something meaningful. There are limits, of course, as I would discover in New Zealand. It's complicated that those lines have to become blurred sometimes. On a union shoot, it's easy to be there and be fresh and give a thousand percent, because union guidelines govern how many hours you can work. But there are times—and *The Lord of the Rings* was a perfect example—when the guidelines become an almost insurmountable obstacle.

All of those things were running through my mind as I absorbed the reality of being a part of this project. Whether or not the film would be a "success," with all that term implies, did not enter my thinking. Wait, that's not quite true. It didn't *dominate* my thinking. After the initial shock and delirium wore off, which took at least a few days, I began to think about the more practical aspects of the job: it would swallow a year and a half of my life, and all the other projects I'd been developing through Lava Entertainment were now in limbo. I didn't want them just to stop, so we generated a postcard for all our current and potential business partners saying, "The volcano is going dormant for a year and a half. Then it will explode again!" I had thought—again, naively—that perhaps when I got to New Zealand, I'd be able to continue to develop projects. The world had become a much smaller place, right? I'd have cell phones, access to the Internet. Most important, I'd have plenty of downtime. Samwise Gamgee was an important character, but not the star of *The Lord of the Rings.* The "story" was the star. This was to be a true ensemble piece, and as such it was likely to provide plenty of opportunities for individual actors to pursue outside interests.

As it turned out, there were gaping holes in my strategy. First of all, I didn't have enough money to be a bi-hemisphere mogul. That became clear right away. Second, and most important of all, there was almost no free time. After the first thirty-six hours of boot camp, it was obvious that my life was not my own. I didn't think that my services would be required twelve hours a day, every day. I was wrong.

I was part of the Fellowship.

CHAPTER SEVEN

I still couldn't read the book.

I tried. Many times. Not having the job or fretting about not getting the job was no longer a valid excuse, so I came up with another one: *There's no time to focus on it.* This was true to the extent that in the month between getting the job and leaving for New Zealand, Christine and I had innumerable tasks to keep us busy.

Even though we were going to be out of the country for the next year and a half, we had made a decision to take up residence, however briefly, in our newly acquired home. That proved to be another major strategic mistake, for it needlessly complicated lives that were already complicated enough. We did this for reasons that were largely sentimental. First, we wanted to convince ourselves that everything would be fine, that I could pay for the house, take possession of it, and treat it like a home. And second, we wanted to teach our daughter, Alexandra, what we hoped would be a valuable lesson—that moving from house to house is a natural part of life, and not necessarily traumatic. We wanted her to see her new room, sleep in it, and feel comfortable there. Christine and I didn't have it in our hearts (or heads) to tell her, "We're going on an adventure, but you'll have your own room in New Zealand." We wanted Alexandra to feel like her real home was in the United States, in Los Angeles. That was probably not as important as we made it out to be, since she was only two years old at the time. But I wanted her to recognize her room when we came back, which I thought would happen far sooner than it did.

We'd been warned that the production would require us to be on location for eighteen months, with very few breaks, but I didn't really believe this. Although I had feigned belief in the warning, I honestly felt that things would work out differently, that at some point we'd all be furloughed for a month or six weeks, and in that time the whole family would return to L.A. and get reacquainted with our new house. The home I felt I deserved to be in, which, I know (and I knew it then), is such a ludicrous idea—it's amazing the power of the human mind, the way you can convince yourself that you are entitled to stuff.

It was a neat house. Situated in the Encino Hills, it had a long, private driveway and a serpentine wall and a courtyard with Spanish tile. It wasn't terribly big, but it was a really cool, interesting house, with white shutters on the doors and a sturdy granite-topped island in the kitchen. It felt like the kind of place an artist would live in, and I was proud to be one of its new owners. Sometimes we'd see deer nibbling outside the window, which in Los Angeles is not a common sight. It's easy for me to understand why people in Nepal or any great mountainous region like to live high in the hills. You wake up in the morning and look out over the vista, and you can't help but feel alive. Such a view can have an intoxicating effect. I'd go out in the morning and stand there like General Patton, looking out over the valley—*my valley*—where I had lived for eight years, and to the hills beyond. The mountain I was standing on was where I'd spent the first twenty years of my life, and I felt some silly kind of power that wasn't real at all but that somehow gave me a sense of security and value.

Had I only known that for eighteen months my dream house would become little more than an expensive and glorified kennel for our dog and a temporary residence for an assortment of house sitters (including my brother Tom, who helped defray some of the costs and gave a real sense of family to the house), I might have exhibited a bit more common sense.

The scripts landed with a *thud!* smacking the granite countertop like a bag of wet cement. It was the first time I had seen them, three great slabs of paper, each bound separately by large metal hoops, each fat enough to represent not just a single film, but a four-hour mini-series, hand-delivered by a studio emissary. This was a sacred moment, one I had anticipated with escalating enthusiasm, the grand unveiling of *the story*. Before the studio would agree to deliver the scripts, I, like all of the actors in the movie, was required to sign a confidentiality and nondisclosure agreement. In no uncertain terms, it stated that the material I was going to read, and the events I would witness while in New Zealand, were industry secrets and thus proprietary in nature.

On a superficial level this was not unusual. Scripts and story lines are the subject of intense secrecy in Hollywood. Warren Beatty wouldn't give a full script to anybody; he would only issue a few pages at a time, and then he'd pull them back and have them destroyed. Why? For reasons known only to him, although one can reasonably presume that it was so that no one would know what was happening in the story. We liked to joke that no one ever seemed to know what was going on with Warren, or what he had in mind with the screenplay, or even if there really was a screenplay. He had an assistant who always seemed to be at his side, and we wondered whether she was privy to information that no one else had—like what the hell the story was about—and if so, did she carry cyanide capsules to be taken in the event she was captured by someone who might want to interrogate her and leak crucial plot points to an eager moviegoing public?

Why such secrecy? I don't know. To maintain the element of surprise, perhaps. On *The Goonies*, Steven Spielberg wanted to promote a sense of adventure, so he and Dick Donner once blindfolded several members of the young cast and backed us onto a set that had been designed to look like a pirate ship. The feeling the two wanted to capture on film was the feeling they wanted the audience to have: the feeling of surprise, of wonder and awe. For Warren, though, I think it had more to do with his political ideas driving the movie, and not wanting other people to sabotage the process. To that end, he keeps everyone involved a little disoriented. For many directors and studio executives and writers, it comes down to the twin issues of privacy and piracy. No one wants their ideas stolen, of course. And it's important to control the flow of information, to mount a public relations and marketing campaign on a schedule that best suits the needs of the people who are most heavily invested in the process. True or not, if word leaks out that a script isn't what it should be, the subsequent wave of negativity can stop a project in its tracks. The paranoia is even more palpable now, thanks to the incredible scope and power of the Internet. Information and misinformation, not to mention actual words from a script, can go worldwide in a heartbeat.

The power of the Internet is best reflected by a man named Harry Knowles, who runs a Web site called Ain't It Cool News. A self-proclaimed (and widely acknowledged) ambassador for the fans, Knowles is a movie lover who somehow manages to get his hands on almost everything: script synopses, the latest deals, actors' and directors' salaries, behind-the-scenes gossip from movie sets. He predicts which movies are likely to be successful, and which are likely to fail, not merely by guessing, but by using the mountains of legitimate information he accumulates. As a result, Harry Knowles, despite living in Texas, is considered one of the most powerful men in Hollywood, and the studios, which once loathed and denigrated him, now actively court him.

As I understand it, Peter Jackson and Harry Knowles are fairly tight. Despite his newly acquired status as a Hollywood titan, Peter remains something of an iconoclast, and I think there is a mutual respect between Knowles and him. Each had a genuine desire to see *The Lord of the Rings* done right, and to sincerely enoble the efforts of the fans. After all, Peter is a fan, too. He wanted to stoke the flames of the fans' passion, so he gave them little things, tidbits of information to whet their appetite. But not too much. Amazingly enough, almost nothing appeared on Knowles's website that Peter did not want to be there. That's one of the many admirable things about Peter: he understands and appreciates the *fandom*, and so he interacts comfortably with people like Harry Knowles. They complement each other in a power corridor, and there's nothing the studios can do about it. Nor should they. Peter and Harry operated in the interest of the fans, and Harry, grateful for a bit of early access, honored his friendship with Peter.

In a much broader sense, Peter develops important relationships with important people based on trust and mutual respect. I don't think Peter gives trust too easily, and yet in my case, once I arrived in

New Zealand, I felt as though he trusted me almost completely—and almost instantly. Of course, he would have known that I had signed the nondisclosure agreement by then, and that knowledge would most certainly assuage any fears that I or anyone involved might betray his confidence. But, I'm talking about a feeling between people, one of openness and honesty, a sense that not only are you free to express yourself, but that your thoughts and opinions are encouraged. Granted, the sword cuts both ways, because what you say counts with Peter and Fran, and if your thoughts are insincere or poorly developed, it won't be lost on them. I say this from personal experience. More than once I've stumbled into a conversation or found myself making utterances that I've not wanted to stand behind upon further reflection. Peter and Fran can be very understanding and forgiving, but I've also seen what happens when people try to take advantage of them or behave too selfishly. I've watched Peter make a mental note and resolve to guard himself more closely in the future. I find it extraordinary that Peter doesn't seem to hold grudges or to act out of malice or revenge. I like to think of him as a somewhat benevolent and more fully evolved creature than most, who by sheer force of will accomplishes spectacular feats and by the grace of his talent can afford to be generous of spirit. He can be exacting when he needs to be and rewarding when it's earned.

Yet I can't deny that I was somewhat nervous about signing this particular confidentiality clause, containing as it did some of the most onerous language I had ever seen. The agreement essentially stipulated that if I disclosed anything I'd seen in the process of making *The Lord of the Rings*, the studio could sue me for the entire cost of the movie, a figure that was estimated to be $270 million! That was slightly more than I had in my savings account, so you can understand my trepidation.

"Jesus! Should I sign this?" I asked my attorney.

"Well, that depends."

"On what?"

"On whether you want the part."

Knowing I was in no position to demand a softening of the language in the confidentiality clause, I adopted the attitude of a soldier in a covert military operation and signed the agreement. However, I made it clear that I would remain true to the spirit of the contract only until the movies were released. I can understand and appreciate trade secrets and rights and all of that, and I did sincerely want to protect the movie. So I signed. But there was an ominous feeling to it. I was on the inside of this organization, and I couldn't help but wonder what would happen if the door suddenly slammed and I couldn't get out. That's a silly feeling, of course, because it was after all just a movie. I was going to work for New Line Cinema, not for the Pentagon or the CIA. Nevertheless, I felt like I was taking a chance by signing that agreement.

Any doubt that the stakes were higher than on a typical film was laid to rest when I got to New Zealand, and it became instantly apparent things were going to be done differently. Great sums of money had been invested, and the result was an unusual alliance between the production and the New Zealand government, from the department of immigration right down to the local law-enforcement officers. It was all done with great aplomb, mainly because Peter has such an easygoing, hippified personality, but you knew, if you were intelligent and reasonably observant, that things were different than they were in Hollywood. You realized when you passed the gate and the guard looked you in the eye that there were people who were not getting in. It didn't feel like the studios in Los Angeles, where I can always talk my way onto a lot because I'm a child of that community and I'm not a threat, and they recognize me or my parents. Not in New Zealand. Uh-uh. When you crossed the threshold that separated the city of Wellington from the city within a city that served as the headquarters of *The Lord of the Rings*, you felt like you were entering the vortex. You felt like you were in Peter Jackson's domain.

I had signed the confidentiality agreement, had agreed to play by the rules. Next came a series of clandestine conversations, the subject of which was the transference of information—specifically, the scripts. Typically, the discussions went something like this: "You signed the agreement? Good. You'll have to talk to Jan next. She's

Peter's assistant. She'll tell you precisely when the scripts will arrive—right to the minute. You'll have to be there to sign for them."

I'd respond with a guttural, "Understood," as if I were an undercover agent. Really, though, what I was thinking was: *What's the problem here? It's just a script.* But there was a culture of secrecy about it. When the scripts arrived, I opened the package and noticed immediately that the title page did not reflect the title of the movie, which caused me more than a little confusion. I spent five minutes trying to figure out the title page, at the center of which, in big bold letters, was the word "Jamboree." Finally it dawned on me that this was a deception: a fake title on a fake page! Why? Well, imagine you're an actor sitting in a coffee shop or some other public place, trying to combine a little work-related reading with some relaxation. That happens, although it's not usually a great idea. The fake page allows for a degree of privacy. A fan might know you're looking at a script, but at least this way he or she won't know the name of it.

All in all, it was an impressive package. Most scripts are held together with brads, but this one had big circular binders, so the pages couldn't be easily ripped out. There were watermarks, too, on every page. This in itself is not all that unusual: important scripts, those attached to "name" directors, or propped up by fat budgets, often have watermarks. But not like this. I had seen Steven Spielberg's watermarks; I had seen Spike Lee's. Usually they're nothing more than a series of numerals: 001, 002, 003. Each person is assigned a particular code. But the watermarks on "Jamboree" were different. Across the first page, in red, were two words: *Sean Astin*

Seeing that watermark took my breath away. The notion that I was literally burned into the work of the director and writers left no doubt in my mind that I belonged in the movie. It's hard to describe how that felt, not just turning each page and reading the story, but also seeing my name, over and over, a constant reminder that I was in the loop. On the first pass I merely looked through the script to see how many lines of dialogue were attributed to Samwise Gamgee, because I really didn't know yet how vital or visible a character he really was. I had heard from others that Sam loomed large in the story, but having not yet finished the books and not having seen the scripts,

I could only guess what that meant. I had agreed to do this movie and accept a specific salary without even knowing who the character was, which was quite a leap of faith, but an appropriate one, I thought, under the circumstances. A quick gallop through the scripts confirmed that belief: "Sam draws his sword and charges!"

Oh, that is so cool! I'm going to get to charge with a sword!

I was giddy, despite the fact that while Sam was deeply involved in the plot and received a fair amount of screen time, it was also apparent that there were huge chunks of story where he wasn't involved at all. At least in the first script. Then I flipped through the second script and the third. Hundreds of pages in roughly ten minutes. I couldn't really engage the scripts at first, so distracting was the appearance of my name, the image of Sam brandishing swords, the secrecy surrounding the whole project, and the thought of what the movie might be. On that first day I could manage no more than a cursory glance, a sizing up, perhaps, of my own character and the decision I had made. And it didn't seem half bad.

Although I lacked a deep understanding of the story, it came as no surprise to learn that inhabiting the role of Sam would require more than mere emotional immersion. *The Lord of the Rings* was a fantasy, Middle-earth was a place that existed only in the mind of J.R.R. Tolkien, and hobbits were tiny, noble creatures with pointy ears and bulbous, hairy feet. Bringing these characters to life would involve not only computer-generated wizardry, but also extensive use of makeup and prosthetics. The transformation, for me, began in Beverly Hills, at the Ma Maison Sofitel hotel.

I had been racing around for days, trying to tie up loose ends and prepare for the trip to New Zealand, when I received a phone call from the studio informing me that I had an appointment with Peter Owen to discuss my wig.

My wig?

This was a surprise only because I hadn't given it much thought. I had seen pictures of hobbits, but hadn't really concentrated on what I was supposed to look like. I was trusting, figuring I'd look like me and get absorbed into it. My body would be there, on location, and I'd give myself over to the process. I wanted to read the scripts when I could really read them (which turned out to be on the plane during the long flight to Wellington). There was so much else going on that I found it hard to absorb the scripts or to worry about how I'd become the character. Six weeks of rehearsal time had been built into the production schedule, so I wasn't terribly concerned. By the time principal photography began, I'd be sharp. Unlike so many movies I'd done in the past, this was a major production in every sense of the word. I understood the importance of having my body and mind prepared, my family cared for, and my personal and professional lives in order. Everything else would be, well, *handled*. And for the most part, that's the way it worked.

Step one on the agenda was my hair.

My own hair, by the way, is substantial. I may be short and I may have a little trouble with my weight, but hair is not a problem. In that area at least, I'm blessed. Follicly gifted, as it were. But I didn't have hobbit hair, which in the movie would be long and matted, carefully crafted to give the appearance of being weathered. Rather than attempt to tame my own hair (or the hair of anyone on the production), it was far easier and more sensible to rely on a set of wigs. Upon hearing this, I reacted like a newcomer to the craft: *Oh, I've heard about these guys. This is going to be cool!* And so it was.

Peter Owen is a wonderfully stylish British gentleman, with baby-fine blond hair and long slender fingers, each adorned with a perfectly manicured nail. He welcomed me into his hotel suite with a flourish, and instantly I sensed something special about him and his place in the food chain. There was something about the way he carried himself, the fact that he was working out of this luxury hotel. He wasn't just a hairstylist. He was an artist, and meeting him was tangible proof that on this production I'd be working with and be inspired by the most talented and successful people in their fields. It was exciting, but also daunting. Every step down the hallway and into the room provoked a feeling of nervousness. My agent had given me a snapshot of Peter's career, including the names of several prominent clients for whom he had designed hairpieces. Not just movie stars either, but towering figures in business and media culture. If these people were willing to give themselves over to Peter, he had to be good. No, check that. He had to be great.

"Why, just yesterday I had a nice little session with Johnny Depp," Peter said. That got my attention. Johnny Depp is not just a terrific actor; he's a treasure. I told Johnny when we met at the premiere of *Blow* that, for an actor, meeting him was like going to Mecca. A bit too fawning? Maybe, but I didn't care. It meant that much to me, in part because his story reminded me of my story. Okay, he's an edgier, funkier guy (who else would show up at a premiere with Marilyn Manson at his side?), but there were similarities. Johnny had first made an impact doing mindless television piffle like *21 Jump Street*. He had earned a lot of money but not much in the way of respect. Then he veered off on a different path, choosing projects based on their artistic merit, and somehow it all worked out. He went from teen idol to respected actor. That kind of stuff strikes a chord with me. You can do one type of job for money and another type of job for art, but whether the business views you as reaching critical mass before you view it yourself . . . well, that's dangerous, that's a gamble. But you really can continue to find yourself and challenge yourself. If you're righteous and believe in yourself, you can come back. You can rise from the ashes.

"Why was Johnny here?" I asked Peter.

He laughed, fanned at the air with a hand. "Oh, we were just having a little play."

That made me envious, the notion that some actors have so much money, and so much time, and so much passion for their craft that they will invest several hours just to see what types of characters they can come up with. Whether Peter was telling the truth or not—whether Johnny was really there, and whether they were "just having a little play," I don't know. I think he was simply trying to earn my trust by sharing stories of his A-list environment. Not that it was necessary, since he had me at "Hello."

Peter was gracious, even eager, as I peppered him with questions. "No offense, but why do I even need a wig?" I asked, running a hand proudly through my own mop. "Can't we just turn this into hobbit hair?"

"Well, maybe if your hair grows out nicely we'll be pulling little bits through the wig lace," he said softly. "But probably not." Then he began talking about "scale doubles," smaller men and women who more closely approximate the size of hobbits, and who would lend an air of authenticity by standing in for the actors in certain scenes. It was the first time I'd heard of this, or at least given it any serious consideration. Peter pulled out a piece of paper and sketched an image depicting Sam's hair, and explained how the wig would make it easier for the actor and the double to mirror each other. That made sense, although upon hearing this news, my first reaction was, *But I don't want a double. I want it to be all me!* Very quickly, however, that sentiment was replaced by an immense appreciation for how much thought and effort had already been invested in the process.

In the interest of full disclosure, I should acknowledge that I did experience a moment or two of anxiety over the issue of size, specifically, as it pertained to my own career and self-interests. I remember whining, half jokingly, to Nikki Mirisch, "Oh, great. I played the ball turret gunner, the smallest guy on the B-17, in *Memphis Belle;* I played Rudy, the smallest guy on the Notre Dame football team; and now I'm gonna play a three-foot-six hobbit. This will be the final nail in my coffin. I'm never going to be a big movie star because everyone will think I'm a miniature guy." To which Nikki replied with a snort, "Get over it."

Impressed as I was with Peter Owen, there wasn't a whole lot to our session. He wrapped my head in some type of cellophane, fastened it with rubber bands to create a skullcap, and then yanked it off. Just like that, he had a model of my head—all that he needed to begin the process of creating Sam's wig.

"That's it?" I asked.

He nodded.

"What about the hair?"

Peter explained that most of it would likely come from female "donors" in Russia, which is, for some reason, apparently the nexus of the hair trade. I didn't get to see or touch the hair that I'd be wearing for the next year and a half, but Peter did present a bunch of ponytail swatches for me to examine. He held them up to the light—as if we were choosing wallpaper patterns or fabric for a new sofa—and we both agreed that matching my natural hair color wouldn't be a problem. And that was about it. We shook hands and I left Peter's suite, emboldened by the feeling that Sam was in good hands.

Fascinating as this meeting was, it wasn't the only meaningful interaction of the day, for while walking through the hotel lobby, who did I meet in person for the very first time? Elijah Wood. I would be Sam to his Frodo.

Elijah's eyes opened wide as I came into view, and we literally ran to each other and embraced. I hugged him like a brother or a long-lost friend. That we had never spoken to each other seemed hard to comprehend in this setting, standing near the front door of the hotel, where each of us had gone specifically for the purpose of preparing for what would be the role of a lifetime (Elijah, too, had an appointment with Peter Owen). I knew enough about the story of *The Lord of the Rings* to know that the friendship between Frodo and Sam was considered not only central to the plot, but one of the most enduring relationships in literature. For the film to succeed, Elijah and I would have to make audiences believe in our friendship. He knew it and I knew it. So we fell against each other and hugged, then pulled back, and I remember just smiling at him nervously, excitedly, the two of us kind of studying each other quietly, as if we both were thinking, *This is a little overwhelming, but we're equal to it.*

Elijah was exactly what I thought he'd be: small, not quite waifish, and friendly. He's a little shorter than I am, and substantially thinner. My agents had assured Peter that I'd expand to the proper bulk before the start of principal photography, and I'd already taken the first sluggish steps down the road to sloth. Prior to getting the offer I was in the best shape of my life. At 160 pounds I was a lean, mean fighting machine, fit enough that I'd actually completed the Los Angeles Marathon. That's the way I thought I looked, almost like a movie star, when I auditioned for Fran and Peter. Interestingly, I got the distinct impression that while Fran thought I was appealing, Peter was less convinced simply because, in his eyes, I didn't look like Sam. That's not how he saw the character. One of the things I discovered about Peter is that he is uniquely qualified to work outside the mainstream.

While he loves American films and is a true student of American and world popular culture (this, after all, is a man who got his start in splatter films and who turned to a remake of *King Kong* as his follow-up to *The Lord of the Rings*), he is no slave to Hollywood convention. I was proud of the way I looked. I enjoyed having cheekbones and a flat stomach. It made me feel like I could be a leading man. To Peter, however, such things were distractions, obstacles to overcome in developing a character. To secure the role, I vowed to do less running and more eating. By the time I met Elijah, I'd already begun to morph into Sam.

Elijah had no such concerns. Wide-eyed and almost elfin in appearance, with an earnestness few actors can project, he was perfect for the role of Frodo. I had known for some time (well before I got the part of Sam) that New Line was involved in negotiations with Elijah, and I was looking forward to having a chance to work with him. I had followed Elijah's career and admired the way he had managed it. He always seemed to be working on interesting stuff alongside major stars, in roles where he was really *acting*. I'm ten years older than Elijah, but I consider him a colleague, and I was at that time old enough to appreciate what he was doing as a young actor rising through the ranks. I looked up to him as an actor at least in part because of his ability to avoid being characterized as a child star insofar as that term is sometimes less than flattering. He had made better decisions than I had in traversing that path. He'd been more adept at choosing projects and negotiating with studio executives. I can recall seeing him in those old Lays potato chip commercials alongside Dan Quayle ("Want a potato chip, Mr. Vice President?"), and thinking, *Wow, that kid is in the zone. He's so smooth.* Elijah conducted himself in a way that was almost unnaturally professional for one so young.

As he matured, it became clear that his youthful precociousness was not just a fluke, not something that would erode with time. Shortly before we met, Elijah had appeared in *The Ice Storm*, Ang Lee's quietly haunting story of domestic upheaval in a suburban Connecticut neighborhood. His career was soaring. Critics and fans alike viewed him as a serious, nearly grown-up actor. But I had appreciated his abilities for some time. Elijah had appeared in *Forever Young* with

Mel Gibson and *North* with Bruce Willis. He'd played Huck Finn and the Artful Dodger. He was still a teenager, but already he had a substantial body of work, and he was keenly aware of it.

I suppose I was a little bit envious, or maybe I just wished I had known what he seemed to know. When I was fifteen years old, I started my own business. I wanted to write, direct, act, and produce. I wanted to be all things to all people—and I still do, as a matter of fact. When Elijah was fifteen, he wanted to work with great filmmakers. That's it. I think he understood the importance of those connections, and thus set out to obtain the best roles he could possibly find.

At that age, I just didn't get it. I thought I was the guy who could be the great filmmaker, the person who could choose the scripts, maybe even write the scripts, and create the great movies. I understood the power of the medium, but when I was Elijah's age, I wanted too much at once, and the thing that got sublimated was the research into other people's film careers. I should have been finding out who was making what movies and figuring out how to get in them. I didn't realize that I could learn about the environment and navigate it in a more sensible way by working with artists who appreciated the value of working with *other* artists. The smart way to approach a career is to realize how talented other people are and figure out a way to work with them.

That's the way I viewed Peter Jackson and Elijah Wood. In fact, Elijah had become a significant component of my motivation for working on this project. There were six really interesting buzzwords or phrases attached to the film: Peter Jackson, *Lord of the Rings*, New Line, trilogy, New Zealand, and Elijah Wood. The importance you attach to something can often be distilled into something as simple as the way you answer a query. When people would ask me what I was working on, I revealed something with the way I responded. Sometimes I'd say something about working on an adaptation of *The Lord of the Rings*, but more often I'd say, "I'm going to New Zealand for a year and a half to be Elijah Wood's sidekick." Why? I guess because it sounded cool, exotic. Who wouldn't want to visit New Zealand? And who didn't know Elijah Wood?

"Are you ready for this?" I asked him at the Ma Maison Sofitel.

He looked right at me, almost through me, with those impossibly blue, almost alien eyes, and smiled.

"Yeah, I am."

It was clear that he wasn't just saying what he thought I wanted to hear. There was an intensity to him, an honesty, that I found thoroughly inspiring, because what I was trying to project to him was an air of responsibility, of confidence, of nurturing: *I know on some level what we're about to undergo. And I'm prepared.* But I was also feeling a small degree of anxiety stemming from not knowing whether Elijah was equally prepared. It turned out, of course, that neither one of us could possibly have known what we were in for, but I took comfort in hearing him say that he was ready and excited. It gave me strength and confidence.

That initial interaction lasted only a few minutes. Elijah was running late for his meeting with Peter, and my ride was waiting by the curb. We hugged again, said good-bye, and went our separate ways. The next time I would see him would be in New Zealand under very different circumstances.

Getting fitted for a wig was one thing; getting fitted for all of the other prosthetic devices that might be needed to create a hobbit was quite another. Central to this process was the construction of a face mold, which the makeup artists could then use to complete the character of Sam. This is a normal part of the preproduction stage of any movie involving characters who will be required to wear a significant amount of special-effects makeup, and to most actors it isn't a big deal. However, if like me you happen to suffer from the occasional bout of claustrophobia, it is a very big deal indeed.

It had happened to me twice in England during the filming of *Memphis Belle.* The first incident occurred during a ten-day, premovie boot camp designed to foster camaraderie among the cast and, no doubt, give us a sort of war-weary look of authenticity. On the last day of boot camp we were taken to the entrance of a dirt tunnel that was nearly filled with water. The object of the exercise, the drill instructor said, was to crawl through the tunnel and exit the other side, several hundred yards away, without drowning.

"If it collapses," he said flatly, twirling a pickax smoothly in his hands, "just try to hang on, mate. We'll come get ya."

This guy was a career hard-ass. His nickname was Bungee, and his skin was stretched so tight over his skull that he looked like a living, breathing cadaver. He'd served in the Falklands, where allegedly his specialty was interrogating prisoners as they dangled from the open door of a helicopter. As often as not, according to set lore, when Bungee extracted the necessary information, he or someone close by would pull out a knife, cut the prisoner's lifeline, and watch him plummet earthward like a stone. Laughing, no doubt. Whether any of this was true, I don't know, but it had the desired effect, which was to shrivel the sacks of a bunch of Hollywood dudes preparing to film a war movie.

We all knew that Bungee was trying to mess with us psychologically, but looking at the tunnel, the potential for a cave-in did seem real. I was the most overtly enthusiastic member of the *Memphis Belle* cast, so I was assigned the task of crawling through the tunnel first. Unfortunately, claustrophobia seized me, and I ended up going fourth. I made it, but not without enduring a healthy dose of anxiety, embarrassment, and humility.

That, however, was merely a prelude to what I experienced during the actual filming of the movie. I knew a time was going to come when I'd have to climb into the ball turret, wearing a heavy wool uniform, a leather jacket, a mask, and a helmet, and stay there for however long it took to film a particular scene. I was terrified I wouldn't be able to do it. I think my claustrophobia stems from my childhood, when my big brothers were messing with me and rolled me up in a big carpet and stuck me in a closet. After listening to me scream and cry for a few seconds, they opened the door and let me fall out. Silly as it may sound, the memory of that brief imprisonment has never left me, and every so often it reaches out and makes life difficult, even now. For the most part I've learned how to manage it. But it takes effort. The night before we shot the ball-turret scene I was in my hotel room in London, barricading myself in a closet with a pile of clothes and blankets, forcing myself to breathe through the panic, hoping to desensitize myself and in that way prevent an anxiety attack on the set. To a degree, the strategy worked.

The turret sat atop some scaffolding, where it could be rotated back and forth, giving the illusion of height and movement, as if the occupant actually sat in the belly of a bomber. There was room for only a few people on the scaffolding, at least two of whom would have to like me enough to rescue me if something were to break, and they were rotating the turret and feeding me stuff through straws, bits and pieces of plastic that were designed to look like frozen saliva, as I fired hundreds of blanks from my machine gun. I was dizzy and tired and nervous when they opened the door and offered me a quick break and a drink of water. Then they slammed the door, resumed rotating and shooting, and suddenly I felt something rising in my throat. Whatever the cause, I felt like I was about to paint the inside of the turret, or at least my mask, with the contents of my stomach.

"Open the door," I pleaded.

No response. Just more rotating.

"Please . . . open the door! Now!"

For just a second I could tell that the director, Michael Caton-Jones, was contemplating filming my distress. I don't blame him, since it surely would have added a touch of realism, but I was nonetheless relieved when the door opened and I gasped for air and the nausea passed.

"Thank you," I said after recovering. "Let's finish."

So, for me, there was considerable anxiety attached to the idea of a face mold. I knew what it was, of course. My father had spent hours in the makeup chair while filming *The Frighteners*, and his scrapbook captured every inch of the ordeal. I knew that in order to make a mold they'd have to put some kind of goop all over my face and stick straws up my nose so I could breathe. And if I didn't calmly endure the discomfort, I'd be forced to go through it all over again. Even though I knew it was coming, I tried to put it out of my mind, but I couldn't, for this time there would be no escape hatch. I had agreed to make the movie for less money than I needed to keep our new house, and by not putting everything into storage and renting out the place, I had painted myself into a corner, where at certain moments I'd experience anxiety that was totally unnecessary. For some reason, probably because I make everything more complicated than it needs to be, I had created a stressful environment, unintentionally torturing myself by trying to reconcile being a father, a husband, an actor, and a filmmaker. I knew that I had lucked into the role of a lifetime, that through my family and career and some quirk of my own talent, I had figured out how to get into this movie, and that was empowering to me. I couldn't back down on needing the house, and I don't know whether the anxiety was based on that dynamic or something else, because consciously I had no anxiety about going to New Zealand. That's our lifestyle. People sometimes say to me, "I don't know how you do that when you've got kids." Well, you do it by not having that attitude. You say, "Fuck it! I'll go where life and opportunity take me. I'll be a global citizen." That was my attitude and bravado, but beneath that swagger, on levels I barely understood, I was a wreck.

Upon hearing that I'd gotten the job in *The Lord of the Rings*, Eric Stoltz said, "My God, Sean, what a terrific break! You'll live off that movie for five years." It was a relief to hear something like that from Eric, a solid journeyman actor, a star, an artist who had always been good to me. Nevertheless, even his encouragement couldn't completely quell the anxiety, which reached a peak on the morning I was supposed to have my face cast.

The appointment was for nine-thirty. I bolted out of bed at six, sweating, clutching my chest, quite sure that I was about to die. I reached over and grabbed Christine's arm.

"Honey, I'm in trouble here."

"Huh?" She was still half asleep.

"I think I'm having a heart attack."

Christine took one look at me and became genuinely alarmed. "Okay, we'll get you to the doctor."

As she scrambled for the phone, I told her to wait. A few deep breaths later, the discomfort began to subside. My chest loosened, and my heart returned to its normal rhythm. After convincing Christine that I was all right, I took a shower, got dressed, and left the house. I hadn't gone more than a mile or so when another wave of anxiety rolled in: shortness of breath, tingling in the arms, a crushing pain in my chest. I sat at a stop sign for a few moments, waiting for the attack to ebb once again. And it did. Now I wasn't just scared; I was pissed! I couldn't believe this was happening, and I was worried that it might cost me the job. I'm not a cancel-the-meeting kind of actor, so I knew I had to get through the makeup process and then visit a doctor. Which is precisely what I did.

A battery of diagnostic procedures, including an EKG and a treadmill test, revealed that I had the heart and lungs of a healthy twenty-eight-year-old man. The cardiologist was thoughtful and considerate, but he made it quite clear that I'd experienced nothing more serious than a panic attack. Both Christine and I were relieved, but when I called my mother to tell her what had happened, she burst into tears. My mother, of course, has had various health issues her whole life, including panic attacks, and the relating of my episode provoked considerable empathy and concern on her part. I think she considered my anxiety to be a red flag, an indication that I was susceptible to the same types of emotional and psychiatric disorders that had at various times made her life miserable. Mom has always believed that her children should be aware of the possibility that such illnesses could afflict them, and while I know there is an undeniable genetic component to bipolar disorder, I have never been quick to embrace it as an explanation for the dynamics or problems in my life.

Whenever something goes wrong, the slightest emotional slip, that's my mother's default. She's inclined to say, "It's a sign of manic depression, and you need to have it fixed." My wife, whose family also has been burdened by mental illness, is more inclined to straddle the fence. She's not so easily convinced, but has on occasion suggested that I should consider evaluation. The truth is, I do a million things at once; the pace of my life is unnaturally accelerated, and an unpleasant by-product of that frenetic pace is an occasional dip into sadness or exhaustion. So it doesn't surprise me that my mother or my wife would feel a certain way, and I am open to the possibility. I'm not blind to it. But I don't like the stigma, and so I often just deflect the concern with humor, patience, and genuine reflection, and then I move on.

God bless my mom. She wrote *Call Me Anna*, a best-selling book about her experiences with bipolar disorder, largely because she wanted to destigmatize the disease, and that was a noble cause for her to have embraced. But there are a lot of things I would like to accomplish in my life, including holding public office someday, and I don't want to have to live with a diagnosis that will shape public opinion before I have the chance to achieve things that will give me the credibility to override that perception—especially when that diagnosis so often seems to be made with alarming speed and ease. A lot of people have anxiety attacks, a lot of people fret and worry. They aren't all manic-depressive.

I've worked very hard to allay my mom's fears, and my wife's fears, while at the same time being honest with myself. Last summer my mother picked me up at the airport in Spokane, Washington, and while we drove to her house she told me that the Arts & Entertainment network wanted her to be the subject of a lifetime retrospective. I was skeptical; sometimes Mom makes decisions that I deem too self-serving. I don't deny that her book helped a lot of people. I've seen it myself. Hundreds of people have come up to me, crying, saying how much the sharing of her experiences helped them. I know her story resonates on deep levels, but I also know that my mother needed money, and I know how adversely her book affected my father and my brothers and our family. So I wanted to be loyal to my mother and supportive of her, and let her tell whatever stories she wanted about me, but I had mixed feelings. My mother's book represented her statement about who she was, and in making that statement she was completely willing to give herself over to the psychiatric community—to her detriment in some ways, in my opinion. I think she largely abdicated certain kinds of personal responsibility, which exacerbated a lot of problems. I'm through the looking glass with my mother on this. I love her and I'm very forgiving of her, but I also don't want to repeat her mistakes. I recognize that there is an ambient perception out there, that as the somewhat hyperkinetic son of a famously bipolar Oscar-winning actress, I am the target of certain presumptions. That's okay. It comes with the territory.

Whether I'd be able to manage my anxiety while having my face encased in plaster, like the Man in the Iron Mask, was a legitimate question, and one I hadn't satisfactorily answered when I arrived at KNB EFX Group in the San Fernando Valley. Like Peter Owen, the folks at KNB are among the best in the business at what they do. Formed in 1988 by Robert Kurtzman, Howard Berger, and Greg Nicotero while the trio was working on Sam Raimi's *Evil Dead II: Dead by Dawn*, KNB had earned a reputation for greatness among filmmakers with a taste for lavish and sometimes gruesome special makeup effects. Among the films on the company's resume were *Men in Black*, *Scream*, *Pulp Fiction*, and *Mars Attacks*. And now they were doing advance work on *The Lord of the Rings*.

More than anything else, I felt inspired when I walked into the studio. It was like another rite of passage. My father had been through this. So had countless other actors. It was a process bathed in trust: you had to put your faith in somebody else—completely. To that end I was offered a tour of the facility designed to set my mind at ease by making the work less mystical and frightening. I was told that a particularly attractive actress had been in just a short time earlier, and that the boys at KNB had to prove their professionalism in making a full-body cast for her. They showed me masks and molds that had been designed for other actors. And then it was my turn; inspiration turned to fear.

"You ready?" Howard asked.

My mouth was dry, so I just nodded.

"Okay, have a seat."

I tried to project confidence, but inside I was dying. While giving me the tour, Howard had related the story of another actor, an action star, who had completely flipped out in the middle of the molding process. He'd started sweating and yelling, and then jumped up and ripped everything off. I laughed at the story and made some joke about how pathetic it was that anyone could let that happen, but at the same time I was thinking, *You know what? That's going to be me in about ten minutes.* Then they told me that Elijah had been in the day before.

"Yeah? How did he do?"

"Oh, he was great, man. Such a professional."

That little shit!

I knew then that there was no way out. If Elijah could weather the process without complaint or incident, then I could, too.

As they stirred the mixture that was to be applied to my face, I asked a question.

"What happens if I have trouble breathing after it hardens? You do a little tracheotomy or something?"

Howard laughed. "Don't worry. You'll be fine."

They kept talking, making jokes, trying to put me at ease. Really, though, I wasn't in the mood for conversation. I tried to be cordial, but what I wanted to do was just close my eyes and get through it. I'd seen makeup effects for a lot of movies, and I'd always wondered how I'd react when it was my turn. Here was the answer: not well.

"Some people tell me it's quite a soothing experience," Howard said, scooping a handful of glop from a bucket.

Splat!

He smeared a patch over my cheeks and forehead. I tensed, and I think he noticed. I'm sure he noticed. "Just breathe. That's it. Nice and easy."

I'd had two panic attacks already, and a third was imminent. Or so it seemed. Then a funny thing happened. The nervousness went away. The more of my face they covered, the more soothing it became, and I realized then that I'd live through it. There was a moment when they were working close to my nose, and I was concerned that my nostrils would get plugged with plaster and I'd choke to death, but that passed quickly. The truth is, they were extraordinarily good at their jobs, and I trusted them. Eventually, as they covered my ears and eyes, everything went dark, and a weird feeling of sensory deprivation took over. Three minutes passed. Four minutes. Five . . .

"We're waiting for it to harden," Howard explained. "Sit tight. It's almost over."

Someone tapped the shell, and it occurred to me then that I had no idea how they were going to remove the mold. Was it like a cast? Would they use a little circular saw on the top of my head? Around my neck? Didn't like the idea of that at all. I hadn't asked enough questions; I had trusted in the notion that if they killed me it would ruin their reputation and upset the studio, and no one wanted that to happen. Still, when I heard Howard say, "It's ready," I felt another small surge of panic. I held my breath in anticipation of the whine of a saw, the sting of a razor, but neither came. Instead, someone reached under my chin and tugged gently on the mold, and I felt my skin pull away from it. The thing had enough elasticity that it could be removed like a ski mask. Just like that, I was in the open air again, breathing freely.

Howard held up the mask and explained how they would use it to create an image of my face, and then make innumerable latex molds from that image.

"You did great," he said.

"Thanks," I replied, feigning nonchalance. "You were right. No big deal."

The molds for the hobbit feet, those giant furry slippers that would be individually applied in a tedious process each morning in New Zealand, were done later, and that was a ball. There's nothing panic-inducing about having your feet molded. In fact, it was while having those molds taken that it first dawned on me that feet were an issue. Even though I had read 160 pages of *The Lord of the Rings*, there was much I simply didn't understand. I just didn't get it: *Hobbits have big feet. So what?* I'm such a pug sometimes. I'm so *pugnacious*, and I don't mean that in the flattering sense of the word. I'm so busy thinking about things and approaching them in a way that gets me where I want to go, that sometimes I just miss the point—you know, I can't see the forest for the trees. I don't always get what's fun or funny or cool or interesting, usually because I'm too busy looking at things from my vantage point, through selfishness, really. In some ways I've been a victim of needing some type of ownership to other's people work in order to really appreciate it. I go to fantasy and science-fiction conventions now, and I see how people spend hours building miniatures. There was a time when I couldn't appreciate that. Oh, sure, I respected their right to play games and build models and be geeky—there are billions of people on this planet and everyone has their own interests—but somehow, as much as I tried to be a student of the business and an heir to a tradition of Hollywood success, I still just didn't get it.

Not until *The Lord of the Rings* did I comprehend the depth of people's work and passion. I'm embarrassed and disappointed in myself for not getting there sooner, for not really appreciating the genius of a man like Peter Owen, and the conversations he must have had with Peter Jackson. What foresight and drive they must have had, what intelligence and sheer artistry! Sure, I admired that Peter found this franchise and devised a way to bring it to the screen, but I didn't appreciate or understand its roots. The success of *The Lord of the Rings* is in a very real sense born out of Peter Jackson's love for making models as a kid. Peter and all these other people who brought the films to life, with their genuine passion and love of interfacing with *stuff* on their own terms. I'd always sort of understood it, but now I was getting it on a big scale. Doing a movie like *Rudy*, the skill set was different. I've always known how to memorize my lines and hit my mark, how to muster the right kind of emotion for the right kind of scene, and how to be comfortable with the director and the other actors. But this realm—*fantasy*—I never had a lot of respect for it. It always seemed hokey to me. Now, though, I realized I was embarking on something where the mission was to make it *not* hokey.

One of the great things about working on *The Goonies* was that Dick Donner and Steven Spielberg made both the set and the experience so real. It was a fantasy, with pirates and treasure, but it didn't feel like a fantasy. It felt like an adventure. Dick and Steven were incredible engines, with different strengths. There was a time when I thought Dick didn't get it, that he didn't understand the real poetry and mystery of the story. In retrospect, of course, I know I was wrong. He did get it. It's just that he was something of a drill sergeant: "Get over here, kid! Hit your mark! Say your line! Now get out of the way." He was a bombastic leader on the set, and I didn't realize that the bravado masked his true sense of the magical. Steven was different. The tenor and the ambience when he was directing scenes (and they really were like codirectors) was much gentler, more whimsical. They're both extraordinary directors, of course, but as a kid I presumed that Steven had a more natural appreciation for the spirit of adventure. I'm not so sure that's accurate. As a wrap gift, Dick presented me with a leather-bound collection of books, adventure classics by Herman Melville, John Steinbeck, Arthur Conan Doyle, Isaac Asimov, and others. He knew.

Unfortunately, it's part of my personality to miss things on the first pass, so when I started reading *The Lord of the Rings*, I barely noticed the hobbits' feet. There's an excuse for that, I suppose: feet aren't a big issue in *The Lord of the Rings*, having been explained and detailed rather thoroughly in *The Hobbit*. But I hadn't read that, either. When they started applying the feet prosthetics, however, it sort of dawned on me: Hey! Feet are of special significance to hobbits! Sounds ridiculous, but that's the way it was. Something about placing my feet in a gelatinous goop caused an awakening, and I thought, *I'll bet Peter and Fran realize how special the feet are, and I'll bet Tolkien gave it an immense amount of consideration.* That was the first moment when I appreciated the tenderness and the sense of humor and the twinkle in the eye of the author. (By the way, when I arrived in New Zealand, I found it immensely amusing that some folks seemed to have little use for shoes, including Peter, who routinely showed up on the set barefoot and bedraggled, much like a hobbit.)

My ignorance of such things, things that are so familiar to fans and devoted readers of Tolkien, might seem incomprehensible, even offensive, but I had only my particular vantage point. I was looking at the role as an actor for hire, so in the beginning at least, I didn't immerse myself in research. That's not meant to be an excuse, merely an explanation. I can recall my stepmother, Val, who had been corresponding with Fran and Peter off and on for years, sending me pictures of the hobbits and of Gandalf via e-mail. She understood the importance of feet in Tolkien's world. And I'm sure my father did, too.

You see, John Astin actually auditioned for a major role in *The Lord of the Rings*. While I was fighting for the part of Sam, he was asked to audition for the role of Gandalf. Ian McKellen now owns the role, of course, and it will forever be hard to imagine anyone else in his place. But my father was in contention for that part, and I wanted in the worst way for him to get it. There had been talk of Sean Connery playing Gandalf, and Ian, of course, was involved in the process from the very beginning. Those two actors are heavyweights, and while on the surface it might seem that any sensible director would prefer either of them to John Astin, that isn't necessarily the case. My father is a classically trained Shakespearean actor. Yes, he's most famous for starring in *The Addams Family* and *Night Court,* for doing the Killer Tomato movies, for being this goofy goober of a guy. And he's good at that sort of thing. But he's a serious man who has given extraordinary and powerful performances. Ultimately, I think I was probably more innately right for Sam than my dad was for Gandalf, although I've totally muted this thought in my interactions with him.

My dad was ambivalent at the time because he was gearing up for his one-man show about Edgar Allen Poe. He is also always fielding offers for TV shows, theater parts, and films. But he knows Peter and Fran, and he respects them immensely. To that end, he was more than willing to prepare an audition for them. I'm a little fuzzy on what took place in the actual room, but according to my dad, Peter gave him a note that represented a real challenging adjustment given the research he'd done and his first take on the character. Peter once said to me that my father was great in the audition. Dad told me that he considered shooting a videotape of himself as Gandalf once he was able to reconcile what he knew of the character with what Peter had wanted. If memory serves, time was short and there was a lot going on. I think it's fair to say that my dad didn't want to complicate matters for me with Peter, because he knew how much I wanted the part and what it would mean for my career. I think he also knew better than I did just how all-consuming an endeavor it would be, and he was reluctant to give up all that he'd been working on. The point of the story is simply this: it is possible for thoughtful, talented people to work and thrive in a complex emotional or "political" environment.

I felt a little awkward when my dad came to my house to congratulate me and celebrate, because I wasn't sure if he was more disappointed than he was letting on. To be sure, he was extraordinarily proud of me, happy for me, and excited for the adventure we were certain to have. If I sensed a little hint of disappointment, perhaps I was projecting my own guilt at having gotten a golden part in a charmed project when he had not. It may seem like a confusing contradiction, but I can also say that I sensed a little relief in him that he didn't get the part. Did Dad know something I didn't know? Something about how grueling an experience it was going to be? Seriously though, I never would have gotten the chance to play Sam if it wasn't for my father—and for the contributions of a lot of other people. But if I had to pick the single most influential person outside of the project, the individual most responsible for my being prepared and capable of doing the job, it would have to be my father.

Dad has spent the better part of the last decade steeped in the richness of an extraordinarily artistic life. He has returned to his roots at Johns Hopkins and the city of Baltimore, where he spent much time in his youth. Now he is a guest lecturer at that hallowed institution. He has a condo near the campus (bicoastal, you know), and he thrives on the energy of his students. He travels with his one-man show, *Once Upon a Midnight: An Evening with Edgar Allen Poe*, and performs in many other plays. I think he is deservedly enjoying one of the most fulfilling and exciting chapters in his life. I'm not sure all of that would have been true if Peter had offered him the part of Gandalf, and he had spent the better part of five years focused on *The Lord of the Rings*. Regardless, I will be forever grateful to him for all that he has done for me and given me, and what is more, I'm probably more proud of him than he could ever be of me.

If you, the reader, learn anything about me in this book, I'll be happy. But I'm sure that my father would prefer that I spend my time developing myself as an actor and not pouring through the subtleties of deal making, money issues, and the mechanics of building a career for the sake of a book. He is a purist when it comes to craft, and in that respect he is wiser than I ever will be. He is my inspiration and my conscience; in a sense, he is my own personal Gandalf.

CHAPTER EIGHT

I arrived with my family in New Zealand on the last day of August 1999, and along with the other actors portraying members of the Fellowship, immediately began an intensive training period. With war movies it's not unusual for actors to be subjected to a ten-day boot camp; our boot camp for *The Lord of the Rings* consisted of six weeks of training, from dialect coaching to fight training with Bob Anderson, one of the great sword masters of Hollywood (he tutored Errol Flynn and Douglas Fairbanks, among others). Then there were canoe training, weight training, and organized bonding sessions with the cast. It was baptism by fire, inculcation into a regimentation, watching Peter and his crew learn how to organize a vast movie machine.

From the second I got off the plane, I knew making this movie was going to be unlike anything I'd ever experienced. Usually if you travel halfway around the world to film on location, you're given time to adjust, to get comfortable. There's a welcome basket and a meeting, maybe a massage or a nap. You talk about stuff and just sort of sit around for a while. You get the movie-star treatment. Not on *The Lord of the Rings*. Basically, we got off the plane in Wellington and were whisked away to an industrial part of town. You would think that with a $270 million trilogy, filming would take place on something that at least looked like a Hollywood sound set. Uh-uh. There were no wrought-iron gates, no Warner Brothers water tower, no Hollywood sign, nothing. New Zealand, especially in less developed areas, is a breathtakingly beautiful place, but Wellington is a city, and like any city, it has its industrial side. And that, mixed with a nearby quaint neighborhood, is where we set up shop. Specifically, in an old abandoned paint factory.

Peter was there on the day we arrived, and the atmosphere was a little reminiscent of Willy Wonka. There was all this ambient energy and nervousness about the arrival of Peter. "Peter is going to be here now, and his schedule is very tight, so don't expect too much." When he came in, bounding around the corner in bare feet and mangy hair and a rumpled T-shirt, looking like a mad scientist who sort of giggles his way through life, I couldn't help but be amused—and impressed. We shook hands or hugged, and he gave us a quick tour.

A few words about hugging. I was raised in a family and in a culture where everyone hugs—a lot! As a greeting, a parting salutation, or a simple expression of goodwill, hugs have been a big part of my life. I have even used hugs as a way to ask for forgiveness or as an act of reconciliation. As far as Peter Jackson is concerned, I think I chose to hug him more readily and more frequently than he may have been initially comfortable with. But I'm proud to say that over the five years of our working relationship and friendship, he has been willing to enjoy more than a few good hugs!

Peter was the proud papa of an extraordinary display of creativity, and every second I was with him, whether I wanted to or not, I found myself studying him. Not just the way he handled the technical aspects of directing a $270 million production, but how he interacted with people, what it was about his personality that prompted people to be drawn to him, what it was in his decision-making process that made him so much smarter than I was. From the moment I met Peter, I thought, *If I can earn the respect of this cat, if I can get him to see me as an equal, I will have achieved what I really want to achieve on this movie.* That he was disappointed in me, or frustrated with me, or not willing to use what I had to offer the process, was at times mortally frustrating to me. But that's more my shortcoming than his. It's funny: as smart as I sometimes think I am, it's amazing how stupid I can be when it comes to the way I perceive other people.

As I see it, Peter Jackson's brilliance, at least as it pertains to filmmaking, stems primarily from his cleverness and his relationship to power, and the way he can exert his power comfortably and with aplomb. I wasn't in certain rooms with him when critical decisions were being made. I didn't see how he built the consortium or how he would build consensus, or how he would strategically machinate toward achieving a particular thing at a particular moment. But I did see some things, and I did hear stories. I know at one point, when he was $11 million into the Miramax deal, he found out that Miramax had misgivings about the way the production would be handled. *The Lord of the Rings* was originally to be divided into two segments, not three, and the studio was questioning the wisdom of that choice; maybe one movie would be enough. So somehow Peter took the project to New Line, which not only agreed to support more than a single film, but a trilogy!

Over time these types of stories become somewhat apocryphal or mythologized, and getting at the truth of them is best left to journalists, film students, or the primaries themselves. Suffice it to say that anyone who could pull off such a miraculous feat had to know something I didn't know. Probably a lot I didn't know. There is an idiosyncratic part of my personality, a flaw in my attitude, that has informed a lot of interactions I have had with extraordinary people. For some reason, when I was a kid hanging around movie sets or sound stages, I wanted to be in charge of everything. I wanted to feel as though I could, to some extent, control the environment. Of course, I couldn't actually compel people to do things, but I developed a knack for being persuasive. People used to say I could sell ice to the Eskimos. I'm not sure where this unctuousness came from, but to a greater or lesser extent, it's been a component part of my life. I used to joke that I suffered from a rare disease called "proximity to scope." Because I grew up in such close proximity to filmmakers who routinely achieved greatness in their work, I naturally assumed that I was capable of doing equal or even better work. Imagine Patton inhabiting the body of a ten-year-old Hollywood brat and you're getting close. Now picture me in New Zealand being exposed for the first time to the brain trust and nerve center of Peter Jackson's outfit. I was in awe and had to admit to myself that I was at least momentarily out of my depth. Then and there, I resolved to learn everything I possibly could about every aspect of this phenomenal enterprise.

Walking through Weta Workshop, I saw ironsmiths working on swords and shields, and hundreds, if not thousands, of orc masks. We toured the digital workshop, where so much of the films' ground-breaking computer-generated imagery would be produced, as well as an editing facility and the aptly named 3Foot6 Limited studio, where the hobbit holes had been assembled. There was an oversized hobbit hole, and right next to it, a miniature one, so that when Gandalf walked into the miniature hobbit hole, he would look and feel like a giant. I was struck by the array of techniques being applied to bring Tolkien's world to life: some of it was clearly on the technological forefront, but some of it was decidedly low-tech. I would learn over the course of the production that anything was worth trying. No good idea would be dismissed as unreasonable.

That the production design seemed to be driven by Alan Lee's art-work was also readily apparent. I'd been impressed by his drawings, but here I was in awe of his imagination. The man behind the art is more subdued, but no less impressive, than the work he creates. We met on that first day in Alan's office, a spare, nondescript little room made distinctive only by the drawings he had tacked to the wall. Standing there, soaking up the atmosphere, I had a sense of under-standing and clarity that I hadn't experienced before. There weren't a lot of drawings in the edition of *The Lord of the Rings* I had purchased, so this was the first time I felt a strong visual sense of Middle-earth. I'd read the scripts on the plane and found them exciting—all the fighting and the spiders and the trolls and everything—but this was something else.

I wondered how we'd actualize this other world I was discovering. Sure, I knew about blue or green screens, but from the smell of fresh-cut wood from the sets, to the paint and the hum of activity of hundreds of crew folks all around us, it was clear that Middle-earth was under construction. And frankly I wasn't sure how it would look. Now contemporary actors have a lot of history and information to draw on. Our collective consciousness is pretty strong for us in the area of special-effects pictures. We've all seen various "making of" videos. I'd seen Sam Neill running away and looking over his shoulder at a tennis ball that would later be replaced by a digital T. rex in *Jurassic Park*. I knew what sort of environment I was entering, and I thought I could do that sort of work pretty well, because I have a good imagination. But here, surrounded by Alan's illustrations, it suddenly felt *real*.

A few of John Howe's paintings were there, too, but somehow I wasn't as drawn to them. In fact, I worried that if they used Howe's color pallet for the set design, it wouldn't be the kind of movie I wanted to see; it would just be a real cool fantasy movie. I didn't know Peter Jackson's work well enough to know which direction he would choose. *The Frighteners* had been visually arresting, but I'd had problems with it. I enjoyed the special effects, but I didn't really like the campiness of some of it, and the third act disappointed me. (Of course, I hadn't yet watched the extended version, which I'm sure is more satisfying.) What came through in the early pages of *The Lord of the Rings* was excellence: storytelling in service of important ideas. Not the world, not the characters, not even the story, but rather the richness of the language and the quality of the ideas as they were being presented. It struck me on an intellectual level, rather than an emotional level, and the challenge, in my mind, was to make sure that my artistry would be able to survive in concert with literary work of that caliber. Ridiculous as it may seem now, I was concerned, maybe even a little worried, that Peter wouldn't understand that aspect of the book.

I was wrong, of course. I underestimated Peter, or at least didn't know him well enough then to understand his cleverness and level of commitment. There's an old saying by Thomas Edison: "Genius is one percent inspiration and ninety-nine percent perspiration." That's Peter. Man, he perspires like no one I've ever seen. And I mean that in the best possible way. He *works* at it. Sometimes I think people fail to recognize that trait in artists. They think it's all about talent or luck or some mystical creative spark. I've experienced it myself; I've found my own creativity muted by other people's genius occasionally, because I look at what they accomplish and I think, "I would never have thought of that. How could they be so smart? How could they be so inspired?" Well, inspiration takes work. I've heard Peter talk repeatedly about using the art of Alan Lee and John Howe to gain inspiration. But what does that really mean? It's more than just saying, "Wow, that artwork is incredible!" It's deeper. It's saying, "I'm going to communicate with that artist, and I'm going to convince him to work with me." That's what Peter did. He figured out what really inspired him.

My read on *The Frighteners* was that the studio wasn't interested in the dark, psychological stuff; they just wanted the really scary set pieces. So they turned the sound way up and assaulted the audience. I missed a sense of universality or an optimism in *The Frighteners*. It seemed designed for people interested in cool effects, and in death and dying. It wasn't a movie for me. Even so, I liked it because my dad was in it and because I could appreciate the artistry. I liked Michael J. Fox, the star, although I was disappointed that he didn't look quite right. Only much later did I learn that around that time Michael was just starting to suffer from Parkinson's disease. I admired that both Peter and Fran seemed to care more about Michael the human being than their movie, despite the stakes being so high. That, too, gave me faith.

Equally impressive was my first meeting with Richard Taylor, whose special-effects work on *The Lord of the Rings* would be honored with multiple Academy Awards. Richard brought me in to see the "bigatures," the not-so-miniature miniature sets the crew had painstakingly constructed, and they were so beautiful, so perfect, so real, that I wanted to cry. I had loved miniatures when I was a kid. Not that I was smart enough to figure out how to fashion them or create them. My mother had an assistant, Elaine, who was one of the most artistic people I've ever met, and when as a kid I had a brief fetish for Smurfs, she made miniatures for me out of cardboard, the most wonderful, elaborate Smurf houses and Smurf garages you could imagine. She made a train station to go with my train set, a lovingly detailed building based, she said, on the station she often visited near her home in Connecticut. Elaine spent hundreds of hours making these things for me and my little brother, and we'd play with them for days on end. Sometimes I'd film them with my Super 8 camera. Elaine wasn't just a model maker; she was like a design engineer. And yet she was working as an assistant for my mother, which I found perplexing. Why, I later wondered, hadn't anyone figured out how to make her a rocket scientist?

Then *Star Wars* came along, and I loved that, too, especially when I saw how George Lucas had created some of the special effects using miniatures. When I worked on *Memphis Belle*, I felt like I really understood the process and appreciated it. Miniatures were used to re-create World War II. There were assembly lines of B-17 miniatures, all destined to be blown up in one fashion or another. And they all looked so real.

So now, walking into this room, meeting Richard Taylor and seeing his miniatures, which were obviously the crème de la crème, I was nearly overcome with emotion. Imagine a kid who likes building models and hanging them over his bed. Imagine saying to that kid, "Where do you build your models?" and hearing him say, "I use the dining room table." Now imagine taking that kid, who loves making model trains or rockets—a kid with an extraordinary attention to detail, for whom building models represents a method of artistic and personal expression—and saying to him, "I'm going to give you a big factory and all the tools and all the time and money you need to build the greatest model ever."

That kid was Richard Taylor.

I tried to build a replica of the USS *Nimitz* when I was a boy, but I failed miserably. I tried to make a glider and failed. I wanted to be good at making models and miniatures, but I wasn't. I did like remote-controlled cars and got fairly adept at making them, but that's about it. Here I was, though, looking at Richard Taylor and a staff of about twenty-five guys who were spectacularly good at it. They'd been hired by Peter and given seemingly unlimited resources. This paint factory was vast, and the miniatures housed within were almost beyond comprehension. I wasn't sure what I was looking at, but I knew it was a representation of a city. I saw orc mines, surrounded by a wall twenty feet high and a couple of hundred feet wide. There was an unbelievable level of detail in these miniatures: like a visitor admiring Renaissance paintings at the Louvre, you could stand and stare at them for hours and not grow tired of the experience. So striking was the level of detail that the cinematographer could take a 35-millimeter camera, put it right next to the miniature, and film it, and the human eye would have no idea it wasn't full-scale.

The experience was nothing short of stunning, and it took my breath away.

Wow! Peter Jackson gets it. He really, really gets it.

In hindsight, that sounds like such an ungracious, stupid thing to say, but everyone has their level of skepticism about how things can or should be done. What got me down to New Zealand was the possibility, not the certainty, that *The Lord of the Rings* would absolutely be done right. It's one thing to look at pictures, one thing to know there's a franchise, one thing to understand the potential of a director. It's another thing entirely to look and feel and smell and hear the results. The armory, the weapons, the leather, the level of detail in every inch of the production was exactly what I would have wanted it to be. The actors were just arriving, and already Peter had accomplished so much. He had assembled a legion of artisans and craftspeople so devoted and committed that you'd get a little wave of anxiety just watching them at their stations: *God, I hope when it comes time for me to do the thing I'm here to do, I can produce a fraction of the integrity, talent, and emotion that all these other people bring to their work.*

There was so much to see and soak up. Richard was talking non-stop; Peter was chiming in whenever the mood struck him. At every stop on the tour, someone would interact with us intensely and briefly, just long enough to provoke a sense of wonder and confidence, to give us the feeling that we were all going in the right direction and that it was going to be an unforgettable ride. So much was thrown at us at once, so many bewildering tidbits of information—"Weta has ordered more foam rubber than any other company on the face of the earth!"—that the effect was almost disorienting. Each person we met seemed to have some specific, almost arcane area of expertise, and each was utterly and completely thrilled to be on this production. They were devotees of the literature, experts in their field, and they were totally committed to the dream of actualizing this movie.

Some people on the production had only the slimmest of connections to the film business, yet they possessed particular talents that merited inclusion. Others used *The Lord of the Rings* as an opportunity to break out of a box, to demonstrate themselves worthy of a land-mark project. Consider the case of Ngila Dixon, who would win an Academy Award for her costume work on *The Lord of the Rings*. Ngila had been working on *Xena: Warrior Princess* and *Hercules*, a pair of campy, good-looking television shows, but representative of a specific type of entertainment. I wouldn't necessarily expect the wardrobe people to take their jobs too seriously on those programs, but you know what? They do. They absolutely do, and you realize after watching them work that the people who do *Hercules* can also do *The Lord of the Rings*, provided there's the right leadership and resources. All in all, extraordinarily talented people were working at every level of the production, but often the lines just got blurred. It became nearly impossible for me to tell who was responsible for something or who deserved credit, because it was such a gigantic, cooperative venture.

"Authenticity" was a buzzword. Peter wanted everything to be based on a kind of history, even if that history existed only in the mind of J.R.R. Tolkien. That's one reason why Alan Lee's illustrations provided more guidance than did those of John Howe. Similarly, the armor worn during battle scenes was not simply the product of a designer's imagination, but was based on real armor. The amount of intelligence and sophistication applied during the research phase of the project, coupled with the money that was invested, allowed everyone to do their jobs at a level I had never seen on a movie set. Still, there was always a sense that cash was being burned. And while $270 million may seem like a ton of money, it goes fast. So fast, in fact, that at each level people felt they didn't have quite enough money to do their jobs. Even so, they were doing more with what they had than anyone else would have been able to do. Why? Because they cared. They knew they were part of something extraordinary.

It was almost impossible not to feel that way. I remember during Peter's guided tour, stopping at a glass case filled with costumes and masks, including those worn by my father as the decrepit judge in *The Frighteners*.

"Look, Alexandra," I said, pulling my daughter close. "There's Granddad."

She didn't respond, just scrunched up her nose disapprovingly, as if to say, *What? That mangy old character?*

It's funny, when you're in the movie business, you cycle through stages: awe, then disillusionment, and then hopefully, a new appreciation for it. And then you get lost in it all over again. You go through waves of how you experience reality and fiction. *The Lord of the Rings*, for me, was a psychological cyclone, an emotional, analytical torture chamber out of which grew something magical: a sense of wonder that I hadn't experienced in a very long time. And I am so very grateful for it.

The notion that I'd have the opportunity to focus on my numerous entrepreneurial ventures during "downtime" in New Zealand was revealed to be pure folly within moments after we arrived in Wellington. As Peter explained some of the logistics—there would be at least three crews shooting at once, using twenty-four cameras at various locations around the country—it dawned on me: *Holy shit! There isn't going to be any downtime.* I realized quickly that work would expand to exceed the time allotted. Indeed, there was never a time, in nearly a year and a half of principal photography, when Peter or any of his assistants were complacent or even satisfied. They rarely, if ever, said, "Great shot, we've got it; let's move on." Instead, we kept going back and redoing things, rewriting and reshooting scenes that, to even a trained eye, seemed to have been captured in a perfectly acceptable manner. Peter had taken all the money and resources he could extract from New Line, and then he went about the business of doing things his way, the way of a perfectionist. Early on I got the sense that no one at New Line truly understood what was happening on location.

Sure, they were getting all the dailies, but that was practically irrelevant, since no one human being could possibly watch everything that was photographed on any given day. There weren't enough hours on the clock. Consider that there were nine hundred-plus days of miniature photography, and every day an hour of footage, maybe an hour and a half, could be shot. And that was just the miniatures. Then you had the insert units shooting a half-day, the second unit shooting three hours a day, and the main unit shooting an hour a day with multiple cameras. So while on most films the dailies usually amount to maybe ninety minutes of footage, on *The Lord of the Rings*, daily footage could average four to six hours a day. That is astounding. At the time, it was also a bit depressing, and not simply because of the exhaustion such a schedule provoked. There was also the nagging feeling that reel upon reel of great stuff would never see the light of day, simply because there was no room for it. Yes, Peter needed a lot of material. We were shooting three movies, not one, and each was going to run for more than three hours. Nevertheless, there was no question that Peter's schedule was so ambitious, and his vision so broad, that only a portion of what we shot would be used in the final movies.

There were times when this presented a problem, when Peter asked for a tenth take, or a twelfth take, or a twentieth take, and I wanted to scream, for I just started losing track of what I had done.

An actor develops a shrewd sense of what's likely to end up on the screen. On the set of *Courage under Fire*, I shot a scene in a bar with Denzel Washington, and in the middle of the scene, in between takes, or when they were turning the cameras around to do my close-up after Denzel's close-up, I had this horrible feeling that the entire plot of the movie was coming to a screeching halt while we indulged in a scene devoted to the backstory of Denzel's character. I walked up to Ed Zwick and said, "Ed, maybe I shouldn't be asking you this, but what are the chances that this scene is going to end up in the movie?"

He laughed. "Pretty much none."

"Then why are we shooting it?"

The reason, Ed explained, was that it was an important piece of the puzzle—not for the viewer, but for Denzel, who was trying to sort out his own character. Actor and director hadn't arrived at a point where they felt comfortable cutting the scene from the movie, so they filmed it, possibly as a courtesy to the star, or as a way for the director to feel the nuances of the scene. I think they needed to shoot it in order to cut it from the movie. Usually, in cinema, you can put a lot more money on the screen if you get to those answers sooner; similarly, as an actor, you don't want to get married to such indulgences. I'm not saying Ed was being wasteful—it always happens, but as an actor, you don't want to show up at the premiere looking for the scenes you fell in love with, only to discover that they've been left on the cutting-room floor. That has happened to me on several occasions, and it would happen with *The Lord of the Rings*.

Not that I was surprised. I knew the movie was going to be spectacular, but I wondered what would become of those little moments, those nuances that were captured somewhere on take seven, eight, or nine, with a C camera or a D camera whirling around the set, picking up reaction shots, when I was fully in character and emoting like crazy, and something magical, but peripheral, was happening. What were the odds a director could find those? One of the director's primary tasks in the editing phase is to tell the story, or to search and destroy those moments that don't work. But finding every little nugget that does work? Who has the time or the energy for that? It's not the way the process is designed.

I hoped that Peter Jackson would know just what to do, but I couldn't imagine how anyone could budget their time and marshal their energy to accomplish the mission. What I did know, from the very first day, was that he seemed excited and inordinately confident. Talent and ambition aside, Peter remained, at his core, a fan. During that first tour, Peter joked that he wanted to have his memory erased, so he wouldn't know how the film was made. He wanted to see it and enjoy it, just like anyone else. That's when I really understood how unique Peter is. Even though he needed to have confidence and faith and be this titanic figure on the set, there was an overriding sense that he was engaged on a purely emotional, almost childlike level. Despite the pressure and the exhaustion and the sheer enormity of the task, he was genuinely happy to be there. I remember looking at Peter one long afternoon, roughly halfway through the production, and saying, "I'll bet you can't wait until this is over so that you can get a good night's sleep."

He laughed softly under his breath. "I'll get a good night's sleep tonight, Sean."

And he meant it, too.

Peter's enthusiasm was infectious, particularly in the early days, when the entire production was bathed in optimism and energy and a sense of limitless opportunity. This feeling extended to the interaction between actors. Each time I met someone, it was like bonding with a fellow explorer. Among the first was John Rhys-Davies, who played the warrior dwarf, Gimli. We met in the Portacom, a ten-by-twenty-foot mobile hut, the kind of thing you might see at a construction site, which initially served as a green room for the cast. I was looking forward to meeting John—I'd been a fan of his ever since I was a kid, watching him as Sallah, Harrison Ford's comic sidekick in *Raiders of the Lost Ark*. John was boisterous and funny, not unlike the characters he's often played. He walked in, extended a hand, and introduced himself. "I'm John Rhys-Davies and I live on the Isle of Man, otherwise known as ten thousand alcoholics clinging to a rock in the middle of the Irish Sea. Hello, my lad!"

Well, this is going to be interesting.

To John's amusement (and sometimes chagrin), I quickly jumped into an accurate impersonation of his voice as Sallah. I'd pass him on the set and say something like, "Indy, they're digging in the wrong place!" And if he didn't love it, he was at least tolerant. One day he did sort of raise an eyebrow and say, "You know, my boy . . . sometimes it borders on *parody*."

I loved being around John, even though we have generally opposing political viewpoints. He's a very conservative man—the polar opposite of, say, Viggo Mortensen, who played Aragorn. I'm more of a centrist, so even though I don't necessarily agree with John, I can appreciate where he's coming from.

It was difficult not to feel for John, who suffered like Job throughout the entire production. His face reacted badly to the makeup—and it took a long, long time for the artists to apply the makeup for Gimli. John spent countless more hours in the makeup chair than I did, and I admired his perseverance, although his discomfort was so great that his double, Brett Beattie, was called on to do an unusual amount of work—so much work, in fact, that there was discussion about Brett getting co-credit for the role of Gimli. He wasn't the voice of Gimli and he didn't appear in close-ups of Gimli, but day in and day out, the amount of time he spent in makeup and on the set was sufficient to prompt consideration of a co-credit from the people who were with him on the set so much. Several more close-ups of John were added in pickups, though, and the controversy, such as it was, faded away. ("I'm not in the habit of giving away the credit for my character," John once said.) And John was a terrific, if sometimes overzealous, promoter of the film.

"Rrrrrrraise your expectations!" he shouted at our first press conference, while thrusting an index finger into the air. "This movie is going to be bigger than STAR WARS!"

To which Peter replied, "Settle down, John."

I absolutely love the combination in tone of what John achieved with his character. He strikes the perfect comic bravado and layers it with gravitas. During the premiere in Wellington, I felt like I had achieved some rite of passage when John and I rode in the same car during the ticker-tape parade.

I met Billy Boyd (aka Pippin) in those first days, too. My first impression of Billy was magical. I was totally enamored of him, in no small part because of his voice. I loved listening to Billy, and even though I could barely understand a word he said through his thick Scottish brogue, I got the feeling (borne out over the course of the production) that he was a really appealing, sweet, kind of guy, the sort of man with whom I wanted to be friends. He was gentle and funny and very cool, very comfortable in his own skin. Both Billy and Dominic Monaghan (aka Merry) have a natural grace when it comes to performing humorous scenes, or when improvising for the amusement of the cast and crew. They worked well together, and that was reflected on-screen. The friendship that developed between Dom and Billy transcends description in any book I could ever write. They are unique human beings with exceptional talent. Living in close proximity to them over the years of making and promoting *The Lord of the Rings* taught me a lot about myself. There are cultural differences between us, to be sure. I think they were much better prepared emotionally to become pop culture figures than I was. Their sense of personal style and their comfort with themselves were qualities I occasionally found in short supply for myself. But the connection we formed was real and permanent.

The same could be said about my bond with Elijah Wood. The

This shot is from our first day in New Zealand. We had no idea about the incredible adventure that awaited us.
PHOTO COURTESY OF THE AUTHOR

The first party at producer Barrie Osborne's home before principal photography began.
PHOTO COURTESY OF THE AUTHOR

Flying from Wellington to TeAnau in a 1942 C-3. This was always a scary flight, but on this particular trip we hit a storm and made an unscheduled landing in Queenstown. PHOTO COURTESY OF THE AUTHOR

(*Left*) As you can see from the party props in the background, this is from the early scenes of *The Fellowship of the Ring* in Hobbiton.

Hanging out at Alan Lee's house.

The amount of detail that went into creating the sets was incredible. PHOTO COURTESY OF PIERRE VINET

...li, Billy, Elijah, and Dom ...uring free time. They are her ...vorite adopted uncles to this ...ay. PHOTO COURTESY OF THE ...JTHOR

Alexandra spending time with her friend, Orlando.
PHOTO COURTESY
OF THE AUTHOR

One of my final scenes: Sam's triumphant return to Hobbiton. PHOTO COURTESY OF THE AUTHOR

Enjoying a yacht in Auckland during the America's Cup.
PHOTO COURTESY OF THE AUTHOR

A day on the links with producer Rick Porras, myself, Elijah and Peter Jackson in Rotorua on the Nor Island. PHOTO COURTESY OF THE AUTHOR

Orlando and I motorbiking in Queenstown. PHOTO COURTESY OF THE AUTHOR

Myself, Elijah, Orlando, and Billy play at a party. We were awful. PHOTO COURTESY OF THE AUTHOR

Alexandra and I enjoy the view in Queenstown. PHOTO COURTESY OF THE AUTHOR

Alexandra and Liv at the Wellington premier of *The Fellowship of the Ring*. PHOTO COURTESY OF THE AUTHOR

Viggo and Phon help decorate for Alexandra's fourth birthday party. In fact, the entire cast and crew (over 100 people) pitched in to celebrate at our home. PHOTO COURTESY OF THE AUTHOR

Billy, Dominic, Elijah, and I on set. PHOTO COURTESY OF PIERRE VINET

That's me bungy-jumping at the world's first
bungy site—Kawarau Bridge. It was a 142-foot
jump.

On set with Elijah right after I defeated Shelob. PHOTO COURTESY OF THE AUTHOR

Lending moral support as Ian gets his tattoo. PHOTO COURTESY OF THE AUTHOR

Orlando and I are all smiles at the tattoo parlor. PHOTO COURTESY OF THE AUTHOR

friendship between Frodo and Sam resonates with audiences because it appears to be genuine. There is chemistry, and chemistry rarely happens between actors who do not care for each other. I can honestly say that I love Elijah like a brother. And like any sibling relationship, ours is at times a complicated one. When we met in New Zealand (which was the first time I'd seen him since our brief introduction at the Ma Maison Sofitel), I had the weird feeling that Elijah was something of a chameleon. It happened at a restaurant called Castro's, where the cast and the "upper echelon" of the production team (including Peter, Fran, cowriter Philippa Boyens, Barrie Osborne, and then producer Tim Sanders) gathered for a preproduction party. Elijah and I shared a big hug, but I sensed something a little bit different abut him, something I hadn't noticed when we met in L.A.

He was happy to be there and happy to see me, but he had a more cosmopolitan air about him. He was smoking his ubiquitous clove cigarettes, and he was dressed very sharply—it was apparent he had a clear sense of his own personal style. In sum, he looked like a movie star, and I remember marveling at him. Here I was, just a guy trying to put a jacket on so I wouldn't be cold or look out of place, trying to figure out what the hell to wear to dinner, while Elijah seemed unburdened by such trivialities, even though it was obvious that in fact he gave such things considerable thought. It just seemed to come naturally to him. He was ten years younger than I, but already he had figured out how to move elegantly in virtually any crowd.

Much has been made of the bond between the hobbits, of the camaraderie that extended from the set to the pubs of Wellington and back again. To some extent, that's an accurate portrayal, for indeed we all got along well and indeed there were nights of debauchery and drunken revelry. For the most part, however, I was on the fringe of this scene. My circumstances were different. Billy, Dom, and Elijah (as well as Orlando Bloom, who played Legolas) are all young, single men, and to varying degrees they enjoyed the status and benefits of being movie stars in an exotic location. On the night of the first party, while others mingled comfortably, I fretted about whether I was stepping on toes by bringing my wife and daughter with me. I worried about things like that. Christine would always just roll with it. She seemed respectful of my concern, but also thought I was a fairly bad judge of propriety.

As much as I wanted to be respectful of other people and the dynamic of the set, I knew I had to carve out a place for myself and my family. I didn't think it was a big deal, since my father had often talked about Peter and Fran and how cool they were when it came to familial matters. He described their hotel room during the promotion swing for *The Frighteners* as being laden with baby paraphernalia; surely they would understand my trying to find the same balance with my family. As a young father I was a little out of my element. As someone who craves a sense of control, I found that the universe was playing a little trick on me. While everyone was getting comfortable with each other, I was eager to fit in. I wanted to prove to myself that I could be a good husband and father, while simultaneously thriving among this auspicious group of artists.

To that end, I tried to make sure that my dressing room on the set was like another room at the house: anytime Christine and Ali wanted to be there, they were welcome. I wanted that and needed that, and I wanted the production to understand. I could work eighteen, nineteen hours a day, but I also knew that I'd be better on the set, better at my job, if my family was there when I got back to my dressing room. Everyone had their own thing. Viggo Mortensen had his artwork, his photography. The "boys"—Elijah, Billy, Dom, Orlando—had their video games and their music and their movies. Such things were considered sacred, for they provided a much needed respite from the endless slogging that the production became. I didn't smoke cigarettes or play as many video games. My diversion was my family—having my wife and daughter there if they wanted to be there.

When we first landed in New Zealand, we felt a little like a military family in a new community, but eventually we got into a pretty comfortable rhythm. Ali went to school with Peter and Fran's children, and everyone found their own routine. Christine took a philosophy class and nurtured a coterie of friendships. She was even allowed to apprentice in the editing room. This was an interesting dynamic. During the filming, the actors weren't generally privy to things relating to postproduction. We all knew that the films were being assembled concurrently, but I think it's fair to say that we didn't have too much access to that realm. Peter or Fran would show us clips if we really wanted to see something, or send us moments to help reconnect us to our character if it felt like we were drifting over time. Also, the cast and crew were treated to edited sequences after the return from a holiday or a given two-week break in order to reenergize and refocus everyone on what we were doing. These screenings were an adrenaline shot to the soul during production and helped keep everyone sane. But beyond that, I don't think many of us in front of the camera spent too much time seeing the stuff we were shooting. I was respectful of the boundaries when Christine started volunteering in the editing room, but I couldn't help feeling a little sneaky every time I would pick her up at the editing facility. I could see the elves working to put the movie together in their workshop, and it was exciting.

That first dinner party went well, but at a certain point Alexandra became tired and started nodding off, so we arranged a chair for her to sleep in. Meanwhile, the boys broke off and were having an intense conversation, the subject of which was, *Which pub should we hit first?* I was torn. I wanted to go out with the guys, but I also wanted to make sure that my wife and daughter were taken care of. Tim Sanders sensed my inner conflict and approached to offer his sympathy. Sort of.

"Oh, it's gonna be hard for you, huh?"

"What do you mean?"

He smiled. "You're the married one."

My first thought was, *Screw you, dude!* But you know what? He was absolutely right. It was hard for me, because I wanted to be able to hang out with the guys and enjoy my time with them, and Christine wanted that for me. And yet my fundamental priority was (and is) my family. For the most part I went home to Christine and Ali, and I found strength in seeing them and holding them every night. There were times when Christine and I would get a babysitter and go out with the gang, and there were times when Christine would stay home and I'd join the guys on my own. But my stamina was nowhere near theirs in terms of drinking or carousing, which I considered a reminder that I was indeed older and at a different place in life than they were.

We were fairly deep into the process of making the first movie before I finally had a night out with the boys, a chance to really bond with the other hobbits. We met in the lobby of the Plaza International in Wellington, in a lounge area where you could get appetizers before going into the restaurant for dinner, and we all sat around with our drinks, talking and laughing and having a good time. In some way, I think I had begun to internalize the Frodo-Sam relationship in the Elijah-Sean relationship. I wouldn't exactly call it method acting, but I liked the idea of playing those roles—at least once in a while—away from the set. I'm older than Elijah, I'm the married father of (now) two children, and I've been in the movie business most of my life. It would be a gross simplification to suggest that I could be Elijah's mentor, because he's quite an experienced and worldly young man himself—and was even then, at only eighteen years of age. Ours is a wonderful and complicated relationship. By the time we met, Elijah had already worked opposite some of the biggest stars in the business. By a creative standard, his career was arguably much more successful than mine, and yet according to some people (Dom, for example), I was more well-known than he was. It's not important, just a little something that provides a fuller understanding of our friendship and professional rapport.

Anyway, we were all having fun that night. I was particularly happy to be experiencing a taste of grown-up, child-free time, and I liked hanging out with my costars. I discovered that Elijah had inadvertently locked his keys in his apartment, and instantly I took it upon myself to say, "Don't worry. Enjoy yourself; I've got it covered." With the help of the hotel concierge, I found a locksmith who went over to Elijah's apartment, got his key out, and delivered it to me. Elijah never had to lift a finger, never had to worry about anything. I did this because I wanted to be Sam, so Elijah could just keep being eighteen and in Wellington. I wanted to serve Elijah, just as Sam might have done for Frodo.

But there were other times when I tried to look after Elijah in a much more serious manner, more like the big brother that I sometimes felt I was. Elijah could be courageous and even inattentive when it came to some of the more elaborate action sequences in the film. If a scene called for a stunt, the crew would wrap something around Elijah's leg and use a cherry picker to haul him up into the sky, and Elijah didn't mind at all. He'd do it in a heartbeat! He just didn't care. He was so trusting. But I did care. I'd grown up on movie sets. I'd seen people get injured. The guy who was my teacher on *The Goonies* also had the misfortune of working on the set of *The Twilight Zone* many years earlier. That film, of course, is infamous for a stunt that went tragically awry, resulting in the deaths of three people, including two children. I believe that on a movie set you have to share the responsibility for your own safety, but Elijah was not concerned about that. He knows that I think he was too trusting of the production. I was perhaps more cautious than I needed to be, and sometimes I'd annoy people. But I didn't want to be the guy on the set who wasn't paying attention when Elijah's leg was ripped out of its socket.

On this particular social night out, however, I didn't think it was important for Elijah to learn a lesson about being careless with his keys. I thought it was more important that he have a good time, courtesy of "Sam." So while I ran around and rescued his keys, he continued drinking, smoking clove cigarettes, connecting with cast and crew, perhaps eyeing the ladies. Not that Elijah was a rake, mind you. He was much more elegant than that with the fairer sex. For an eighteen-year-old, I thought, he was remarkably graceful and sensitive and thoughtful.

CHAPTER NINE

All right, I admit it. I took a shortcut. Tried to, anyway.
Before we moved into the rented house in New Zealand that would serve as our home for the better part of a year and a half, Christine and Ali and I stayed at the Plaza International Hotel, in a nice suite with a lovely view of Wellington harbor. One evening, just a few days into our trip, I filled the bathtub and settled in for a long night of reading.

Listening, actually.

While Alan Lee's three-volume tome sat unopened on a nightstand nearby, I tried to absorb an audio version of *The Lord of the Rings* that had been recorded for the BBC. It featured, among others, Ian Holm, the esteemed British actor who, of course, played Bilbo Baggins in the film trilogy. I settled at first for listening to the story because I was afraid people would ask me questions that I'd be unable to answer, and this would allow me to complete it more quickly.

Even after reading the scripts, I still didn't have a firm grasp of the story. I understood my dialogue and what the story was supposed to represent, but I wasn't emotionally invested in the nuts and bolts of the screenplay, partly because I felt guilty about not having read the books. Quite a conundrum, huh?

Granted, the solution was obvious: sit down and read the damn books! As had often been the case when I was a child, though, I found the task intimidating. More than a thousand pages, hours of time, when I didn't really have the time to spare. And I must admit that in those early days and weeks I found it difficult to toggle back and forth between what I wanted to do and what I *had* to do—between my responsibility as a professional actor, someone who wanted to be thoroughly prepared, and my desire to have fun with my family in an exotic locale. No one was telling me what to do. I don't think I had to read the Tolkien tales in order to do my job (in fact I know that some people, most notably my partner in crime, Elijah, never read the books in their entirety), but there were expectations. Peter knew from the way I presented myself in our meetings that I would be totally committed to the project, which meant studying hard and being pre-pared. I had if not a professional obligation, at least a moral mandate to take up residence in Tolkien's universe.

Eventually, within the first few weeks of principal photography, I would complete the entire trilogy, as well as *The Hobbit*, which served as a neat introduction and made the task of reading *The Lord of the Rings* not only easier, but more worthwhile. This wasn't exactly a unique experience, since several million people had come before me, but once I picked up *The Hobbit*, I found the books to be enthralling, enrapturing, like nothing else I'd ever experienced. I finally enjoyed them as a reader; as an actor assigned the task of interpreting one of the story's key characters, I felt enlightened, emboldened.

Before that moment of illumination, though, came the shortcut—and the doubt and anxiety and, yes, the abject fear. Not so much from the audio version, which was enjoyable and elegantly performed and permitted a degree of effortless absorption that mirrored those early "reading" sessions with my mother. No, the panic set in when I made the mistake of watching a videotape of Ralph Bakshi's 1978 ani-mated version of *The Lord of the Rings*. Seeing how Bakshi portrayed the hobbits—as predominantly fat, bumbling, stupid characters—I nearly had a heart attack.

Please, God, don't let Peter Jackson approach it this way.

I should have had more faith, but it was too early in the process. I wasn't sure what Peter had in mind, and I knew that Bakshi was far from a hack. He had his devotees, and I'm sure he knew the story and felt that his was an entirely appropriate interpretation. Moreover, the animated version had its moments. The ringwraiths, for example, were spectacularly depicted. I could appreciate what Bakshi was trying to do as a director and an animator and a storyteller, but I was concerned mainly with Sam and how he would be portrayed. Not having read much of the books, I couldn't help but feel that I might have made a critical mistake in agreeing to play the part; I had no respect for the bumbling idiot that Samwise Gamgee appeared to be—at least in the eyes of Ralph Bakshi. At that point I didn't understand the importance of the hobbits and what they meant to the story. I didn't have a grasp on their sense of nobility. They just seemed like frightened nitwits: *"Oh, Mr. Frodo, help me! I don't know what to do!" Pleeeeeease!* I wanted Sam to be heroic and strong, to have integrity. He was a gardener, a working-class man. That's the Sam I wanted to portray. Admittedly, there are a lot of interpretations that can be gleaned when you read the books, so bringing it to the screen is not an easy thing. There are probably thirty valid ways to depict the hobbits. But I had my own idea of how I wanted Sam to be perceived, and it was set in concrete. What I had in mind wasn't that . . . that *thing*, that animated oaf on the videotape.

At times during the production I felt isolated and rigid in my beliefs about how the hobbits should be depicted. Even the other actors were more willing to embrace the silly or whimsical side of their characters. Dom, for example, enjoyed being a bit more hokey, playing up the notion of hobbits as little people, almost like leprechauns, or at the least, childlike. I resisted. By putting on oversized feet it would be easy for clumsiness to rule the day, but I wanted the character's gait to be comfortable. I wanted it to be honest and real. I was pleased the first time I stepped into the complete hobbit ensemble, replete with backpack, and Sam's walk emerged naturally.

That I wasn't alone in striving for authenticity was something I found immensely reassuring. In fact, that goal, while perhaps open to interpretation, was paramount in the minds of everyone on the production. The nature of our six-week "boot camp" prior to the start of principal photography was such that it left us all with a feeling of excitement and preparedness. We'd receive marching orders each evening, detailing how every moment of the following day would be filled. From seven in the morning until six at night our bodies were required to be in specific places, for specific tasks.

Dialect training was particularly intense, at least for me. I'd meet in the Portacom with Andrew Jack and Roisin Carty, the dialect coaches, and we'd make small talk just to loosen up, and then I'd get a lesson about how sounds are made. You don't think about it much in everyday conversation, but there are specific ways to use the tongue and the teeth in order to achieve certain sounds. They'd give me booklets to read, audiotapes to review, and my job was to practice speech patterns. There was a laundry list of things that needed to be done in order to get the dialect just right. The cockney accent I had employed during the audition was deemed inappropriate for Sam; they wanted me to do a "Hobbiton," which they saw as a Gloucestershire-inspired accent.

It was hard for me to get it right. I could do the thing that Elijah was doing as Frodo, a standard British accent: *"No problem for me whatso-evah."* I'd done that a hundred times. But to push it into West Country . . . well, that was harder. It's very hard to do *"thaaaaat."* Andy and Ro kept trying to get me to elongate the sounds, and I struggled mightily to do so. It felt like emotional warfare, even though I was completely inspired by and respectful of their expertise. I didn't really know who Sam was, so I wanted to give myself totally to them. At the same time, I wanted to feel good about what I was doing.

"Come on, Sean, extend the word *that,*" the dialect coach would instruct. Say 'Thaaaaat.' '

"Thaaaaat."

"No . . . Stretch it out. *Thaaaaaaaaat.*"

"Thaaaaaaaaaaaaaaat."

"Again! *Thaaaaaaaaaaaat.*"

"Thaaaaaaaaaaaaaaaaaat."

"Good!"

I feel like an idiot.

For a while it seemed that Andy and Ro were a little nervous, concerned that I wasn't ever going to nail the dialect. And I'm not sure that I did nail it, but I tried, and I think the results are good enough.

The production team did a thorough job of filling our days with valuable instruction, so it was up to us to manage our own energy level, and to muster the requisite strength and courage and acumen. We had access to a personal trainer, Dave Nuku, for an hour and a half each day.

There was, depending on the species you were playing, horseback training, archery training, canoe training, and sword training. It seemed as though whenever there was a free moment, we were sent back for more sword training. I think our endurance was being tested as much as anything else. We had to be battle-hardened, and we all accepted it.

We also accepted the idea that we were down there and we belonged to the studio. I got the distinct impression that if I wanted to do something with my wife and my child, I was expected to work it out on my own time. That didn't bother me, not in the beginning anyway, simply because I was so excited. I thought, *This must have been what it was like for Errol Flynn, or Jimmy Stewart, or any of the legendary stars in Hollywood who worked under the studio contract system and whose every move was dictated.* There's an aspect to that kind of control that's creepy, yes, but there's also something weirdly reassuring about it. I mean, I had dancing lessons during boot camp! This was to prepare me for a brief scene (trimmed to be even briefer) in which Sam dances with his future wife, Rosie Cotton.

Such devotion, such support, was exhilarating. It was an actor's dream. I felt at times like I was at the peak of my career, that nothing could ever hold a candle to what I was experiencing on *The Lord of the Rings.* I liked that these people understood everything about making a great movie, including the notion that an actor's body had to go through certain motions in preproduction so that he'd be ready to perform at a high level. Simply waking up in the morning and going to work felt good, like I was involved in something important. Something hard, yes, but also something that had the potential to be extraordinary. There was just one problem: I was getting fat. The weight lifting, combined with a diet that consisted of whatever the hell I wanted to toss down my gullet, left me feeling thick across the back and shoulders, and ample in the belly. Not an inappropriate state for Samwise Gamgee, I suppose, and I know Peter approved, but I found the transformation to be exhausting and depressing.

There was, as you might expect, considerable bonding between cast members. *The Lord of the Rings* was a male-dominated production, and the atmosphere often mirrored that of a football team's locker room. Conversation routinely was reduced to the most vile and base sort of talk—male bonding taken to its most ludicrous extreme. I remember thinking, *I hope the driver has a confidentiality agreement, because if anybody were to hear what we're talking about in this van right now, no one would ever respect us again. It's appalling. If my wife could hear me, I would be in grave danger of never being able to even hold her hand again.* We were all equally responsible for our sophomoric behavior, for telling raunchy jokes and heaving filthy insults at each other. Billy and Dom were particularly effective at this little game—not as good as I was, but close. Of course, their strength was impeccable comic timing. But we all played a part.

As I look back on it now, I realize that the point of preproduction training was not simply to get us ready for the hard work ahead, but to toss us all—hobbits, dwarves, elves, wizards, and men—into a cauldron and see what bubbled to the surface. With any luck we'd forge friendships and alliances, and the strength of those friendships would be reflected on screen. Elijah led the way. "We're going to be friends forever!" he'd say. Inside, I was more jaded. I was older and had been on numerous movie sets where I had felt similarly enthusiastic about my fellow actors. Inevitably, though, over time we drifted apart.

I wanted to believe Elijah was right, but he was young, and I thought he hadn't been around quite as much, so I had my doubts. However, at this writing, in the spring of 2004, I can honestly say that we do remain friends. But it's been easy so far. Looping and various postproduction obligations, as well as the seemingly endless publicity tour that has accompanied the trilogy, have made it easy, even necessary, to get together. We shall see what time holds. I hope the truth is closer to what Elijah believes than what my experience tells me is likely to happen, because we really did go through something special. The actors on *The Lord of the Rings* were closer than on any other movie I've ever been on—probably closer than on all the other movies combined.

Before the start of principal photography, Ian McKellen and I found ourselves at Peter Jackson's house viewing *The Lord of the Rings* in animatic form. An animatic is basically a crude animated version of a film, almost like storyboards set to music. It's a relatively cheap but effective way of presenting the complete story in visual form.

Arriving at Peter's home was like arriving at the modest castle of a king, or at least one of the noble lords of the manor. I had been to

Steven Spielberg's house; I'd been to Richard Donner's house. I'd seen a lot of different mansions. I'd toured throughout Europe and visited ancient castles, and in my estimation Peter was the kind of feudal lord or captain of industry who would live in a way reflective of that spirit. Well before *The Lord of the Rings* phenomenon, I'd read a news story about him being one of the richest people in New Zealand, and when you meet people like that, you can't help but gauge how they wear their wealth, or whether they're worthy of their riches. I remember feeling as if Peter and Fran were like the king and queen of New Zealand. They were connected, and it reinforced my idea of them being masters of their domain. Peter is accurately depicted as a favorite son of New Zealand, someone who has pioneered an industry and given work to thousands of people—tens of thousands by extension, when you consider the money pumped into this film. He's a part owner of the movie theater in Wellington, and part owner of a film laboratory and special-effects company. He is a man who has had, and continues to have, a huge impact on the development of his country.

But the house . . .

The first time I saw it, I was struck by how little it resembled the house of a king. It was beautiful and sprawling and all of that, and the view toward the harbor was breathtaking. But it wasn't a mansion in the traditional sense of the word; it wasn't a monument to the ego of its owner. It was, well, comfortable. It felt like a home, rather than a museum, which I found extraordinarily appealing and impressive. I liked the idea that Peter and Fran weren't obsessed with their house; instead, they were more interested in work and family. Part brick, part wood, three stories high, it was an appealing, funky house that looked like a lot of older New Zealand homes. A very warm, unpretentious kind of residence. It didn't draw attention to itself. Yes, there was a playful coat of arms, but it wasn't like Bruce Wayne's house, where the coat of arms is standing there, and you feel like, *Ooooh, it's marble, maybe I should salute.* The house was lived in; even the couches were worn from having welcomed so many friends. The one thing that did concern me was accessibility. Peter and Fran were so reluctant to relinquish their normalcy and their comfort with people that they sometimes failed to understand the magnitude of their own celebrity. I once told them they needed a security buffer, and Peter looked at me rather disdainfully, like he was annoyed that I didn't understand New Zealand culture, that kind of Kiwi spirit, and that I was an elitist Hollywood guy. But I had a few glasses of wine in me, and I didn't mind telling him what I thought.

"You've got kids; you need to be careful. You shouldn't worry about preserving an image of being cool and down to earth."

Peter dismissed me with a wave and a chuckle, but a few months later, when media and fan attention became oppressive, they made sensible adjustments to their entranceway.

This particular night was my first opportunity to spend a fair amount of time with Ian McKellen. When I had first arrived in New Zealand, the role of Gandalf had not yet been cast. Or, if it had, the news hadn't been leaked to the media. Gossip and innuendo had been circulating for some time that Sean Connery was going to be offered the part. I had asked Peter about this a couple days into my stay, and he merely raised an eyebrow and feigned disinterest, like someone enjoying the fact that the rumor mill had gotten going. Peter understands the value of such things; he knows that when the fan base is vibrating with that kind of noise and energy, when there's so much genuine interest—when Tolkien purists debate the merits of a given actor and question the director's wisdom—it's beneficial to the production, provided it's managed correctly. Sean Connery is a hero of mine; nevertheless, I thought he would have been distracting in the part, and I wanted to share with Peter my take on that. But he didn't bite.

Peter once said that New Line had told him to make an offer to Sean, and another time he said no such offer had ever been made, so I really don't know where the truth lies. I did find the process fascinating. It seemed that in the upper echelon of the business, it was all about saving face: Did someone make an offer? Did a brilliant and famous artist extend himself across the world? Did Sean Connery say, "This is something I would like to consider?" Obviously, Peter Jackson, when building a project of this magnitude, wanted to both capture and trade on the success of other people. Certainly, he wanted to include the core talents of incredibly gifted artists, while managing their egos and dealing with the ancillary business dynamic that is attendant with hiring world-class artists. Given all of that, did Peter reach out to Sean?

In other words, what the hell happened? How do you get sophisticated enough to do it? Do you fall in love with somebody's talent and say, *God, he's so right for my project that I'll put up with any amount of shit to have him here?* Or do you say, *I recognize that this person is a legend in his field, and he would bring a certain level of energy and distinction and credibility, but is he right? Is he really right?*

A fair question. My father has such a nobility of purpose and philosophically realized attitude about human nature that I think he might have tried to impose that on his Gandalf. Sean Connery has a kind of rugged persona that has been honed and magnified over decades. Everybody knows Sean Connery and what his thing is. I wondered whether anyone would be able to see past that, past the fact that he was Sean Connery. Would the audience accept and believe him as Gandalf?

The only reason I mention this is that I'd like people to know that actors, like fans, are susceptible to curiosity and intrigue. I think there's a perception that once you're on the inside of the project, you get to know everything, but that's just not true. I suppose if any of us really wanted to know something on *The Lord of the Rings*, all we had to do was ask, but that's not the way it worked a lot of the time. The movies were a huge operation with many people, many egos, and a lot at stake for everyone involved. Some of us were on a need-to-know basis, and some of us had better or quicker access to information than others. Elijah was funny about this stuff; he always seemed to know everything that was going on a nanosecond before everyone else. I was generally a few beats behind everyone. We were deluged with such a mountain of paperwork, a seemingly endless stream of constantly updated information about locations, call times, crew lists, schedules, traveling itineraries, script pages, invitations to various events, publicity stuff, and so on. The data stream was like Muzak to me. I was focused more on the practical implications of what I was doing or would be required to do on a given day.

Unlike most productions, this project could nimbly adjust everything to accommodate for radically changing conditions in weather, set construction, or a myriad of other scheduling exigencies that might arise. Since I saw myself as a low man on the totem pole (at least in terms of having an impact on the schedule), I resisted staying too up to date with production logistics. I probably would have enjoyed myself more if I had treated the dynamics of the shooting schedule like a parlor game and played at getting inside the heads of the producers. But I experienced something on *The Lord of the Rings* that I'm not proud of. To anyone who happened by, it was obvious that the people in charge of the movie were engaged in something unique. I had so little decision-making ability on anything relating to the bigger picture of the films that I was, in a word, jealous. I envied the hell out of Barrie and Peter, the two most visible decision makers around. They got to make decisions every day that affected the movements and fortunes of dozens if not hundreds of people. They were focused on the business and creativity of the pictures, but in a larger human sense they were exerting a kind of power over others; in a very un-Sam-like manner, I wanted to share in that. But it was not to be. For obvious and more subtle reasons, I endured a kind of torture, watching people doing the very thing I had dreamt about my whole life— and doing it better than I probably ever would.

Peter and Elijah and virtually everyone who knew me well could sense that I had a hard time bottling my enthusiasm and desire to, if not be in charge, at least have a say. Again, I'm not proud of this, and even while we were shooting, I knew how inappropriate my feelings were. But it was such a long time commitment that I couldn't just tell myself, *Hang in there; soon enough you'll be able to get back to the business of try-ing to accomplish a modicum of what these geniuses are doing.*

I got to watch and learn and be patient and suffer. I read dozens of books on filmmaking, even while sitting off to the side of the set waiting to be called in. I wanted Peter to see me reading, giving myself the kind of education that he clearly gave himself as a devotee of cinema. But his learning was purer than mine. He genuinely loves everything about movies. While I do, too, I'm trying to share a different driving force in my personality. I wanted to understand how the power I could behold in Peter and Barrie and the studio heads was born and nurtured and built. I wanted to earn Peter's respect and admiration as a contemporary and as a thinker. It was so stupid—all I really needed to do was focus on my acting, and everything else would naturally have flowed from that, the way Elijah or Andy Serkis or Billy Boyd did. But I couldn't. I had too much of a certain kind of experience as an actor. The very reason it was good for the production that I played the part of Sam—namely, that I didn't need too many technical things explained to me—was the root of a lot of discontent for me. Peter and others didn't have to get me comfortable with the language of filmmaking the way they might have if they hired a less experienced person to play the part. I knew pretty readily what I needed to do for Sam, and it didn't take up too much of my time to be ready. I didn't have too much control over the direction of my character, in the sense that it was clear that the right thing to do was just be ready to give Peter whatever he might want for the part. But I couldn't help it. Ambition burned in my belly, and professionalism and courtesy and survival compelled me to swallow my silly pride and twitch with the knowledge that, *Man, if only I could be let loose in this arena, I could accomplish extraordinary things!* I would watch as thousands of extras assembled, or listened as people communicated somewhat inefficiently, because the protocol mandated waiting for access to Peter before moving ahead. Suffice it to say that for me this kind of patience is nearly unbearable.

But getting back to my first night at Peter's house . . .

The question about who was "right" for Gandalf was irrelevant. Ian McKellen had arrived in Wellington. He *was* Gandalf, and that was that. On this night and afterward, envy and insecurity often permeated my interactions with Ian. I found him at once inspiring and intimidating. I wondered why I wasn't smart enough to know what he knows, like how to create a character: deciding on the size and shape of the nose, the length of the hair, the beard, the ears, and turning to Alan Lee's illustrations not just for enjoyment but for guidance and meaning and inspiration. Everything about Ian and the way he approached his craft was so thoughtful and evolved and considered that it was obvious why he's the caliber of actor that he is. And I was in awe of him.

That said, there was also a part of me that sensed some artifice in Ian's approach to acting. I wanted to arrive at the creation of my character in a more organic, honest, ground-up way, rather than from the brain down. It would be hard to argue that my approach makes more sense than Ian's, given the caliber of his work and the plaudits that have been heaped on him over the course of a long and distinguished career. And, yes, I know it may seem insulting for me to compare my style with his. But I want to share the way that I felt. Certainly I know, deep in my bones, that Ian has probably forgotten more about acting than I'll ever know.

But there we were, watching the animatic together, with Peter sitting right behind us. This, for me, was an important experience. I had always wanted to be in that environment, where you're at the house of the filmmaker, getting into his head, having conversations at a place close enough to the source of the Nile that you might affect how the river will be shaped at the other end; where there is the real possibility of having a substantive impact on your character or even the film itself. Acting is more fun when you feel like your ideas matter. You feel valuable, and you have a greater investment in what you're doing. So to be in Peter Jackson's house, just a couple of weeks before shooting was scheduled to begin, sharing dinner and conversation with Ian McKellen, well, that was like Christmas coming early for me.

Sort of.

I had seen and admired Ian in several films, most notably *Gods and Monsters*. By anyone even remotely knowledgeable about movies, he was considered a very important actor. So I studied him that night. I tried not to be too obvious about it, but that's what I was doing. At the same time, I was trying to act like I belonged in the room, reminding myself that I had talent, too; that I was right for the part; and that while I could learn from somebody who was a little bit older, somebody who had succeeded so completely in his craft, I wasn't exactly chopped liver. I wanted to absorb the conversations around me while communicating ideas of my own, but I knew I was swimming in deep creative and intellectual waters.

Much of the conversation centered on the animatic. I found it hard to concentrate on the actual story because I was so intrigued and inspired by the thought and technology behind it. To help shape the movie experience for his actors, the studio, and the crew, Peter had gone to the trouble of spotting the soundtrack or choosing musical accompaniment from *Braveheart* and other movies. I know what it takes to put together coherent storyboards, and the animatic was essentially storyboards set in motion. So much energy had been expended, so much time. The way it was photographed, the way the camera panned across the images—I was as intrigued as much by that as by the story.

Not that the animatic wasn't a valuable tool. It was, for it helped illuminate and clarify certain things in terms of rhythm and pacing, and pivotal moments. I had finished *The Fellowship of the Ring* by this point, and I had read the beginning four or five times. And yet I remained confused. That whole bit about *Three rings and the Elvin kings under the sky*. I didn't really get. I got it on a poetic level, that it set the tone in terms of language and style, but as far as the story, I just couldn't comprehend it. Why were there this many rings or that many rings? The animatic, however, contained the prologue that was more or less used in the movie, and seeing that helped me understand the books. To his credit, Peter had allowed for the fact that some people hadn't read the books, and for that I was grateful. As a serious, interested, and invested party who had engaged the books and failed to grasp their meaning, I felt frustrated. Peter's sense of composition and story, combined with the work of the artists, helped me see the story. That, in turn, made me more excited about reading the books. I was determined to have finished the full trilogy before we started principal photography. I missed my deadline by a couple of weeks, but I did finally complete the books, which is a good thing, because I'm sure my performance would have suffered if I hadn't. Moreover, I would have felt like an idiot and a slacker.

There was one thing about the animatic that I found frankly terrifying: the realization that in assembling the presentation, Peter and Fran had clearly allowed other actors to read the screenplay. After all, someone had to read the lines, right? So there was someone playing Frodo, someone else playing Aragorn, someone playing Bilbo and Merry and Pippin and Legolas—and someone playing Sam. My role! More than anything else, this stirred within me a feeling of competitiveness, as if I were getting ready to play a baseball game. Granted, I already had the part, and it was perfectly reasonable and even kind of cool that Peter had such a community of friends in drama that he could just pull them together and do the equivalent of a table reading. But there was something else. The way the actor read the lines for Sam in the animatic, the way the character was portrayed in the Ralph Bakshi cartoon and the BBC audio version—all three were similarly deficient in portraying Sam as the heroic character I wanted him to be. Not one of them lived up to my expectations. The feeling that maybe the book lent itself to a particular type of reading concerned me because I had committed a year and a half to the project. If it turned out to be just a show for kids or for fans of the genre, and not something that I would want to see, then that just wouldn't be acceptable to me. I had faith in Peter and the process, but something happened in my skin when I was sitting there watching the animatic. Afterward, I tried to demonstrate for my boss that I was respectful and had the requisite amount of inspiration. At the same time, I didn't want to fake it.

Ian, as far as I could tell, experienced no such inner turmoil. On the drive back to the hotel afterward, he said, "Isn't it great to be working for a couple of hippies who have the business so wired?" That was it! He'd put his finger right on it. There is such a quality of whimsy and ease and confidence surrounding Peter and Fran. This movie, this trilogy, was going to consume their lives—it already *had* consumed their lives—and yet on some level they didn't take it too seriously. It was, after all, just a movie.

Yeah, the biggest movie in history . . .

Hour after hour, day after day, week after week, Peter would display a preternatural grace. I became exasperated at times, just as almost everyone did. But I never saw Peter panic. I never even saw him get angry. Not really. I've since come to the conclusion that his is a rare type of confidence, the kind that can only be possessed by someone who knows exactly what he's doing, and how it's going to turn out.

I think Ian figured that out before anyone else. He knew how to exploit Peter's generally laid-back nature, and how to communicate with him on an intellectual and creative level. He'd done his homework. He knew who Peter was as an artist and a filmmaker, and he used that knowledge, in conjunction with his own status as a beloved icon of the British stage, to get deep inside Peter's head. Ian's portrayal of Gandalf was enhanced as a result.

Not that Peter was blind to the machinations. There is no chance of that. I think Peter genuinely respected Ian's intelligence and dramatic sense, but I was awash in awe and envy and frustration that Ian was so clever at understanding the issues, and idea, not just within the movie and the story, but behind the scenes as well. He brought to the project and to the role a breadth of experience and a depth of knowledge unmatched by any other actor. He was a decorated Shakespearean stage actor; he'd costarred in the Hollywood blockbuster *X-Men*; he'd compiled an impressive and eclectic body of work in contemporary cinema. In short, he had gravitas. He had power, and he leveraged that power in negotiating with the studio, and in communicating with Peter and Fran and Philippa, so that their rewrites affected how his character appeared on the page, and subsequently on the screen. I was smart enough to recognize all of this, but not smart enough to figure out how to mimic Ian's style in the best interest of my career or in the development of Samwise Gamgee.

More to the point, I wasn't sure I wanted to follow his lead. My relationship with Ian was then, and remains to this day, somewhat of a disappointment. That's my responsibility as much as his.

Ian is a brilliant man and obviously a serious actor, but he has a great sense of humor, too, which he'll act on once in a while. There's some great footage tucked away somewhere of Ian doing wardrobe tests, where he's dressed as the venerable Gandalf the Grey in his long gray cloak, and suddenly he snaps out of character and launches into this little raunchy catwalk, with a glimpse of underwear, a flash of thigh—just a flamboyant gay guy having fun. And he did it fully aware that what made the performance amusing was that the star was *Sir* Ian McKellen, one of the greatest actors of our time.

Ian is complicated, though. He was perpetually annoyed at having to share a makeup bus with the boys. Elijah is the most passionate music lover you'll ever want to meet, and our long days on the set usually began in the makeup trailer at 4:30 in the morning, with the ritual of Elijah taking out his CD binder and deciding what everyone would hear. Sometimes he'd take the temperature of the room and entertain suggestions from the other hobbits, and sometimes he wouldn't. Many mornings I just wanted to read—I brought thirty-seven books with me to New Zealand, and used my three hours in the makeup chair to digest each and every one of them—but there were times when the choice of music made it difficult to concentrate. I just endured it quietly, because I knew it was important to Elijah and the other guys to get in the right frame of mind.

But Ian was less tolerant. He actually had himself removed to a different makeup station because he couldn't take it anymore. The music, he said, was giving him a terrific headache. Ian had no problem registering his dissatisfaction with what he considered to be absolute rudeness on the part of the other actors. How did he do this? Well, when you entered the truck from the back, you'd see four makeup stations, then a door (almost a partition, really), and then a fifth station. Ian took this last station, and whenever he needed privacy, he would simply close the door.

I love and respect Ian. I think he's an incredibly brave and articulate advocate for gay rights. I recognize his talent and his success for what it is. That said, I also know he can be selfish and self-centered. For example, I could write an entire chapter in this book called "Sir Ian McKellen Stole My Makeup Artist!" Because he's *Sir* Ian McKellen, and because he's smarter and funnier than I am, and because he's farther ahead of the curve on most decisions than I am, Ian figured out how to work the politics of the corporation so that he could poach at will someone with whom I had developed a long working relationship. He didn't ask for my opinion or permission; he just made sure that he was taken care of. Frankly, of course, he was entitled to this sort of treatment, and I got over it, but it was painful for a while. Now, changing makeup artists may not sound like a big deal, but when you're spending three hours a day in a chair, you do develop a certain rapport with the person assisting in your transformation. One of my three makeup artists was a gifted, world-class craftsman named Jeremy Woodhead. We became good friends, hung out a lot, played tennis. But when Ian's makeup artist quit to take another job, Jeremy greeted me one morning with the news that he was being reassigned. "I'm going to be working with Ian," he said matter-of-factly. There was no debate, no negotiation.

When the Academy Award nominations came out in the spring of 2002, after the first movie, my publicist asked me to call a Los Angeles radio television station. *The Lord of the Rings: The Fellowship of the Ring* had received thirteen nominations, including a best supporting actor nod for Ian McKellen, and I was asked to provide a few sound bites. So I called in and they put me on hold, and while I was listening to the show, guess who called in live from London? Ian McKellen! They congratulated Ian and chatted for a few minutes about his nomination and the film's success, and then, to my great surprise, the host said, "So, Ian, what do you think of Sean Astin's performance in the movie?"

Ian paused for a moment. Then he said cooly, "Oh, well, to be fair, he didn't really have much to do now, did he?" The way he said it . . . well, it seemed they hadn't told him I was on the phone, and they hadn't told him that he was going to be answering that question, so it was an honest reaction. And yet it allowed for the possibility that he might have been kidding. So afterward the host said, "That's funny, Ian, because guess who's on the phone? Sean Astin! Sean did you hear what Ian just said?"

What could I do? I laughed. "Oh, Ian and I know exactly how we feel about one another. I just wanted to call and congratulate him. Congratulations, Ian, on an extremely well-deserved nomination."

"Why, thank you so much, Sean. Good to hear from you."

As I said, he's complicated. While I was working on a television show in Vancouver in the summer of 2002, Ian was filming the X-Men sequel nearby, and I called him one day just to say hello. He invited me over to his place and we talked and had tea; then he drove me to the theater and introduced me to Dame Edna Everage, who I had never seen before, and we had a wonderful, interesting evening. We parted with an embrace and a kiss and a fare-thee-well. Unfortunately, it's not always like that with Ian. He's a towering presence, and when we see each other I always feel a bit disappointed that he's not nearly as interested in me as I am in him.

Then again, I'm sure he has a lot of incredibly interesting people to choose from.

CHAPTER TEN

Peter broke the news toward the end of the six-week prep period, in a quiet, private conversation at his house, probably because he sensed my anxiety.

"You know, Sean, Sam is not going to be that big a character in the beginning. He's going to grow with each film."

Sadly, he wasn't referring to my girth. No, Peter was trying to let me know that I would have to be patient, that Samwise Gamgee would have his moments, but most of them would come late in the game. Very late. This was not an easy message for Peter to deliver, and it wasn't easy for me to hear. In fact, it nearly broke my heart. I felt that in order to have earned the emotional impact of the third film, it was critical that the character, in all of its sweetness, sincerity, and earnestness—in all of its integrity—needed to be clearly established early in the first film. Also, on a much more selfish level, I couldn't imagine that if we were going to be shooting for eighteen months, that I'd spend six or seven of them inhabiting a weak and underdeveloped character. And then I'd have to endure two years of press cycles following the release of *The Fellowship of the Ring* and *The Two Towers*, knowing the impact it would have on my career if my character was little more than a shadow.

Of course, as the director and cowriter of the screenplay, it was Peter's prerogative to shape the story and its characters in whatever manner he deemed appropriate. And, after all, I had begged him to be in the movie. I had written him a very specific letter, wishing him well and offering my services at any level. When I reflect on the sentiment expressed in that correspondence, and the fact that I used it to get a seat at the table, it seems unfair and selfish of me to second guess how much or how little Peter wanted to include me. But there were times in New Zealand when reflection wasn't my greatest strength.

Peter earned my respect by being honest with me, by revealing his vision for the film and the character, and asking me to trust in him. But I disagreed with him in my heart, and I was devastated by his decision. I remember hearing him explain the rationale behind his decision, and I remember feeling my eyes dilating, and a tightness in my chest. I didn't want to cry in front of him, but I very nearly did. I just couldn't understand his logic, and his words went in through my ears and straight to my heart, provoking that flood of adrenaline, or whatever it is, that occurs when you hear bad news, that hot rush of blood that you can feel in your fingertips. Knowing full well that if I responded badly, it would send the wrong message to my boss—it was, after all, my job to weather such decisions with calm professionalism— I swallowed hard and blinked back the tears.

"I understand, Peter," I responded, even though I didn't want to.

There was a sense on the project that rampant egotism would not be tolerated, that no one was bigger than the film itself. This was an ensemble piece in the truest sense of the term, and each of us was expected to accept and perfect his role as a cog in the machine. If you couldn't meet that standard, for whatever reason, you could and would be replaced. The most glaring example of this dynamic occurred on Day One of principal photography, when the hobbits were sequestered and informed that Stuart Townsend had been dismissed from the production.

Stuart is a talented Irish actor who had been cast in the role of Aragorn, even though at twenty-seven years of age he was surely too young for the part, at least as it was written. Aragorn is a mature man, closer to middle age than adolescence, scarred by loss and weary from years of battle. It was obvious why Peter and the producers had fought for Stuart—he was charming and handsome and was no doubt going to be a big movie star—but it was also apparent that he was wrestling with the notion that he was perhaps too young and lacking the physical stature for the role.

We were all getting to know each other in those first couple of months, and on a fairly intense level, since we understood that the right thing for us to do was to become real friends, and to do so quickly. To that end, we opened up to each other almost instantaneously. The family element for me made it different, but not really difficult. The other actors were open to the idea that I'd show up with my wife and daughter, and Ali would sit on everybody's lap, and they'd be the uncles and the big brothers and we'd all have a good time. Inevitably, though, they'd pull away and go off to the pubs or the clubs, and I'd go home. But I'll say this: the natural half-life of the interaction with a youngster ended sooner for a lot of other people than it did for Stuart. He was young and single; he'd never been a parent and had no intention of becoming one in the near future. And yet he was great with my daughter. He was just really cool. If Elijah had that *thing* that I was studying—what to do if you're an A-list movie-star type—then Stuart had something else. Stuart reminded me of Bono, the lead singer for U2. He fairly dripped cool.

Maybe it's because I have Irish blood in my veins that I'm drawn to the Irish sensibility, that lust for life, that honesty you see in an Irishman's eyes. I know he drives a lot of people nuts, but I think you get the same thing from Colin Farrell. It's unique, it's real, and he has it. Stuart Townsend has it. But there is a difference. I think Colin might have more of a sense of humor about himself, a more playful attitude toward his work and life. Stuart isn't going to sell out on any level, whereas Colin is willing to sell out a little bit because it's fun and will give him a more extraordinary ride around the planet. Stuart isn't like that. He seems to torture himself and submit to his own demons more readily than is good for him, I think. That's the feeling I got in New Zealand. So when Peter and the producers broke the news that Stuart was gone, no one was shocked. Mortified? Yes. Saddened? Deeply. But shocked? No.

My wife and daughter had a lot of affection for Stuart, as did I. My heart ached for him. But insomuch as it was possible to consider anyone being dismissed from the project, it wasn't a surprise. My wardrobe fitting occurred at approximately the same time as Stuart's, so I saw firsthand some of the trauma he endured while trying to inhabit his role. The guy was absolutely beside himself with discomfort, both mental and physical. He just didn't look right, didn't feel right, and he couldn't explain what needed to be done to correct the problem. Even Ngila Dickson, who is a genius at costume design, couldn't figure out what to do. Neither could Peter. They were all trying to work toward a solution, but Stuart wasn't helping matters. He was a black hole of negative creative energy.

I kept wondering why he couldn't just relax and enjoy the process. This was supposed to be the fun part of acting, the dressing-up and playing. When I tried on my costume, a couple of things were not quite perfect, but by and large it felt right. I liked being Sam, and I felt a sense of ownership with the character and the clothes. It felt *good*. There were similar problems with Orlando Bloom's costume, but Orlando was so keen and so obviously right for his part that no one was overly concerned. They just kept working at it until they got it right. But a combination of factors for Stuart—primarily his own fear—proved insurmountable. There was one time in particular when I could see how hard it was for him, and how heavily the job weighed on him. We were eating at a great little bayside restaurant called the Chocolate Fish—my family and I, Stuart and Orlando and the other hobbits—all of us having fun, praising the production, sort of toasting the adventure of a lifetime. At some point during the evening I found myself alone with Stuart, and I could sense his anxiety.

"This is a pretty awesome opportunity for you, isn't it?" I asked the question almost out of empathy, as a way to give voice to that great pink elephant in the living room that no one wants to talk about. Stuart was so intense, and yet so clearly agonized by what was happening. He wasn't enjoying the experience in any way. And yet he wasn't false. He wasn't manufacturing the pain. This was almost like a personality trait for Stuart, a genuine recurrent theme. As much as I liked him, I could tell that others, particularly those in charge of the production, found him challenging. There were, for example, times when they wanted him to do sword training, but he was focused on something else. You could just see him struggling to figure out the character, and he was so connected to the nature of the struggle that the solution wasn't presenting itself. Now, I carried no position of authority—we all had moments of insecurity about our own capacity as actors—but I think in my Zelig-like personality, I instinctively try to have something in common with whoever it is I'm talking to. So, when Stuart projected trepidation, I probably manifested my own trepidation about myself as a way to connect. And he responded to it.

"A pretty awesome opportunity..."

His head snapped around, and on his face was a soulful, almost pained, expression.

"Yeah," he said, and as he spoke, the breath seemed to leak from his body. I waited for more. But that was it. A single, sad word.

That image came back to me a few weeks later when we were told of Stuart's departure. There was something about his acknowledgment of the magnitude of the role, which carried with it the promise of making him a major bona fide motion picture star and serious actor for generations. Maybe he just couldn't handle it. Or perhaps Peter determined that Stuart's way of handling the role would have been inconsistent with the spirit of the production. Regardless of the reason, and regardless of whether it was a surprise or not, it was a terribly unnerving development. Suddenly you got the feeling that things had changed, that job security was not to be taken for granted, and thus a prudent man would know better than to whine too loudly whenever his ego was bruised. I had been reluctant to advocate passionately for my position regarding the character of Sam, and now that seemed like a wise course of action. You have a survival instinct as a person who's been hired to do a certain job, and the efficacy of that awareness was made all too clear when they told us that Stuart had been fired.

Already, Peter explained, they were out looking for the next Aragorn, and I knew why. Stuart hadn't been capable of doing what I had done, and what most of the other actors had done, which was to sublimate his own desires about his character to Peter's vision of the character, and to say with your whole consciousness, "I'm going to lean forward like a skier at the top of the mountain and give myself over to the process. I'm just going to trust that I'm the right guy for this job, that it's going to work, that Peter is that good and that talented, and he'll take care of me."

That's quite a leap of faith, but it was necessary if we wanted to survive on such a sprawling, at times incomprehensible, production.

While in New Zealand, part of my research for the project involved renting and viewing much of Peter Jackson's early work, most notably *Meet the Feebles*, an almost impossibly raunchy and funny movie. Let's put it this way: I'd never seen a movie in which the characters curse like longshoremen, drink and vomit like frat boys, and engage in sex acts that would make a porn star blush. At least, not one in which the characters are portrayed by puppets! Imagine if Jim Henson had been kidnapped and raped and forced to do LSD—*Meet the Feebles* would be the nightmare that experience provoked. Written by Peter and Fran, the movie tells the story of an eccentric, demented acting troupe in all its self-indulgent, pseudoartistic glory. While watching it, I experienced a number of reactions: laughter, shock, revulsion, and outright fear. *Meet the Feebles* demonstrated that Peter and Fran were so sophisticated about the egos and set politics of actors that there would be no pulling any crap with them. There were no little theatrical, drama-queen tricks that you could play to elicit a response. They were through the looking glass. They absolutely understood the nature of vanity in the actor, and the nature of self-serving comments coming from actors trying to jockey for position in a show.

One of the great, unspoken trump cards between them (Peter and Fran) and us (the cast) was, in fact, the very existence of *Meet the Feebles*. I know it helped keep me in line. You see, I have this little self-pity mechanism that I can click into; I don't know why or how it developed, except that maybe sometime in my life I used it once or twice and it was effective, so I keep it in the repertoire as sort of an emotional escape hatch to deal with situations that make me uncomfortable or unhappy. With Peter and Fran, though, I wasn't allowed to use that mechanism. Oh, sure, I indulged in a bit of self-pity at times, but nobody responded to it. Like screaming in the wilderness, it was a thankless emotional exercise, and unfortunately the brunt of it was taken out on my wife. I thought then (and still do, although as time passes I'm less inclined to rationalize my own bad behavior) that there was a legitimate reason for my frustration. Christine, though, tolerated only a small amount of whining.

"Open your eyes!" she'd say. "You're part of something unbelievable."

Then she would run through a list of, oh, twenty-five or thirty anecdotes that reflected varying degrees of feedback and recognition for the work I had done. Unfortunately, my inability to exorcise the egocentrism from my personality spectrum led to a good deal of unnecessary, self-induced misery during the making of these movies. Elijah absorbed a lot of it, too, because we talked about it. Most of the time he was really positive. He would indulge my self-pity to the extent that it made sense to honor it, and then he would joke with me about it, or not honor it when it was destructive to do so. Or he would have a visceral, knee-jerk kind of reaction: "You're being an idiot; don't do that." All of which was fine. I needed him and I needed Christine to help me set limits to my own selfishness. And I did try to reciprocate. If Elijah went negative (which rarely happened, by the way), it was like flipping a switch: I turned into the most optimistic, most tireless, most aware, self-realized, inspired individual on the planet.

These were the types of psychological games I played to keep myself entertained, because we were down there for so long, imprisoned in this spectacular, but sometimes spectacularly tedious, process. If you talk about it with people in casual conversation, you seem ungracious, totally out of touch with reality. I remember at one point chatting with Dominic about my feelings, and he just scoffed. "Listen, man, you need to get some perspective. Are you out of your fucking mind?"

I needed a cold slap in the face like that every once in a while, and Dom could always be counted on to provide it. Dom is, by degrees, a tougher guy than I am. He'll fight with little provocation, and he'll not tolerate bitching that stems from self-induced misery. I don't mean to completely dismiss my own suffering on this production, because it was the hardest job of my life, but the truth is, there were people in close proximity whose suffering far exceeded my own.

Stuart Townsend was the first and most obvious example. Peter was getting feedback from a lot of different quarters that it wasn't working out well with Stuart, so I think Stuart has to bear the brunt of the responsibility for that himself. I'm sure Peter would love to have had a crystal ball, so that he might have foreseen the consequences of his decision. New Line did not want to hire Stuart, but Fran and Peter used their influence with the studio to help him get the part. They reasonably felt that Stuart could overcome his youth and make the part his own. And maybe he could. Maybe Stuart could be a great Aragorn. I suspect he could. Certainly there is no reason to believe he can't be a major leading man in Hollywood, but given the particular dynamic of this film, I think Peter and Fran believe they did Stuart a disservice by rallying around him to get him the job, only to discover several weeks later that it wasn't going to work out. The studio sometimes gives notes that are completely antithetical to what the artist is trying to do, so the artist develops a defensive posture with the studio. It takes a pretty sophisticated mind to absorb the good and bad of studio notes and elevate the nature of the work to a level that is consistent with those notes. Peter is as good at that as anyone I've ever seen. He picked his battles and gave the studio plenty of victories along the way, but ultimately he remained true to his vision.

Stuart was a casualty of one of those battles. And when he was gone, he was simply gone. Vanished. There were no long good-byes. By the time we found out, he'd already left the country. I left a message for Stuart on his cell phone, but never heard back. Everyone was really worried about him for a while. What happened to Stuart, to be presented with a major opportunity and then have it taken away, is almost cataclysmic for an actor. I haven't talked to him since, but I know several of the other actors have. He's recovered nicely and done a bunch of movies, but it's obvious based on interviews he's given that he has sour feelings about the whole thing. I don't know if Stuart is capable of taking responsibility for his part in why it worked out the way it did, but I like to think that everything happens for a reason. Eric Stoltz went through something similar with *Back to the Future*, in which he was replaced early in the production by Michael J. Fox. Now, Eric is a dear friend of mine, and he's told me the story of his firing on more than one occasion. I know how painful it was for him. As his friend, I could offer only empathy and understanding; as a moviegoer, my honest feeling is this: it's hard to imagine anyone doing a better job in that role than Michael J. Fox. (When I first saw *Back to the Future*, I wanted to scream when the movie was over. I enjoyed it so much that I didn't want the experience to end. I understand fans who get attached to a particular movie, like *The Lord of the Rings*, because that's the way I felt about *Back to the Future*.)

Things just happen. I don't think anyone had nefarious motives or was operating with ill will in regard to Stuart's dismissal. For this production, Viggo Mortensen was the right choice for the character of Aragorn. I wouldn't go so far as to say that it's difficult to imagine anyone else in the role, for the simple reason that I worked with Stuart for the better part of two months. There are certain elements of his persona that would have been interesting in Aragorn. There is a brooding romanticism to Stuart, a genuine pathos you see in his eyes; your heart wrenches when you see him on screen. Viggo is a much more austere actor, and that is reflected in the way he portrays Aragorn. His strength and beauty and sex appeal derive from some other place, so it's pretty hard to compare the two of them. Stuart would have been a very different Aragorn. He might well have been a very good Aragorn. Given the fan and critical reaction to Viggo, however, it's hard to argue that the wrong choice was made.

The story of Viggo Mortensen's entry into the fray has become the stuff of legend—how he was told of the project one day and flew to Wellington the next morning without seeing so much as a word of the script, and jumped immediately into heavy sword training with Bob Anderson. By this time we'd spent nearly two months learning some of the key concepts in swordplay. Bob would teach us fifteen different moves or techniques, assign each a number, and then choreograph a fight scene using those numbers: "Okay, Sean, I want you to do two, seven, eight, five—in that order." Viggo arrived and had to instantly learn a specific fight sequence, the Weathertop battle with the ringwraiths, from *The Fellowship of the Ring*. We had been choreographing the scene with stunt doubles, and one day Viggo just showed up, in costume, sword in hand. He was strong and athletic, and very serious. And clearly up to the task. I never doubted for a moment that he'd be able to handle the role of Aragorn, despite the circumstances under which he'd gotten the part.

Not long after his arrival, Viggo and I had a meal at a restaurant called the Green Parrot. Actually, it was more of a burger joint than a restaurant, the kind of semigrungy place that oozes character. The Green Parrot quickly became known as Viggo's hangout, and one night we went there to talk. I wanted to share with him how badly I felt for Stuart, but also to let him know that I was looking forward to working with him. I wanted to understand from Viggo how he was approaching things. Part of my motivation was to establish a genuine rapport with a fellow actor, and part of it was to make myself feel better about what happened to Stuart. Also, I was trying to get a bead on the leadership style at the top of the pyramid. Not just Peter's style, but that of the producers, as well; I thought I might be able to get inside by talking with Viggo, simply because he'd been approached to join the production, and I'd be able to test the veracity of what had been said to us regarding Stuart's dismissal.

That was a big learning experience for me, and it left me wondering whether I'd have the ability to fire somebody I liked for the greater good of a production. It left me with a healthy fear of the authority behind *The Lord of the Rings*, but also a sense of doubt about my own ability to do what they were doing, because some of it did seem ruthless. I could rationalize it by saying that it was ruthless in service of the ultimate goal of making the movie the way Peter wanted to make it, but it was painful nonetheless.

Not that any of this was Viggo's fault or responsibility. He was simply the new man on the job, and I sensed right away that he was a decent, worthy person. I was intrigued by his idiosyncrasies, like the way he would carry his sword around to different restaurants. Viggo has that kind of brooding aura, as if he's always in character. He wasn't carrying it the night we met, by the way, but he did carry it a lot. Peter was somewhat amused that Viggo did that, but given the results on screen, it's hard to question his strategy. Aragorn, as played by Viggo, is an impressive and thoroughly believable warrior.

Different parts of Viggo's personality emerged in different ways. When he first showed up, he carried himself with an obvious grace and intensity, and the intensity heightened as time went on. At first, I couldn't believe how he just appropriated the role, how he made it his. I would expect that it would be enormously difficult to step in on short notice and take over from someone who has just been fired, but perhaps it's possible to overthink these things. Maybe jumping in with both feet is the best approach. Maybe Stuart had too much time to think about it, too much time to fret over character development and to dwell on the career ramifications. It's also possible that Viggo was uniquely suited to the task. He has a reputation, enhanced during this production, for being somewhat eccentric, and I think that's probably an accurate assessment. I also think he enjoyed the notion that other people were perpetuating that reputation on his behalf. Viggo has a definite self-awareness and amusement about those kinds of things. This is not to suggest that there is something false about him. Viggo does at moments lose himself in whatever it is he's doing. He's very smart, and he's very passionate and sensitive. He's committed to his poetry and photography; he also paints and sings. He has an enormous amount of energy, and he applies that energy in unique and interesting ways.

Viggo was utterly devoted to the production—not merely to being the best Aragorn he could possibly be, but to helping others understand what that meant. He and I were different in this regard. Viggo lived with Tolkien's books. He was constantly reading and coming up with new ideas and existing in an ongoing, contentious creative discussion with Fran and Philippa and Peter. For his part, Peter seemed to enjoy it, or at least was willing to accept that there was nothing personal or mean-spirited about it. That's who Viggo is, and occasionally, when it was convenient, or if he agreed (and maybe sometimes if he didn't), Peter would incorporate the actor's suggestions; I presume the same was true of Fran and Philippa. But there were moments when Viggo's advocacy produced a few chuckles. There was one time, for example, when he wanted to bring in a deer carcass and flop it down on the hobbits' campfire.

"How the hell are these guys eating?" Viggo had wondered aloud. "They're traveling all the time, and we never see them eating."

Viggo's intentions were noble. He wanted realism. He didn't want this to be one of those movies where nobody ever goes to the bathroom or has to reload in the middle of a fight, and so he argued in favor of things that would give the story sweat and blood. Unfortunately, they were also things that would command time away from the spine of the story. I'm sure Viggo knew that, and yet he was tireless in the communication of his ideas. I tried once or twice to get an idea into the movie that I thought would serve the story well, and when it didn't fly, my ego was bruised and I backed right off. I didn't want to bang my head against the wall. For me, something happens in those situations. If I try to float a good idea and it doesn't get incorporated, it's too painful to try again. I give up. And I stew about it for a while. Not Viggo. He's relentless.

He's also extremely political and politically extreme. Viggo is a Noam Chomsky guy. He gave me Jim Hightower's left-wing screed *Thieves in High Places* as a gift one day. He gave me one of Michael Moore's books. Viggo would just do things like that. I wanted to talk with him, share ideas and thoughts and philosophy, but I sensed he wasn't comfortable relating with me on that level. He'd rather blow through a party handing everybody a copy of three different books that he'd read, and then move on. If you read one of those books, which I did, and you talk about it with him later, it's almost like trying to communicate with a humming-bird: he sort of hears you, says something, then flitters away. Viggo is not a ranter, at least not in that kind of setting. He doesn't dominate the cocktail party scene. But when he has a microphone in front of him, watch out! Michael Medved, a conservative columnist and author, wrote an essay attacking Viggo not so much for his political views, but for using his celebrity status as a platform for expressing those views, since that expression intrudes upon and colors a fan's interaction with the film. I happen to disagree with that assessment, since actors, like anyone else, are entitled to their opinions. But there is no denying that Viggo is a rabid, radical, political activist. This is a guy who appeared on Charlie Rose's rather sensitive, erudite PBS talk show wearing a T-shirt bearing the inscription "No Blood for Oil"; he showed up at a premiere for the third film wearing a United Nations patch (actions which I admire, incidentally).

In many settings Viggo used *The Lord of the Rings* as a pulpit. At some point he decided that he was not going to promote the film purely to promote the film. Instead, he was going to use it as a platform to espouse his political discontent, in service of his humanitarian ideals. And he really is an idealist when it comes to his commitment to peace, which is somewhat ironic, considering he's done more than a few movies that seem to contradict that stance, *G.I. Jane* and *Crimson Tide* being the most notable. But I know he is genuinely committed to a liberal ideology, and I feel a kind of kinship with him in that. Emotionally, I'm pretty close to where he is. Politically, he wants to be one of the voices on the fringe, someone who is committed to pushing the extremes of the discussion; he doesn't really want to make his views accessible to the broadest number of people. Viggo probably thinks I sell out too quickly or drift too close to the middle, but that's okay. I think the world is big enough for guys like Viggo and guys like me to operate.

As an actor, it's hard not to admire Viggo. Ninety-nine percent of the time, he was totally in character. And he was a constant body in motion. If I was a sedentary blob because I was fat or had the feet on, or because I was depressed about not having enough to do, Viggo was always moving, creating things, stirring up shit. He was a catalyst, and people enjoyed his spirit and energy. Sometimes, just for the sheer hell of it, he'd pass out chocolate to the hobbits, because he knew it made us happy. He was like the chocolate fairy. And he was always coming and going. He'd jump on a plane and fly back to Los Angeles to go to his son's graduation, then turn right around and fly back—a thirty-six-hour trip!—and go right to the set. If this left him exhausted or grumpy, you'd never know it, in part because it worked for the role. Viggo was Strider, right? The valiant warrior on an endless journey. Who cared if he had bags under his eyes? It made sense.

From the beginning, Viggo seemed pretty comfortable and confident about what he was doing. That night at the Green Parrot, we didn't talk too much about the part of Aragorn. Rather, we focused on the fact that we were both approaching the craft with confidence and goodwill. Once that was understood, there wasn't much left to say. When I heard that Viggo would be joining the cast, I thought back to the first time I had seen him, in a film called *Perfect Murder*, starring Michael Douglas. Viggo was the villain in that movie, but his character was also an artist. I remember thinking not only that he was going to be a star, but also that there was a connection between actor and character. I remember thinking, *Wow, I'll bet he's a lot like that in real life* (the artist, I mean, not the murderer).

And so he is.

CHAPTER ELEVEN

I've frequently used the word "faith" to describe the attitude required to survive the filming of *The Lord of the Rings*. Faith in the process, faith in the adventure, faith in the director and writers and producers. Faith in fellow cast members. Faith in the technicians and artists and crew who brought Tolkien's Middle-earth to life.

Faith was required because, for the actors, at least, there was no control whatsoever. There was simply an eighteen-month roller-coaster ride that we hoped would somehow result in a film worthy of the work that had gone into it. Sometimes it was hard, if not downright impossible, to envision the outcome or to imagine that anyone, including Peter Jackson, had a clear picture of what the finished product would look like. I'm quite sure now that that wasn't the case, that in fact Peter knew exactly where he was going and how he wanted to get there. Like soldiers in a battle, though, the actors were more concerned with the mundane task of placing one foot in front of another, slogging onward day after day.

In a typical production, once you complete a scene and break a set, there is no going back. It's in the can. It's history. If you don't get it quite right (and it's *never* quite right, incidentally), well, too bad. Time is money, and rarely does it makes sense to reset the scaffolding, reposition the camera, the crew. So if you're not happy as the director or the actor, once you break it down, you're out of luck. That was not the case with *The Lord of the Rings*. We'd go back again, and again, and again.

Sets would be rebuilt, cast and crew dispatched, scenes rewritten.

Sometimes this would happen days or weeks after the scene had been originally shot; other times it would happen months, even years later, when we returned to New Zealand for pickups. There was constant reworking, and thus a constant sense that it was never, ever going to be finished. You'd finish a scene, get it right, or so you thought; then you'd look at it in dailies, and if it wasn't perfect or almost perfect, you'd go back. This approach was at once exciting and frustrating, because as an actor you had to reprogram your internal clock, your truth meter, your way of knowing if the director is shooting straight with you. We've all been asked many times, "How did you keep everything straight?" The answer is, we didn't. Or at least I didn't. Certain people kept certain things straight at certain moments, I'm sure, but a lot of stuff seemed to me impossible to comprehend.

A normal day for the hobbits involved getting to the set at, say, 4:30 in the morning and spending a couple of hours in the makeup chair, having prosthetic feet applied, as well as ears, wigs, and costumes. Then, as on any movie set, there was a lot of "hurry up and wait," as the crew prepared sets or as thousands of extras marched into place. Then, all of a sudden, you were thrust into Middle-earth, ready to fight a Balrog or a cave troll or a giant spider or ten thousand orcs. Although we set out to shoot chronologically, that approach was essentially discarded early in the process. Every site, every location, was used in every possible way. So it wasn't unusual to be filming three scenes from three different movies in a single day.

As an actor you want to exist "in the moment." That's a cliché, I know, but such a philosophy was absolutely crucial to the success of this production. In fact, since so much was happening at once, there was no other option. You might be at the top of an active volcano at sunrise, and then later in the afternoon find yourself on a tennis court, surrounded by polystyrene boulders, with each scene requiring a completely different set of skills and emotions. A Zen-like approach to acting was required: take a little snapshot of your mind and your soul right before you start whatever it is you're to do at any given moment and ask, *Who am I? Where am I? What am I doing here?* And then accept the idea that you're going along for the ride of your life, and that everything will work out in the end.

"Controlled chaos" is a phrase that accurately describes the filming of *The Lord of the Rings*. The logistics accomplishment alone was staggering, as thousands of people had to be moved around the country. At any one time we would have five helicopters ferrying people to the top of a mountain, while Peter monitored three or four different televisions with a satellite link so he could see what the other crews were doing. Meanwhile, he would be talking on the phone and on the radio, calmly and patiently issuing orders and directions. It was almost unfathomable. What started to develop over time was a sense of righteousness and inevitability about the quality of the work, that the whole project was moving inexorably in a direction that was going to yield something magnificent. And that sustained us even in the murkiest of times.

One of the things fans sometimes fail to grasp about the making of the three movies is that we used the entire *country!* You say that to some people and they don't quite get it, for they think of New Zealand as a dot in the South Pacific, located somewhere in the vicinity of Australia and probably encompassing a landmass no larger than Rhode Island. Wrong. Way, way wrong. New Zealand is three thousand miles off the coast of Australia, and it's as far south as you can go before hitting Antarctica. It's a diverse region spanning two islands and more than 103,000 square miles. As a point of reference, it is larger than the United Kingdom and only slightly smaller than Italy. And yet somehow we experienced much of what New Zealand has to offer. True, the production was based in Wellington, and we filmed a good deal of the movies on sets and soundstages in and around the city. But we were also all over both islands, and as we traveled I was repeatedly struck by what a wondrous and unique place the country is, with its tropical rain forests, desert expanses, snow-capped mountains, rain-swollen rivers, even active volcanoes. Think about it: we filmed for six weeks on a rumbling mountaintop! How amazing is that? By the time we left the country I'd seen so many spectacular vistas, and said so many wonderful things about New Zealand, that I felt like a poster child for the Ministry of Tourism.

New Zealand was the perfect place to film *The Lord of the Rings*. It's almost as though there's a tunnel through the center of the earth connecting England and New Zealand, as if Tolkien were alive in one place and wanted to create this mythology in another place. And while that place may have existed only in his mind, it's hard not to notice the similarities between Middle-earth and New Zealand.

Tolkien devotes thousands of words to vivid descriptions of the land, incredibly rich and evocative prose about topography. He brings the region to life. You know, you can fly from Seattle to Miami in three hours, and in that time you barely notice the country passing beneath you in a blur. Cities are specks, and mountain ranges are but lumps on the landscape. Imagine, though, what it would be like to actually walk across the Rocky Mountains or to hike the Appalachian Trail; imagine the impact on your feet, on your back, on your mind. Imagine the things you would see and feel and hear. I'm hardly a Tolkien expert, and God knows there are countless scholars who have devoted their life's work to analyzing such things in far greater detail than I ever could, but I do know that Tolkien loved the natural environment.

I actually saw more, and experienced the grandeur of New Zealand more acutely, because I was studying *The Lord of the Rings* closely. I might not otherwise have appreciated the varieties and textures of the land if I hadn't read the exquisite descriptions of similar places in Middle-earth.

Peter Jackson articulated to us in a very passionate and specific way what he thought Tolkien was trying to say, that indeed an underlying theme of *The Lord of the Rings* is something of an anti-industrial message, an appreciation for preserving the integrity of the environment. At the same time, Tolkien couldn't have written about the dwarves and their industry and their innovation and their capacity for creating mechanical devices if he didn't appreciate the value of such things. But it's quite clear that Tolkien believes the dwarves have lost something, that they've become preoccupied with things mechanical and technological—to their detriment. A careful reader senses from the books that a heartless commitment to technology may not be the most fulfilling or meaningful way to live. Certainly in battle, the Fellowship is able to use certain elements of technology to its great advantage, but I think Tolkien understood that there's more to life than that; it's equally important, if not more important, to appreciate the magic and the poetry of something as simple as tilling a garden. I think *The Lord of the Rings* is a celebration of the importance of that sentiment, as well as a stark and grim reminder of what can happen if you forget how important it is.

I like the notion that people shouldn't be afraid of the simple, that they need not look beyond their own homes and their own earth to find happiness. There are certain heroic characters in literature and film who fascinate me, characters who travel the world over, fight to defend their way of life, and meet all kinds of fascinating people, but who ultimately discover that what is important is to have a little piece of earth, a place to work the soil. Sam is absolutely a symbol of that realization. Frodo has a great speech at the end of the book: *I have been too deeply hurt, Sam. I tried to save the Shire, and it has been saved, but not for me. It must often be so, Sam, when things are in danger: someone has to give them up, lose them, so that others may keep them.*

You can't have paradise saved without having something else lost, and so it's the journey that really shapes the reader's commitment to what has been preserved once the battle is over. The irony, of course, is that while demonstrating a commitment to Tolkien's vision, and a thorough understanding of his message, Peter Jackson presided over the most technologically advanced production in movie history. Nevertheless, one of the great benefits that I received from *The Lord of the Rings* was the privilege of discovering the literature, and feeling like I was in some way participating in an homage to Tolkien's appreciation of nature. I'm a city kid. I mean, I've traveled around a lot and I've camped out, but basically I grew up in Los Angeles. I haven't really lived in the outdoors, or in a frontier land like New Zealand is to a certain extent, or a place like Middle-earth is described in the books. So to be able to sit in a beautiful hotel in the south island of New Zealand, looking out at the Remarkables, the aptly named mountain peaks rising above us, and to be reading these descriptions of land masses and what it was like for the hobbits to walk barefoot across rocky shale, and then to be able to put the book down, go to sleep, and wake up at four the next morning, put on my prosthetic feet, and go for a long, long, walk . . . What a gift!

It didn't happen this way, I know, but it seemed as though Tolkien had strolled across New Zealand and then sat down and started writing. And here we were, interpreting his vision, in the most appropriate of places. It was honorable work.

And it was hard work, of course, not just for the cast, but also for the crew, which did a commendable job of making sure that we could actually get to some of the more remote locations. They would use helicopters to transport sling loads of equipment and four-wheel-drive vehicles into otherwise impassable places. There always seemed to be several stages to each journey: a chopper ride, followed by a drive, followed by a hike. Once you got out of the van (or the Jeep or the Humvee, or some other similar rig), there would be a long walk—sometimes as much as an hour—in prosthetic feet. The studio tried to protect its investment (and by that I am referring to the fake feet, not the real feet) by having us wear big green plastic boots, but these looked ridiculous and made walking even more of a challenge.

Complaining, however, was hardly encouraged. Somehow it seemed generally in the spirit of things to grin and bear it. Not that I wasn't concerned. I was. Our bodies were put through a lot as a function of making these movies. We all had bumps and bruises and minor injuries; some of us incurred injuries that were a bit more than minor. It was part of the job. But Elijah often seemed uniquely oblivious to the possibility of disaster. I used to call him "Plastic Man" because he looked like a little doll or something; they could do anything with him—fling him from the top of a crane or push him off a cliff or dunk him in ice-cold water. Nothing bothered him. Elijah went through an unbelievable amount of physical stress without uttering so much as a peep. That was left to me, the "Nervous Nellie" hobbit, always driving people nuts with my worrying and fretting that something terrible might happen.

And not just to the actors. At one point, for example, there was something of a crew mutiny fermenting, which got me really excited, because, hey, I played Rudy! I like to believe that my heart is in the right place, that I'm informed by a working-class, solidarity kind of philosophy. So when I saw the sheer exhaustion of the crew (and to a lesser degree, the cast), I became concerned, and I hoped in my heart that they might rise up and protest. This was a legitimately dangerous production; that no one died making these movies is a fact I found frankly stunning. I was sure we would lose crew members, because there were thousands of people working on *The Lord of the Rings* at one time, and it just seemed like it wasn't the safest environment in which to work. I'm not sure what the workplace regulations are in New Zealand, but my guess is they must be less stringent than they are in Hollywood. The kinds of fumes and chemicals that the special-effects people routinely subjected themselves to—my God! Take, for example, Richard Taylor, the special-effects guru, who is one of the most brilliant men I've ever met. He's an absolute genius and the movie could not have happened without him, but the man made enormous sacrifices in the name of his art. When he and his wife (and working partner) had a protocol done on their bodies to test for toxins acquired over the course of their careers, the results were staggering. I know this is hyperbolic, but I felt like they were in *Silkwood* territory. But these people were so committed to their craft, their art, that they just did it willingly, knowing the risks.

(Please remember, these are just my thoughts and impressions, not necessarily reality as experienced by everyone else. Furthermore, I'm not suggesting that Peter, Barrie, and the rest of the leaders on the production were reckless or inhumane or foolish. There were extraordinary precautions taken for safety, and everyone in New Zealand that I came into contact with had as much love for life and safety as any people I've ever known. But standards and regulations in an industry historically develop over time as a result of accidents and lessons learned on the job. The film industry in New Zealand is newer and therefore less developed in many regards. So all I'm saying is that during my time on the movies I witnessed smart, hard-working, good people take calculated risks in an endeavor to push the envelope of creativity. Admirable in success to be sure, but dangerous nonetheless and worthy of mention as the industry goes forward in time.)

I thought about the Taylors as I watched the rebellion among the crew, most of whom had been working an endless string of twenty-hour days. I saw drivers taking catnaps behind the wheel moments before trying to guide massive trucks along rugged mountain precipices, with death on either side of them, and I kept thinking to myself, *Somebody is going to die here!* My concern (some called it paranoia) became the butt of jokes, but I honestly believe that it was legitimate. As someone who would like to be a director, as a social activist—as someone who would like to be thought of as a leader—I was worried about the conditions people worked under, and what they did without question or complaint. So I was happy when the crew got together to take a vote on whether to shut down the movie. The producers knew what was happening, and they responded with a small increase in overtime compensation—not much, really—and I was expecting the crew to close down the movie for a while because what everyone really needed was about three days of sleep. But that's not what happened. To my amazement, they voted to keep working at the same pace for nothing more than a nominal bump in their pay. Perhaps they realized that once the movie was over, that was it; the giant teat that everyone had been suckling would go dry, and they'd go back to their ordinary lives. This was their chance to be part of something special, and nothing was going to get in the way.

But then that's typical of the Kiwi mentality. I was in New Zealand during the American election debacle of 2000. I remember having my prosthetic feet applied as I filled out my absentee ballot in the makeup bus, and then calling my father on a cell phone and asking him to deliver my ballot to a polling place when it arrived. And I remember the New Zealanders having a ball at the expense of the stupid Americans who seemingly couldn't figure out how to hold a free and fair election, despite spending an immense amount of time going all around the world, telling everyone else how they should embrace democracy and capitalism.

As a self-appointed ambassador for the United States, I was in a difficult position, trying to advocate for the process in my country while grappling with its obvious and oh-so-public shortcomings. One night in the aftermath of the election, I came home late, bleary-eyed after another eighteen-hour day on the set, and instead of going to bed, I got on the Internet, downloaded the sixty-four-page Supreme Court ruling that ultimately led to George W. Bush becoming president, and read the entire document before going to bed. I thought it was important to have an opinion when I showed up on the set, so that when the grips and the gaffers and whoever else started asking me questions and giving me shit, I'd have a response. I didn't want to be dismissed as yet another uninformed American. It was really interesting: I was getting an American civics lesson while visiting a foreign country.

What I like most about New Zealanders is their universally high standards. While they undoubtedly suffer from a bit of "little brother syndrome" (with Australia the big brother), and thus took some snide satisfaction in seeing a superpower such as the United States wallow around in ineptitude, they're equally demanding of their own icons. When politicians or athletes or other public figures fail in New Zealand, it's a serious matter.

If I could make one generalization about New Zealanders, it would be this: they work much harder than most people in order to achieve something. In Hollywood, frankly, the working-class mentality is a little bit softer. It's harder to get the unions, or some members of the unions, to work for less or to work harder. At least, that would be the producer's perspective. Even for an actor, it's frustrating to see that the mentality is to go a little bit slower, all the time, and to have a chip on the shoulder about the corporation that is employing you. I wouldn't say American movie crews are lazy, but let's put it this way: American crews are more experienced, and probably have more talent bred historically into them, but New Zealand crews work harder. And it won't take Peter Jackson and his squadron of willing, able-bodied filmmakers long to compete with anyone on the planet. I just hope a global balance of opportunity can be struck, whereby filmmakers the world over are inspired, work hard, and share in the fruits of their labor.

They're extraordinary people, Kiwis. They're frontier people who've learned how to survive away from much of the Western world, and they've managed to create a First World country with all the bells and whistles of contemporary civilization, despite existing a vast distance away from most of it. It's an amazing accomplishment. And while they are ruthless on their homegrown heroes when they fail, they take the appropriate pride in the accomplishment of their native children. Consider that the New Zealand five-dollar bill bears the image of Sir Edmund Hillary, the famous Kiwi mountaineer. On May 29, 1953, Hillary and his climbing partner, the Nepalese Sherpa Tenzing Norgay, became the first men to set foot on the peak of Mount Everest. Think about that. You know, only a handful of people can look up at the night sky and see the moon and say, "Been there, done that." Guys like Neil Armstrong, Buzz Aldrin. Same thing with Sir Edmund Hillary. He was the first to be able to look up at Everest, the unreachable summit, and say, "Been there, done that."

Peter Jackson is now a huge favorite son of New Zealand, and I just love the fact that Hillary came to visit Peter on the set. Nobody made a big deal out of it, at least not far in advance. We just showed up one morning, and one of the assistant directors said, "Hey, Sir Edmund Hillary is coming to the set today." He might as well have said, "Oh, by the way, God is going to come over and have a bite of lunch." I mean, Hillary is one of the most remarkable men on the planet. He'll have a seat in the hereafter at a table marked Greatest Accomplishments of All Time.

And he's coming to the set? Today?

I remembered that Hillary had recently written a book, so I started asking around to see if anyone had a copy. Or, at least, a New Zealand five-dollar bill. I wanted something meaningful for him to autograph. That's how excited I was. Regardless of how many famous people I meet, I'm always impressed with the accomplishments of others— from the mundane, though undeniably heroic accomplishments of, say, a single mother to the greatest accomplishments known to man, like walking on your own power to the top of the tallest mountain. I'm totally inspired by people like Hillary, and when I find myself around them, all my self-flagellation just goes out the window and I act like an excited little kid meeting one of his heroes. So I was giddy as a schoolboy when I found out that Hillary was coming. And when I told Peter that I was bummed out because I didn't have Sir Edmund's book, Peter got one of his assistants to go to the bookstore for me. I don't know who paid for the book, but an hour later I was holding a copy of *A View from the Summit* by Sir Edmund Hillary (as well as a five-dollar bill).

That may seem like a small thing, but it really wasn't. Peter Jackson gave me that book, and I felt like it was his way of saying, "Come down to my land for a while." And I was humbled that I'd been invited. Whatever disappointment I might have felt from time to time, the truth is that Peter Jackson invited me down to New Zealand to play in his paddock, and extraordinary things happened in that paddock. You know, it's like in the United States when jazz started, or in any great place on the planet that enjoys a renaissance. Peter is drawn to greatness, and he draws greatness to him. He's comfortable communicating with great people, and once in a while he opened the door to that sacred chamber of greatness to me. This was one of those days, the day a hulking giant of a man named Sir Edmund Hillary came to the set.

I had lunch with him, and while it was fun, it was also kind of awkward because I just didn't know what to say. Eventually, the title of his book popped into my head, and I used that as a way to start a conversation: "Well, how was it?"

"How was what?"

"The view."

"Oh," he smiled, "pretty good, actually."

After lunch he autographed my book and my five-dollar bill. Then he stayed for a little while and watched us film one of the many "walking" shots in the trilogy, a scene of the hobbits trekking through the forest. That was cool. When you're going in front of the camera after doing eight trillion walking shots, there is a tendency to take it for granted. Not always, of course. When you've been helicoptered to the top of a mountain, you feel like, Oh, this is beautiful! This shot is being preserved for all time, and it's showing New Zealand in all its splendor. But when you do a walking shot that's closer to the city and to civilization, and you know there will be twenty takes, it takes a bit more work to get excited.

But not on this day. Not with Sir Edmund Hillary sitting behind a monitor. I wanted the scene and my work in it to be worthy. Somehow, with Hillary looking on, that simple walking shot became more important than all the other walking shots.

CHAPTER TWELVE

Few men are more impressive upon introduction than Christopher Lee. Tall and elegant, with a sturdy baritone and the history of cinema fairly etched into the creases of his face, he is a formidable presence on a movie set.

This was especially true on *The Lord of the Rings*, not simply because Christopher came to the project with more than two hundred films on his résumé, but also because he was regarded among cast and crew as perhaps the most learned student of Tolkien. Just about everyone involved in the production had read the books, or at least claimed to have read them; some had read them multiple times. Christopher, however, was in a league of his own, having read the entire trilogy each year for more than twenty-five years. It was, for him, a tradition, a way to connect with great literature and great storytelling. I know he had always dreamed of participating in a project such as this, of having a chance to portray one of Tolkien's characters. That he was now too old for the role he had once relished—Gandalf—seemed only a minor disappointment. Saruman, the evil handmaiden of Sauron, suited him just fine.

Though separated by nearly five decades, Christopher and I developed an extraordinary rapport; he allowed me to enjoy a friendship with him that became almost as close as my friendship with Elijah. It happened pretty early on, in part because of my admiration not only for Christopher's acting, but his familiarity with Tolkien's writing. He knew the books cold, and in fact had a far deeper understanding than

I did of Sam and his importance to the story. Not only that, but he made it clear that he appreciated and agreed with the choices Peter and I had made in my portrayal: namely, that Sam is a heroic character. Christopher understood this more than the other actors, or at least more than Ian McKellen or Ian Holm (who played Bilbo Baggins) did. These gentlemen—Christopher and the two Ians—were *legends*. You couldn't help but look to them and wonder if they grasped what you were doing, because if they did, that was validation.

Christopher and I would occasionally sit together in the dressing room, smoking cigars and talking about acting, art, politics—almost anything. Because of being raised by two actors, I've long felt a particular kinship with mature actors. I'm part of an acting tradition, and so I look at other actors and think, *We're fellow travelers along a common road.* I look to the generations that have come before me with a kind of respect that I think they've earned, and I feel like I'm ready to assume the mantle of that tradition with younger performers. I say this despite the gnawing feeling in my gut that, all else being equal, I'd rather be behind the camera directing than in front of it. It's weird, but that said, acting does give me a sense of belonging, and it's because of my parents, of course. I wasn't necessarily comfortable staying in the living room at their parties, conversing with the adult actors, but knowing they were there was comforting; it made me feel like I had a place in the world.

Christopher Lee tapped right into that. His reputation preceded him on the set. I'd never met Christopher, but I knew that Peter Jackson absolutely revered him for his work as Dracula, Rasputin, Fu Manchu, and other dastardly villains in the classic Hammer horror films of the 1960s. I had seen some images of him and had heard about him, so I had an idea of what he would be like. And he was pretty much as advertised, a rangy, almost regal man in his late seventies, with long thin fingers and a slow, steady, purposeful gait. This is a man who moves with stature, who moves, come to think of it, not unlike Treebeard. When Christopher Lee enters a room and turns around, it's a *choice*. He's a very dramatic, almost theatrical man.

We met for the first time in the wardrobe area. I introduced myself after watching him for a few moments, sizing him up and waiting for the appropriate time. And I remember thinking while shaking his hand, *Here's somebody who wants you to know that he's capable of determining that you're not worthy of extended interaction.* He had a commanding presence, which I found simultaneously appealing and intimidating. I knew he had read *The Lord of the Rings* trilogy every year, and that was the context of our first conversation. The subtext was, *I know you're a substantial performer deserving of respect.*

Once I'd earned his trust and our friendship had begun to blossom, Christopher would occasionally indulge in a bit of griping in my presence. Actually, that may not be the best word. He wasn't griping so much as fretting. A healthy amount of commiserating went on among the actors, as happens on almost any production, although perhaps more so on *The Lord of the Rings* because of the sheer scope of the project and the demands it placed on cast and crew. For Christopher, a primary concern was the number of takes Peter routinely required to film a scene. Christopher was a "working" actor in the purest sense of the word. He'd made a career out of stacking one role on top of another, and always delivering exactly what was asked of him. The bulk of his filmography consisted of genre fare produced on tight budgets and squeezed through the smallest of windows. He was accustomed to filming scenes in a single, flawless take (and if it was flawed, so be it). On a couple of occasions he'd been asked to do three or four takes, but I got the impression that probably happened in the late 1940s on a lucky day when the cinematographer had an extra roll of film. Now, though, a different set of demands was being heaped upon Christopher, and he didn't like it. On the one hand, he was angry at Peter; on the other hand, he was experiencing self-doubt.

"Why, I've never had a director ask me to do it this many times in my life!" he exclaimed one day, after filming a scene that required some fifteen attempts. "This is ridiculous! I've done fewer takes in an entire movie!"

He was almost posturing, trying to project a sense of righteous indignation, but I could tell he was also looking for reassurance that everything would be all right, and that there was nothing inherently wrong with his performance.

"That's Peter's style," I said. "It's not about you. It's just the way he works."

While I was trying to comfort Christopher, I also meant exactly what I said. Peter had so much on his mind, and he was juggling so many different things at once—the story, the technology, the finances. Whatever frustrations I may have experienced, they are mitigated by the realization, crystallized in hindsight, that simply by completing this project, Peter accomplished one of the great miracles in the history of cinema. That his creation is artful and entertaining and accessible is a wonder almost beyond comprehension. (Think about it: in *The Return of the King* there is a swashbuckling scene in which Orlando Bloom's Legolas surfs gallantly down the trunk of an oliphant, a smile on his face, bow at the ready, as Howard Shore's musical score reaches a crescendo. How many movies could get away with a scene like that and still be deemed serious enough to merit eleven Academy Award nominations?) Although I know he tried, Peter hadn't the time to dwell on the myriad insecurities of actors. I think Christopher sometimes felt that the production was not making enough accommodations for the fact that he was elderly, resulting in a game of tug-of-war. Peter expected Christopher to be able to do more than he wanted to do, but not more than he actually could do. Maybe it came down to this: Peter didn't want Christopher to pull a star trip on him. I know firsthand from my mother that actors can and do use their infirmities to get attention. (Sorry, Mom. Please don't kill me!) Perhaps Christopher hadn't had the benefit of watching *Meet the Feebles;* he was used to being the grand pooh-bah on pictures. He enjoyed that status, he had fun with it, and you know what? To a certain extent, he had earned it. On *The Lord of the Rings,* however, the story was the star; there wasn't time or space for coddling.

Another aspect of the process troubled Christopher (and almost everyone else at one time or another), and that was the constant changing and rewriting of lines. It wasn't at all unusual to be presented with a ream of new dialogue just minutes before a take, with the understanding that instant memorization and clarity of purpose weren't possible, and so it was okay to work through the bad stuff for a while, over the course of maybe a dozen or more takes, on the path to capturing something worthwhile on film. Most of the actors, especially those of us who'd been on location for a while, understood that. But each time a new actor arrived, he or she was subjected to baptism by fire. Many of the more familiar names in the films, such as Liv Tyler, Ian McKellen, Ian Holm, and Cate Blanchett, spent much smaller blocks of time in New Zealand than did the Fellowship. Some handled the demands better than others. Christopher's work in *The Lord of the Rings* is stellar, but it was not achieved without some pain. This was a production that required nimbleness, elasticity. Most of us accepted that we'd look dreadful while churning through the disposable takes, but Christopher didn't like looking bad. He wasn't used to it. And I felt for him during those moments.

I also felt for Peter, who loved Christopher's work and wanted him—*needed* him—to shine in the role of Saruman, and who also wanted to be respectful of Christopher's age and experience and stature. And yet, Peter had to contend with the much more practical, pressing matter of filming a $270 million trilogy. He had been weaned on the Hammer films and had been mesmerized by the repeatedly and consistently creepy work of Christopher Lee; but now he was dealing with a sometimes cantankerous old bastard who didn't want to do more than three takes, but Peter wasn't going to leave until they got it right.

The writing process made this challenging. Christopher is from the old school. If he had a speech to deliver in a scene, he wanted to see the pages well in advance—at the very least, the night before filming—so that he could commit the words to memory. He wasn't as quick to embrace the notion that on this production the smart survival strategy for an actor was to learn it, be willing to totally forget it, and know that if they write you a new scene ten minutes before you're scheduled to perform it, somehow it will all work out. If you screwed up on the first ten or fifteen takes, that was all right. Peter would give you thirty. And by the thirtieth take, you'd have learned the lines. This was not just a one-way street, incidentally. To his immense credit, Peter understood the demands he placed on his cast, and he was willing to reciprocate. If you wanted another take, Peter was, within reason, willing to give you another one. To a large degree, he trusted the actor to be the ambassador of his character, and he expected him to communicate what was working and what was not working—above and beyond what he could sense.

Everything was fluid, especially the writing. There is no such thing as hyperbole or overstatement when talking about the constant nature of the rewrite process on *The Lord of the Rings*. Let me be clear about this, because Peter and Fran would doubtless be hurt, or feel their reputation was being impugned, if I were to suggest that there wasn't a sense of professionalism about delivering pages on time. There were very real-world, budgetary consequences to having pages rewritten beyond a certain point, and Peter was always aware of such things. In fact, another area of expertise he demonstrated was knowing what needed to be written (and shown to the studio) in order for certain budgets to be drafted, for sets to be constructed, illustrations of the sets to be commissioned, and so on. But he also knew how to time everything so the writers could apply the best part of their creativity to the reworking of language at the right moments. Peter was deeply respectful of the screenwriters and the screenwriting process (and not simply because he is a credited writer on the screenplay and a coauthor of the original draft). He respected their autonomy, and was deferential to what they had done—unless, of course, push came to shove and he had to change something. Generally speaking, it's fair to say that the standard response to suggestions made by the actors regarding dialogue was, "Oh, we can't change that—the script girls will come in." Peter jokingly referred to Fran and Philippa as the "script Nazis." They were fiercely protective of their work. Understandable, really, since they bled for each and every word.

I recall feeling for them as we were prepared to shoot the Council of Elrond sequence, which was arguably the hardest scene in the book for Peter to film, because it involved so many main characters in one place at one time. With the exception of the closing scene of the final film, such crowded scenes were avoided. Like the characters in the movie, in fact, we were all scattered about New Zealand and Middle-earth. Just as Sam and Frodo, while marching to Mordor, have no way of knowing what is happening to Pippin and Merry, Elijah and I spent great stretches of time isolated from the other actors. The Council of Elrond, however, is a break from that style of storytelling, a pivotal moment in the first film that presents to the viewer the formation of the Fellowship. It's an enormously complicated scene, one requiring significant exposition in the face of monumental technical challenges. I'm not sure the writers ever got it quite right, although God knows they tried. Tolkien devotes some seventy pages to the Council of Elrond meeting and its implications, and yet the scene as filmed lasts only a few minutes.

That only magnifies the challenge, for this is a scene that sets the tone not just for the remainder of the movie, but for the entire franchise. The story repeatedly refers back to the idea that it's Frodo's *mission* to carry the ring. That is the fundamental quest at the core of the trilogy, and the reasons for Frodo being assigned and accepting this burden, as well as the motivation of the other members of the Fellowship, are all established at the Council of Elrond.

Talk about a plot point!

In addition to the formidable task of communicating the information necessary to understanding the story, Peter was also dealing with the expectations and skills and egos of a score of world-class actors, all sort of jostling for space and screen time; at the same time, he was wrestling with the scale issues endemic to a production in which some of the characters are three and a half feet tall, and others are twice that height. It's challenging enough to put Gandalf and Bilbo in a room together, and make it believable when the actors who portray them are roughly the same size. But when you put everyone in one place at one time—elves, dwarves, men, hobbits, and wizards—and ask the camera to sweep across the screen, scale issues become a point of great concern.

Many of the artful ways Peter devised to introduce various characters—like Boromir arriving in slow motion at Rivendell—hadn't been completely determined at that point. The script called for ways of introducing characters and handling exposition, but changes were often made at the last second. This, of course, was one of the ways they struck terror into the hearts of studio executives: that $270 million had been committed, and the director wasn't going to shoot the script. Well, he was shooting the script. And he was shooting so much more than the script. The script was a very real, living and breathing document, but Peter wasn't a slave to it. While he was respectful of the script, he knew intuitively that when we'd get to a particular sequence and shoot all day long, the process would evolve organically. Each page of a script typically results in one minute of footage. On average. Well, Peter would shoot so much footage that each page could have filled fifteen minutes on screen. But he did it without going over budget, and he did it largely without incurring the wrath of his cast and crew, which speaks volumes about his managerial style and wisdom, as well as everyone's faith in him.

The Council of Elrond, however, tested everyone's patience and creativity, most notably Fran's and Philippa's. In the weeks leading up to that sequence, they worked tirelessly, like orc slaves locked in the mines being whipped and beaten every day. And they weren't mining coal or ore; in a sense, it was harder than that. The sweat and blood and tears of having to continually go back into their imagination and back into the text, while trying to keep a macro vision of the movie in mind—their mental slogging, day in and day out—is hard to fathom. The kinds of things they were asked to do are almost incomprehensible. *Listen, this set is going to be built in three days. We're going to have fifteen actors show up on the set, ready to go, and right now the scene isn't good enough. Make it better.* Such requests happened all the time. That had to be maddening. Not that Fran and Philippa were wandering blindly. The original scripts, 150 pages apiece, were always available; there was always a blueprint. But Fran and Philippa understood that the blueprint was flexible, and what shocked me was their level of commitment to this kind of attitude and process. They were unflappable.

As we rehearsed the original Council of Elrond scene, it seemed that most of the actors were struggling with it. We had the rough rhythm of the scene, the emotions and information it was intended to convey. But we all knew it wasn't quite right. A lot of people pitched ideas: some floated; some plummeted. For me, it was a rare occasion when something I suggested ended up in the film, although not in exactly the way I had envisioned. The idea that Frodo would stand up

and shout, "I'll do it! I'll carry the ring!" when everyone else is screaming and yelling at each other wasn't initially written in the script, and
I don't recall exactly how it appears in the books. I know when we were
talking through the scene one day at Peter's house, I made a suggestion, and Fran responded with, "That's a good idea." A small contribution, I admit, but I was proud of it, and I especially liked the idea
that they were open to it, which is not to say they wouldn't have come
up with it on their own. They probably would have. I just happened to
be invited into the process for a while, and Peter and Fran were open
enough to include things. That was the cauldron of creativity that
boiled and bubbled throughout the production.

I don't want to give the impression that we engaged in improvisational filmmaking. We didn't. This wasn't *Waiting for Guffman*. Fran and
Philippa (and Peter) were quite open to suggestions, as long as their
authority wasn't questioned. Which is the way it should be, because if
their authority is repeatedly questioned, then at other critical low
moments, when people aren't offering ideas, how are they going to do
the triple lutz and nail the landing? It was their process, their baby,
their screenplay. There was never any question about that. There were
times when they solicited ideas and nothing came, so they went back
to work. And there were times when suggestions came unsolicited. I
know Viggo was relentless with them about his character. Absolutely
relentless. He would go to them every day, it seemed, with thoughts
and ideas and suggestions, things the script apparently missed; he
constantly whittled and chipped away at what they were doing and
tried valiantly to put his imprimatur on Aragorn.

Was this helpful? I don't know. At times it seemed like they wanted
to kill themselves, or Viggo, because it was so maddening that he was
doing this, and then twenty minutes later they would turn around and
honor his suggestions. There were times when it was unnecessary, and
other times when it was unproductive, but overall he was a great
ambassador for his character. Viggo helped them forge things and
kept their feet to the fire. They hated him for it, and they resented it.
They also loved him and appreciated it. If they had to do it over
again, they probably wouldn't change a thing, because that was the
process they had invited.

On *The Lord of the Rings*, the door was always open, but I didn't really take advantage of it. Why? That's a complicated question, and I'll offer one of my typically strangled explanations. At one point during the shoot Fran shared with me a story about the making of *The Frighteners*, and how the star, Michael J. Fox, who was away from his wife and children, spent enormous amounts of time at Fran and Peter's home. The tone in Fran's voice and the wistful look on her face revealed just how much she liked Michael and how much she enjoyed providing him a home away from home. But I also detected a bit of sadness, as if she felt sorry for him. There's an openness about Peter and Fran, a family dynamic to them that is wonderfully appealing, but I always worried about pushing the boundaries. For some reason, after hearing her talk about Michael, I tried to be vigilant about not overstaying my welcome. I would have been there all the time, watching movies in their garage and borrowing videos even more than I did, but I found myself not wanting to overstep the bounds of propriety with them. This is what sometimes happens with relationships: you'll pull back a little bit, just because you think that's what you're supposed to do, and then as a result the others pull back, too, until you reach emotional détente. The icebreaker for us was our kids. Our children created a common ground. I enjoyed the quiet confidence of knowing that Peter and Fran were such good parents and loving people that my daughter and their children were bonding in a way that would keep us communicating with each other. The movie was important, but our kids are our kids, and they're more important. Being a parent allowed me to establish a connection with Peter and Fran that few other people on the film enjoyed.

That said, I wasn't always sure how to approach Fran or Peter on professional or creative matters. The night before we filmed the Council of Elrond, I called Fran, fortified by the knowledge that Viggo had done this essentially every night, and said, "Look, the way it's written, I don't come in until the end of the scene. If you read the book, Sam is there throughout; if you look at Alan Lee's illustrations, Sam is there. I think it's critical that I'm visible as the scene plays out."

Granted, the way the set was designed, with a dozen or more chairs up on the stage area, was very awkward. Where were they going to put me? With the visual aesthetic Peter was trying to capture, there was no way to accommodate my request, but I felt I had to say something. As I had with Warren Beatty, when he asked me to do some writing for *Bulworth*, I went out on a limb and built a case for myself. Sam belonged there. It was based on the text and my understanding of the narrative, and a legitimate desire to act as an audience surrogate. As the movie progresses, Sam demonstrates a clear understanding of everything that happens in that council meeting. Therefore, some explanation for this awareness must be proffered. He can't stroll into the frame at the last moment.

Ultimately, we reached a compromise: to have Sam pop out of the bushes and shout, "Hey! Nobody's going anywhere without me!" which lets the viewer know that Sam overheard everything. But it was where the rubber met the road for me, in terms of Peter wanting Sam to be comic relief and me wanting him to be serious. Peter, I think, would have been thrilled to have me say the line differently, to add a touch of comedy to it. Instead, I chose to frown a bit, to play it softly, proudly, which I think makes for a sweeter reading of the character and his motivation. Seconds later, of course, the other two hobbits, Merry and Pippin, come bouncing into the frame as well, smiling goofily, proclaiming their bravery and allegiance, and taking their place alongside Frodo.

Naked admission: I hate that part of the scene. When I see Billy and Dom come scurrying out, stumbling and bumbling like circus clowns, I just want to cringe. I'm being disrespectful, and I don't mean to be. I love them both. I think Billy is a more talented actor than I am; I think Dom is braver than I am. And I was willing to appreciate Dom's willingness, in service of the movie, to commit to the light-heartedness of hobbits more than I was. He and Billy both deserve a lot of credit for that. I was unwilling to pull on that thread, to embrace an undeniably legitimate reading of the characters of the hobbits as gentle, oafish, little creatures. That's in there. No question about it. It's not a mistake that Ralph Bakshi came up with the film he did and the characterizations he did. Nevertheless, I resented and rejected that particular characterization.

That's why I called Fran and made an impassioned plea for Sam to be there from the beginning of the scene, even if my presence was merely alluded to with a quick, single shot of Sam listening off to the side. "You could do it with a B cam," I suggested. "It won't even change the way you set the shot." Fran listened to me, said she understood, and promised to mention it to Peter. I wouldn't say that my request fell on deaf ears; that would be unfair. I think it just fell on ears that were overwhelmed.

I remember almost wanting to cry at the outcome. Granted, there were a lot of actors in the Council of Elrond scene who wanted to cry, simply because there were so many people locked in a tight space for such a long time. There were too many performers, too many monologues, too much to do and explain. Several days were required to film that scene. We shot the same thing so many times that people were ready to scream because they were so sick of it. So I guess I was lucky in that sense. I placed out of the exam by being the guy who pops up out of the bushes at the end of the show. There I was, in my feet and ears and wig, just standing around for hours on end, day after day, like a pitcher in a bullpen, waiting to be called in for my shot, wondering if they were going to acknowledge my suggestion in any way, shape, or form. When I was finally called out onto the set, Peter was entrenched in his position, tucked behind the monitor, obviously battle-weary from hours of sparring with fifteen strong-willed actors—each trying to do the best job possible—but also trying to assert himself. For any director, that's a daunting task, a process that wears you down, inch by inch. I could tell it was a low moment for Peter, and that filled me with sadness. I wanted Peter and Fran to respect me and appreciate me, and I'm sure they did. But not getting the feedback I wanted led me to indulge in self-pity, and I think traces of that existed for the rest of the project.

Not always, of course. There were numerous times when I was smart enough to take a good look around at the work being done and the almost unbearable pressure that Peter (and Fran) seemed to handle with uncommon grace and dignity, and to say to myself, "God, how stupid was I to have ever felt that way?" But other times, I'm almost ashamed to admit, it would bubble to the surface again.

I wanted two things professionally out of the experience: I wanted Peter Jackson to respect me as an actor and as a peer—as a filmmaker, a cinema artist. And I think I wanted him to do it in a way that allowed me to help shape the overall product. To an infinitesimal degree, I suppose I did that. To expect anything more would have been impractical, even unrealistic. For example, in the early days of rehearsal, when we discussed some of the scale issues, and presentations were made to us by digital-effects people, it was easy to see the genius behind the ideas, and to gauge the level of comfort and confidence that people felt with given strategies for achieving certain visual effects. One of the most spectacular things I've learned from Peter is his passion for achieving illusion. Remember, this is a man who tricked much of New Zealand into believing that they had the right to be proud of having flown before the Wright Brothers. And yet, he's not merely a master illusionist; he's also a storyteller. But he loves the early days of film, and he loves special effects—within context. He loves the original *King Kong*, so it's not surprising that he's doing a remake. I can picture him studying the early version of *King Kong*, trying to figure out how they achieved some of the miniature effects and perspective effects. Peter's favorite movies, though, are older Hollywood comedies. What a clever guy! A lot of filmmakers love the early effects of Hollywood, so they devote their entire lives to raising the bar on those effects. And there are a lot of filmmakers who appreciate the power and sophistication of the comedy of Buster Keaton and Charlie Chaplin. Peter falls into both categories. He's assimilated many elements of special effects and comedy, and is leveraging that to help shape cinema culture.

One of the great things about *The Lord of the Rings* is that Peter built into the structure of the film a flexible process that would allow for true innovation. I'm sure there were scale effects that had been achieved in Hollywood movies that were superior to what was done on this production. Peter's goal was not to set a new standard for scale effects, but rather to apply them to a different context: a sprawling, emotionally rich epic. Often it seemed that Peter was guided by a simple, almost childlike philosophy: *How can I make it fun?* Fun for himself, fun for the audience. Peter enjoyed getting down on his hands and knees, taking the little lipstick camera inside the miniatures, and moving it around. He liked talking to storyboard artists and presenting his ideas. He'd even get sketches of the props and then start making them himself. He was a grand puppet master, always moving, inciting, and inspiring.

It occurred to me on this particular day of rehearsal that you could simply have two characters of different size in the same shot and sell the scale. So I got down on the floor and said, "Peter let me show you this one thing." I could tell he was a little impatient, and perhaps I was overstepping my bounds, since that wasn't how he wanted to drive the rehearsal process. But I was eager to impress him and also to test my idea.

"Look," I said. "You can put the camera right behind me, and if Strider stands there, and you don't see his feet, and you film it, we can both be in the same shot, and the audience will believe it." It was a decidedly low-tech solution to one of the seemingly endless string of scale issues, and a pretty effective solution at that. Peter was at first reluctant to believe it would work, but then he looked more carefully, smiled, and agreed that I was onto something. Now, that's not to suggest that Peter and his effects staff hadn't already discussed a similar approach, or that they wouldn't have come to it on their own anyway, when it was organic and right. In fact, I'm sure they would have, because everything was tried a thousand times. But I was excited anyway, because I had figured it out in my way, at a time when it seemed as though the solution was unique, and I wanted some type of validation from Peter. I wanted him to say, "Well done, Sean," and then invite me to a private dinner, at which he would ask me questions and want to know my thoughts and opinions and ideas. We would sit there together, two titans of the cinema, one recognized for his genius, the other on the cusp of such recognition.

As I've said, this was my problem, not Peter's. It's funny. I'm so emotional sometimes. My feelings get hurt so easily. Maybe I need to toughen up a bit.

The dull ache of frustration was often a result of letting my exuberance get out of hand. I'd throw myself out there to Peter and compel him to take a natural step back and sort of qualify me in his mind as someone who needed to be *handled*, which is just about the worst thing you want to do as an actor, especially if you're an actor whose career has been built on a foundation of professionalism. I didn't want to be handled. I wanted to be patient and quiet and trusting. It just sometimes didn't work out that way.

Part of the problem, if you can call it that, is cultural. In general, the Kiwis are a reserved, almost stoic people. And Peter is a true Kiwi. He embodies a lot of the New Zealand mindset. If his feelings are hurt, he internalizes it, and if he wants to express himself, and it's not met in the right way, he's visibly but not hysterically disappointed. He's had to find a way to guard and shepherd his own vision. I've watched Peter hundreds of times take a deep breath when things weren't going quite right. There's a particular look he gets: his chin drops, almost like he's looking through his forehead, and he seems to be thinking, *I don't like the way this feels right now, so I'll have to figure out how to make it stop*. If you're a person who wants to be near Peter or to work with him, you find a way not to provoke him. It's not callous or mean. He's a gentleman. He's polite and thoughtful and generous. But he is formidable in a quiet sort of way.

I was raised differently. In our family, everybody talked about everything. We were a talky family. We'd have family meetings where we'd spent hours clearing the air until the air was so clear there wasn't enough oxygen left to breathe. We were clumsy and dysfunctional in so many ways it's almost comical, but one of the things that helped us survive was that we talked. *Talk-talk-talk.* Even now, when we get together for the holidays, there's no shutting us up. The sun goes down and comes up three times, and the wives' heads are splitting because the husbands are still in the living room, talking endlessly, torturing each other with laymen's psychoanalysis. It's sweet, it's endearing, and it's absolutely insane.

CHAPTER THIRTEEN

Some people came to *The Lord of the Rings* without the weight of expectation, as a virtual blank slate. Andy Serkis was one of them. It seems strange to say that now, for if any single actor is likely to be associated with the trilogy for the remainder of his career (and perhaps well beyond), it's Andy, the man who so vividly and brilliantly portrayed the doomed hobbit Smeagol and his duplicitous, computer-generated alter ego, Gollum.

"Portrayed" is precisely the right word, for while Andy's face appears only in the prologue to the third film, *The Return of the King,* it would be unfair to say that he did not contribute as much to the development of his character as the other actors on the project did to theirs. Indeed, he may well have contributed more. Certainly his wasn't simply a "voice-over assignment," as such performances are too often described. In many ways Andy's was the most demanding and rewarding role in the trilogy, and there's no question that he earned the adulation of fans and the critical acclaim that came his way in the wake of the final film. But I don't know if anyone expected him to be quite as good as he was. In fact, I'm not sure anyone even thought he'd be that important a player in the grand scheme of things.

The story often told is that Andy was originally hired for three weeks of work, that he received a call from his agent asking him if he was interested in providing the voice for Gollum in a new adaptation of *The Lord of the Rings.* Andy's response? "There must be a lot of proper parts in there; can't I get one of those instead?"

An understandable sentiment really, since Andy is a classically trained actor. I mean, if you heard that *The Lord of the Rings* was being made into a movie, Gollum wouldn't necessarily be the role you'd want to play, now would it? Sure, he's one of the best characters in the book and one of my favorites, but how do you bring him to life? Andy couldn't be faulted for wanting something apparently more substantial and serious. As it rather famously turned out, however, Gollum was the flashiest role in the franchise, providing Andy with the star vehicle of a lifetime and not just three weeks of employment, but three years! He returned to New Zealand on several occasions, far more frequently, in fact, than did the rest of the cast.

While Gollum is a computer-generated (CG) creature, he is very much based on the movements and expressions of Andy Serkis. This was apparent to Andy from the outset, and so he quickly became a powerful and emphatic ambassador for the character. I'm sure the CG animators would cringe if they read here that they somehow contributed less to the character of Gollum than Andy did, or that they were less enthusiastic about the character. I know they worked tirelessly and looked at Gollum as a great literary character and scene-stealing cinematic creation. Nevertheless, I'd be shocked to discover there has ever been a moment in the history of movies when an actor has gone to the workstations of the animators—some two hundred in all!—hunched over their computers for hours on end, and talked through the emotional nuances of each and every scene. Andy did that, and he was demonstrably frustrated and disappointed if he met even one animator who seemed not to match his own level of commitment, or who failed for some reason to grasp the real drama of the performance. Without Andy there—flopping about in ice-cold streams, rolling down the sides of mountains, and torturing his body and voice for the sake of a performance that would not even reward him with the actor's most profound currency, face time on screen—Gollum might have been little more than a two-dimensional foil for Sam and Frodo. But Andy wasn't about to let that happen. Nor was Peter.

We were deep into the production process by the time Andy arrived in New Zealand, or at least by the time I first met him. A lot has been written about how Andy was with us (and by "us," I mean the hobbits) every step of the way, but that's not really true. Because of the intense nature of his postproduction work, it's quite possible that if you added up the total number of days on location, Andy spent more time in New Zealand than we did. But there were great chunks of time when we did not see him and did not work with him. In terms of scheduling and shooting, the films were approached in roughly chronological order, but then a lot of things were added and moved to take advantage of locations and travel schedules. By the time Andy arrived, the *über*-movement of the production had gotten roughly to the second film, although that didn't really mean anything. For example, I met Andy at the Grand Chateau, a spectacular hotel at the foot of Mount Ruapehu in the Tongariro National Park. We usually stayed at the Grand Chateau while we were filming scenes set in and around Mordor. Such was the case on this day, when we were scheduled to shoot a scene involving Gollum, Frodo, and Sam—a scene intended for the third movie. I don't even remember the precise scene, but I do recall quite vividly the impression made by Andy.

For one thing (in stark contrast to my portly self), he was in terrific physical condition. Andy is an avid and accomplished rock climber, so he's extremely sinewy and strong, and really intense. Shaking his hand, feeling his grip, staring into his wide and expressive eyes, I couldn't believe how focused he seemed to be—it was almost like he was ready to explode. While Gollum provides a good deal of comic relief as well as pathos to *The Lord of the Rings*, the man behind the character is not exactly a laugh a minute.

"Pleased to meet you, Sean," he said, his face inches from mine, so close I could feel the heat coming off his skin. It wasn't just a normal business introduction. It was an *interaction*. "Looking forward to working with you, mate!"

Whoaaaaa. I'd better say something good here, because this guy is paying attention.

It was clear that Andy was extraordinarily fired up about being part of the production, which I found somewhat fascinating, because after all he was only Gollum. The way I saw it (incorrectly, of course), the poor guy was doomed to be disappointed, for he was going to be replaced by a digital image. Little did I know—little did *anyone* know—just how impressive an actor Andy would be, and what a groundbreaking performance he would achieve. What I did know was this: he had come to work. He understood that this was a big, important project, and he wanted to make it clear that he was equal to the task.

Although there was an element of mystery surrounding the computer-generated effects so heavily employed in *The Lord of the Rings*, I thought I had a reasonably good handle on how these things were done, at least on a fundamental level. I knew there would be blue screens and a stick with a tennis ball attached to the end (simulating what would later become a computer-generated image). I felt in my gut that I was probably better equipped to adapt to the circumstances than most other actors. Not because I had a wealth of experience in similarly effects-laden projects—I did not—but simply because I had a pretty good imagination and I'd seen enough movies to know how it was supposed to be done, or at least how it was *not* supposed to be done. You can tell when an actor is uncomfortable playing alongside a CG image—he's never looking quite in the right direction. I knew that much before the start of principal photography, and I quickly figured out how to be a part of the technology, instead of struggling against it. I liked doing mime work, which is basically what CG work is. So I was confident about what we were going to do.

As it turned out, none of the actors, including me, had any idea about how it was going to work, or how much of our trust was placed in the hands of the animators and the tech wizards (and the editors, and the composer, and so on). By and large, it was a lot of fun, and I felt privileged to be there, to be a part of something so revolutionary that it would change the way movies were made. I think we all felt that way, including Andy, who seemed in the first few days content with doing dialogue off camera. But then it became clear that Peter wanted us to rehearse, to make the scenes stronger, and to work out any kinks in the story or dialogue exactly as we did in other scenes.

In theory, this was fine; in practice, it dramatically altered the level of participation expected of Andy. Suddenly he was no longer just a guy standing off to the side, out of the frame, shouting lines of dialogue for a computer-generated Gollum. Now Andy was in the scene, rehearsing the part of Gollum. Andy naturally enjoyed this, but the intense nature of his personality and his relentless pursuit of artistic perfection eventually caused a strain. A horribly awkward dynamic developed wherein Andy looked at his work in the movie as the definitive portrayal of Gollum, as opposed to merely a model of what Gollum was supposed to be like. He was passionate about it and committed to it, and he wasn't going to let anybody be dismissive of it.

Andy was no wallflower, either. He wasn't about to just sit quietly, playing cards or napping, waiting for someone to call his name so that he could step up to a microphone and deliver his lines off camera. Not at all. He advocated for his character and for himself as an artist. Andy felt the best way to bring Gollum to life was to act out each and every movement, to give the animators as much ammunition as possible. The voice might have been enough, because the voice is absolutely stunning, so raspy and haunting and tortured. So utterly creepy. (By the way, that *is* Andy's voice. It's not a technological trick. It's all him. I've said to him, "Andy, you may get sick of it, but no one else does. How does it feel to know you can kill in any room the rest of your life?" Long after the rest of us have stopped signing autographs at science fiction and fantasy conventions, Andy will still be getting invitations to do Gollum. The split personality is perfect for functions like the MTV Awards—"Smeagol *loves* MTV; no, MTV *sucks!*"—where he can insult people and then apologize for insulting them. He's got a built-in gimmick, applicable to any setting, any routine.) But Andy wanted to provide more than just a voice; he wanted to embody the character, just as I had embodied Sam or Elijah had embodied Frodo. Even more so, in fact, given the psychological complexity of Gollum.

You can't blame him for feeling that way, and you can't possibly dispute the results. Gollum is an unforgettable character, and Andy deserves an enormous share of the credit for that accomplishment. Getting there, however, was a clunky process. For one thing, there was no comfortable lexicon for how to communicate. So we'd rehearse a scene—we'd shoot it with Andy—and the director would call that shot, the one with both Andy and another actor, the "reference pass." The original motivation for shooting Andy on-screen with us was simply to give the animators something to watch and then recreate on their computers. It was beneficial for the other actors, too, because it facilitated the performance to have another actor standing in front of you. In most movies, though, that approach is cost-prohibitive. You have a crew on the clock, and with each take, each rehearsal, resources are diminishing. Time, after all, is money. But the truth is, the performance is infinitely better when you rehearse the action before miming it. Elijah and I would have the scene choreographed and coded in our minds when Andy would step off, and we were grateful for that. Unfortunately, Andy's feelings would inevitably be crushed because Peter or one of the assistant directors would say something like, "Okay, nice job on the reference pass. Now let's do a real one."

"What do you mean, a real one? That's my performance!"

Even though no disrespect was intended (everyone admired Andy's work, as well as his work ethic), I felt for him. He acted his heart out. It was a challenging and unique situation: I wanted to honor my fellow performer, this guy who was crawling around on the floor in his green Lycra bodysuit, trashing his voice, screaming and crying and emoting, giving it his all on every take—but it was almost distracting at times. I wanted to recognize and applaud Andy's work, but it was difficult to throw myself into the scene, to not hold anything back, when I knew I'd have to do it again for "real" a few minutes later. Virtually every word uttered by Gollum was recorded by Andy off camera, or added later during looping sessions (or both). It's fair to point out, however, that an enormous percentage of the dialogue in *The Lord of the Rings* was looped—probably as much as ninety percent. On a normal film, that figure is closer to ten percent. On any project there is an eternal battle between the sound mixer saying, "Hey you don't have a clean track," and the director saying, "Well, I want the performances to be natural and organic, so let them go and we'll overlap later." Bits and pieces from different tracks are eventually spliced together and layered, until something close to perfection is achieved. It's a painstaking process, complicated even further on this production because of the presence of Gollum.

I don't know if Elijah would agree with this, but over time I found myself trying to conserve my energy during both rehearsals and first few takes, so that I could give it my all on the reference passes, not so much for the animators, because they weren't going to be animating me, but simply out of respect for Andy. It was a point my mother drove home when I was just eight years old and working as a professional actor for the first time, on an Afterschool Special called *Please Don't Hit Me, Mom.* My mother was the star of that movie, and at one point she became infuriated with me for relaxing a bit too much during another actor's close-up. I didn't know any better at the time. My job, I thought, was to sit there quietly, out of frame, and listen to the other actor. No big deal. Mom thought otherwise.

"You should be better off-screen than you are on-screen, do you understand me?" she admonished. "That's your responsibility to your fellow performer."

She taught me at that moment that you give just as much, if not more, when you're off-camera, and to this day I'm always better off camera than on. I don't know why, whether it's because I don't have to worry about how I look, or whether it's just a point of pride. I do know that something happens on camera; if you're sophisticated and aware of the camera, you want to be good at that and lose yourself in the part. It's highly egocentric. When you're not on camera, and you really emote and play the part, it's just the opposite: it's all about the other actor. The degree to which you are willing to open an emotional vein in support of the other actor is directly related to the amount of respect you have for him or her. I felt like I needed to be there for Andy, to honor the energy he emitted—and by the way, it was a level of intensity that was about five thousand degrees hotter than anything I'd ever experienced. White hot. I don't doubt for a second that Andy's strength and focus, his seriousness of purpose, improved the performances of everyone who worked with him.

I hear people talk about intensity all the time within the context of sports. There are very few athletes capable of peak intensity every day. Some days, it just isn't there. They're still professional, they still do the work, but they're just not quite as intense. Well, it's the same thing in acting. There were days when Elijah and I—I point to him only because I did just about every scene with him, and we both did an enormous amount of work with Andy—lacked intensity. Not merely because of the extended length of the production, but also because of the way our characters were approached, the way certain shots were designed. It was clear that we were doing a lot more work than would end up on the screen, and even though we wanted to do our utmost for Peter and the movie, it was impossible not to slow down and take a deep breath once in a while.

When Andy showed up, though, it was like, *Holy shit! Who is this guy?* Peter, in particular, wanted to reward Andy for his commitment, for his unflagging approach to the character of Gollum. Unlike Ian McKellen, who was so clever in his ability to encourage Fran and Peter and Philippa to bend the story based on his ideas, and unlike Viggo, who would just engage in creative trench warfare by continually coming at them with suggestions until he whittled them down, Andy was the sturdiest and most loyal of soldiers. He was willing to do whatever was asked of him, so long as everyone understood that he was not just providing the voice of Gollum. He was a real actor. He was an artist.

Fran loved writing for Andy, especially the schizophrenic stuff, and Peter liked having fun with that. He liked it for all the reasons the audience likes it: the arguing back and forth, the humor and the pathos. But it didn't come easily to Andy, regardless of how effortless it might appear to be on the screen. He suffered perhaps more than anyone else on the film (with the possible exception of John Rhys-Davies), and he did so willingly. I think Peter loved that about Andy, and I can't say that I blame him. Billy Boyd and Andy Serkis have something in common: they're both serious actors, and they're both really happy practicing their craft. There is something unique about the way they approach acting—and their lives. There is a selflessness about them that I envy. Andy is honest about when he's feeling competitive, or when he needs to assert himself. He's never sneaky or underhanded, and he's thoroughly devoted to doing the best work he can possibly do, and to helping everyone else rise to the occasion.

Billy has a similar attitude and drive, although it feels different to be around him, probably because he's slightly less intense, at least on the outside. In both cases, though, there is an admirable and palpable commitment to acting, and it was clear that Peter liked and respected it (as almost any director would), and wanted them to shine in the movie because of it. I think Peter recognized my talent and honestly knew that I wanted to do well, but I also think my level of awareness about how movies are made and the politics behind the making of movies prompted him to view me in a different light. That's a round-about way of saying that at times I was a pain in the ass, which isn't quite as worthy a thing to honor.

My two favorite characters, as written by Tolkien, are Treebeard and Gollum; in the movies, they're showy parts that provide almost limit-less options. But to be the other guy in the scenes with those charac-ters, well, that's a challenge, too. When Fran and Philippa started writing for the complexity of the emotional triangle between Frodo, Sam, and Gollum, when they started fleshing that out, it felt good. But sometimes we'd do scenes that were basically excuses for Gollum to perform a monologue, and that required patience on the part of the other actors. Most of the time I didn't mind, and in fact wanted to do whatever I could to assist Andy, to make his seemingly thankless on-set task easier. I must admit, however, that there were other times, when I was feeling downtrodden and underappreciated (and fat, too, really fat, which exacerbated my mood swings) because my character was getting short shrift, that I suffered from a dose of Gollum envy.

There is, for example, a scene in *The Two Towers* in which Gollum stops Sam and Frodo as they're about to try to sneak through the Black Gates of Mordor and says, "There's a better way. We'll take the stairs."

Well, Andy is a strong guy, and he's also a littler bigger than I am, so when we'd do fight scenes it wasn't unusual for him to inflict actual pain. Even apparently benign scenes, such as this one, held the poten-tial for discomfort. As Andy grabbed me by the collar and pulled me back, he caught a fistful of hair and yanked my wig off. Now, this was not an easy thing to do. This was not a "hairpiece"; it was an anchored wig. The makeup artists would slick back our hair and glue the wiglace on. They'd twist the real hair on the top and in back, and tie it off with rubber bands. Then they'd put a wig on top and insert pins through the wiglace and anchor those into the rubber bands. The end result was a wig that wouldn't move in a hurricane.

But there I was, sitting on my fat butt in front of the stunned cast and crew, wigless and white and wounded, looking and feeling suddenly like a star from the silent-movie era ("I'm ready for my close-up, Mr. DeMille!"). What I should have done was laugh it off. I should have given Andy a pat on the back and said, "No hard feelings" or "Dude, lay off the caffeine!" I mean, it didn't hurt that bad. It was just embarrassing. But I was tired and frustrated, so I got up and, without saying a word to anyone, walked off the set and headed for the makeup area. In truth, it was the most efficient way to get back to working, but I did walk off in a bit of a huff, which was pretty silly, considering Andy hadn't done anything wrong. He was *supposed* to grab me hard; I *wanted* him to grab me hard. It wasn't his fault that my wig came off, and I should have said so. I didn't, though, and my lack of courtesy really pissed him off.

"Sorry, man," he snapped. "It wasn't on purpose, you know?"

I did know, and I told Andy as much when I returned, with a new wig and a better attitude firmly in place.

CHAPTER FOURTEEN

As the production slogged along, and days turned into weeks, weeks into months, and months finally gave way to years, it became apparent that we were, of course, in good hands after all. We realized that Peter had a vast sprawling image in his mind, and somehow he had the talent and ambition to transfer it to the screen in a way that would make sense to audiences, even Tolkien purists. Moreover, I began to get the feeling that the patience Peter had requested would be rewarded, and that Samwise Gamgee would have his moment (or moments) to shine.

Not that I understood the entire story; I don't think any of the actors, even those most familiar with the books, had a clear grasp of Peter's adaptation. I couldn't tell from reading the scripts how the first movie was going to end or how the second movie was going to begin, and I wasn't terribly concerned with figuring it out; that wasn't my job. My job was to trust Peter and Fran and Philippa, to have faith that they knew exactly where they were going and how they were going to get there. It wasn't until the premiere of the first film, in which a complicated story unfolded so eloquently, that I truly appreciated the depth of their genius. But there were signposts along the way.

For example, take the Bridge of Khazad-Dum, where Gandalf fights heroically before falling to his (apparent) death, and the grieving of the Fellowship that followed. That scene felt pitch perfect even as we filmed it. We took a chopper to the top of Mount Nelson on the south island, where the view was nothing short of spectacular.

Being up there in this pristine, rocky place, unaccessible to most people, felt fresh, exhilarating. It was one of those days when the work came easily, not because it wasn't difficult, but because it just felt right. I remember nailing the crying scene, and hoping that it wouldn't be lost in translation. And it wasn't. A few months later Peter screened a small amount of footage for some of the cast and crew, as well as for an executive who had been invited. This wasn't something I'd seen Peter often do, but obviously he felt pretty good about the material. With good reason. The scene was the aftermath of Khazad-Dum, and it was absolutely breathtaking. The swirling slow-motion footage captured the beauty and majesty of the setting, as well as the emotional power of the scene. I still think it's one of the most evocative scenes in the entire trilogy, and even when viewed out of context, as it was in this case, it gave me confidence. I felt very proud of the work. For perhaps the first time since I'd been in New Zealand, I felt like I had been nurtured—encouraged to soar and allowed to flourish—and it felt permanent, unmistakable, and just plain great!

The roller coaster continued afterward, and at times I felt adrift and frustrated, but always I knew Khazad-Dum was in the can, and that gave me strength. I only hoped there would be similar opportunities to come.

Which there were. The first involved the ending to *The Fellowship of the Ring*, which depicts the splitting of the Fellowship at Amon Hen. We made several trips to the Mavora Lakes region to shoot this and other sequences. At one point John Mahaffey, the second unit director, filmed a scene in which Frodo and Sam paddle away together, only to be attacked by uruk-hai, who rise out of the water. I don't even recall the nature of the relationship between that fight and the escape from Boromir that preceded it. I just know it was one of a couple of endings written for the first film, and that it felt a little awkward and clunky. As always seemed to happen, however, the scene was revisited and rethought and ultimately improved to an astonishing degree. There was no room for complacency on this film, no settling for just okay.

Elijah and I were introduced to what turned out to be the final version—the definitive ending of the first film—during dinner with Peter and Fran and Philippa. They had invited us to an Italian restaurant, and although no reason was given for the meeting, I knew it had to be important; they didn't often extend such invitations, not because they weren't gracious or accommodating, but simply because there was far too much work to be done. If a meal was scheduled, there usually was a reason for it. On this occasion, the reason was made clear before the appetizers had even arrived, when Fran presented us with two typewritten pages on which were printed the final scene of *The Fellowship of the Ring*, in which Sam, loyal to the end, marches into the lake and very nearly drowns in an attempt to prevent Frodo from going off on his own.

Fran and Philippa were justifiably proud at having figured out a moving, logical conclusion to the first film, and they wanted us to know how good they felt about it. I presume Peter also wanted us to understand that this was a critical transitional scene, one that would leave viewers eager to see the second movie, and as such it required intense focus on our part. I do know that that evening was among the highlights of the entire production for me, sitting in that restaurant, reading this beautifully rendered scene, and thinking, *See, we're all just colleagues after all; they really do care about me and want to spend time with me.* Such are the insecurities and neuroses of my sometimes feeble mind, and they were easily magnified on a production of this scale. Peter and Fran and Philippa were so busy and were being pulled in so many different directions that it wasn't unusual to go weeks on end without having a substantive conversation with them. In fairness, though, it wasn't Peter's job to be my friend or mentor, even if that's what I wanted. But I remember feeling like my value as an actor was perceived as important that night. There were so many times when I lost sight of what we were doing, when it felt like we all were just grinding it out—putting on the makeup, the ears and feet—and that we were somehow disconnected from the big picture. Now, though, Sam had a purpose—I had a purpose—and it was germane to the overall project.

This was one instance, however, when circumstances conspired to make filming the sequence a physical as well as emotional challenge. It was early in the morning, and I felt pretty good about the work ahead, maybe even a bit cocky, because I knew I'd have something important to do. Christine and Ali were with me in the dressing room, and I gave them both a quick kiss before heading out to film the scene. It wasn't a complicated shot. Elijah would sit in a canoe, some twenty feet off the shore, and shout to me an explanation for his departure, and for leaving me behind. I would respond by telling him that I understood, while simultaneously declaring my intention to follow. The fact that Sam doesn't know how to swim does not dissuade him in the least, and ultimately Frodo must paddle back and rescue his friend, sealing their bond for the duration of the journey: they will go together to Mordor, regardless of the consequences.

I had taken only a few heavy steps into the water, however, when I felt a searing pain in my foot, the kind of pain that instantly signals a severe injury. If you smack your funny bone or stub your toe, it hurts, but the pain passes almost instantly. This was different. It felt as though something had gone right through my foot. The shot called for me to walk into the water and swim—or flail—out of frame, but I stopped immediately, frozen in my tracks by the pain. It hurt pretty bad for about ten seconds, and then I turned and limped out of the water and stumbled back up the beach. I was surprised by how quickly everyone seemed to realize the gravity of the situation. Of course, the blood streaming down my prosthetic foot was an indication that something bad had happened. I'd been stabbed, as it turned out, probably by a branch or a shard of glass, although I can't be sure of that, since we never found the offending object. The likely scenario is that when the crew prepared the lake for this scene, they ran a rake along the bottom to smooth things out and make sure nothing was there. Unfortunately, they might have churned something up that had been buried. Also, I was putting such force into the way I was march- ing into the water, while wearing just my hobbit feet, that anything with a sharp tip was going to do some damage.

I discovered on this day that you can determine the severity of an injury by looking at the faces of the people around you. If it's really bad, they squint or scrunch up their faces, or even turn away in revul- sion. That's the reaction my wound seemed to provoke. Not from everyone, mind you. Elijah walked over as one of the emergency med- ical technicians was cutting off my prosthetic foot, an act that dislodged a huge blood clot, which landed on the ground with a *splat!* This naturally disgusted most everyone in proximity, with the possible exception of Elijah, who simply said, "Cool!" and then began poking at the blood clot with a stick, an act that disgusted even Peter Jackson, whose background in splatter films ought to make him immune to such things.

"Come on, Elijah. Don't do that!" he admonished.

"No, that's okay," I said. "He can play with my blood clot."

Elijah just laughed. On some level, I think, I enjoyed the attention, especially once the pain began to subside. But it was a bit of a carnival atmosphere. The DVD crew was shooting close-ups, and everyone was gathering around, and it was becoming clear that while this wasn't a life-threatening injury or anything, it was going to be a major inconvenience.

"Oh, yes, it's bleeding quite freely now," the medic said as he dressed the wound.

Freely . . .

Not a word you want to hear associated with your own blood. To me that meant, *Whoa, I'm losing a lot of blood.* But that's not what he meant. He was referring to the fact that it was a clean, empty wound, that dirt was going out with the blood, which was a good thing. Relatively speaking.

Everything happened pretty quickly after that. Ali and Christine showed up, and the three of us were flown by helicopter to a small hospital. Christine doesn't like helicopters, so she sat in the back. Ali was up front with me and the pilot. She was only four years old, so she naturally looked to me to see whether she should be afraid.

"Don't worry," I said. "It'll be fun."

Ali smiled. Meanwhile, in the back, as the chopper left the ground, Christine closed her eyes and turned a little green. The pilot, I had been told, once worked with Jacques Cousteau, flying in and out of some of the most remote locations in the world, so I figured he had to be pretty good. And he was. The flight was bumpy but uneventful.

Ali wanted to stay with me while the doctor treated my injury. As he pulled out a syringe filled with novocaine, I wondered if I had made a mistake.

"Oh, Daddy," Ali said sympathetically, "that's a big needle!"

So it was. But I was determined to look like a tough guy for my daughter, so I swallowed hard and held my breath as the doctor inserted the needle.

There was a brief rush of pain, followed by numbness, and then it was a party. That night, of course, after the novocaine wore off, the pain returned, but some of the cast and crew got together for dinner, and I made a point of joining them, mainly because I didn't want to be regarded as a guy who was laid up. I wanted to be heroic like Sam!

The very next day I returned to work, although on a completely different scene in a completely different location (a few weeks would pass before we returned to the Mavora Lakes region to film the conclusion of the first film). At the end of the workday, Peter presented me with a Maori walking stick.

"This is from the crew," he said with a smile. "They wanted to give it to you for coming back to work right away."

I have to tell you, when Peter handed me that stick, I felt like the king of New Zealand. It was one of the best moments of the entire production. I let it roll around in my hands for a moment. Later, Gino Acevedo (supervisor of prosthetics for Weta) and I carved the date, place, and some Tolkien runes around the top of it. It would become the single most unique and memorable treasure I brought home. I looked in Peter's eyes when he handed me the walking stick, and even though his admiration wasn't for my prowess as a filmmaker, it was enormously meaningful. It was clear that he and the crew were grateful I didn't use my injury as an opportunity to get any star treatment. As a guy, Peter respected me. Maybe I wasn't as tough as Viggo (who merely asked for a dab of superglue when his tooth broke off), but I had weathered a little punishment with dignity.

"Thank you," I said to Peter, and pretty much left it at that. For a change, I was practically speechless.

CHAPTER FIFTEEN

You think it's easy to wrestle with a giant spider? Trust me, it's not. One of the most exciting scenes in *The Return of the King* is Sam's battle with Shelob, the massive arachnid who guards Mordor and at one point captures and nearly kills Frodo. It's a thrilling and artful sequence, one that allows Sam's courage to percolate to the surface and effectively stamps him as the hero of the third film. He is an ordinary man in an extraordinary circumstance, and he rises to the occasion in epic fashion, as so many of the great literary and cinematic heroes have done. That the scene works as well as it does is testament to Peter Jackson's vision and talent. When film critics repeatedly pointed out that Shelob was the most realistic and frightening giant spider ever depicted on film, it wasn't faint praise. A creation such as Shelob, in the wrong hands, might well have resulted in a messy, laughably implausible climax to a movie that wears its heart on its sleeve. In other words, if not done properly, it might have been a disaster.

My job, as I saw it, was to not screw it up. Seriously. Shelob was so good, and the action sequence so well constructed, that I had only to make sure that I followed the choreography and emoted properly and energetically. But it proved to be more challenging than I had anticipated. Throughout filming I'd been reasonably adept at playing make-believe, at visualizing the story's numerous computer-generated creatures; my imagination was good, and I could act opposite my imagination with relative ease. People would sometimes ask me, "Isn't it hard to look at a piece of tape or a tennis ball and envision the thing it represents?" Well, no, not when you have Alan Lee's and John Howe's illustrations as models. They helped seed my imagination.

Something happened with Shelob, though. The sequence took a great deal of time to film, and at one point, when the camera was supposed to cut to me, and I was supposed to deliver the strongest line of the scene—"Let him go, you filth!"—I had a moment of crisis. Suddenly, for some reason I still can't explain, I couldn't see the spider anymore. Shelob had disappeared. It was as if my imagination had dried up.

"What's wrong?" asked Peter, who directed the scene.

"I don't know. I can't see the spider."

"What do you mean?"

"I mean . . . it's gone. Shit!"

I started panicking, having an internal meltdown, which is kind of funny when you think about it. I'd held it together through all the bad moments, through all the dull and frustrating times when I wanted only a chance to show what I could do, and now, here I was, starring in the climactic action sequence of the whole trilogy—in a scene that was supposed to have the audience rising out of their seats and pumping their fists—melting into a puddle of anxiety.

The truth is, we had actually filmed the Shelob action sequence during principal photography, and most of it was handled by John Mahaffey. I had fought and killed Shelob years before. Now, during the pickup shooting for *The Return of the King*, I had lived with Sam for four years. I had seen the first two movies countless times and traveled around the world promoting the movies. Thousands of people had told me what they thought about my performance, and I'd read innumerable articles about every aspect of the films. In a sense, I had all of that wisdom and experience at my disposal when Peter brought me back to New Zealand to shoot, among other things, this climactic moment. I think I'd even seen a rough version of the sequences immediately preceding and following the Shelob cave stuff.

If you think about George Custer and Ulysses S. Grant, and what they knew and when they knew it, you can begin to appreciate my wee dilemma. I just couldn't quite drop into this moment—or it didn't feel "Sam-like." I loved the cinematic heroism of it, and I certainly had wanted for years to get this kind of opportunity on screen. But I'd already gotten to do the boat scene with Elijah and the unfathomably special scene in the ruins of Osgilith with Frodo, where we talk about the great stories that really matter, and the fact that there is still good in the world worth fighting for. So, could I get a grip and do the relatively simple "hero shot"?

For a few long seconds, I really didn't know.

After a brief respite, a drink of water, a few words of encouragement, and a pat on the back, we tried again. And again. And again. Ultimately, I got it right, but it was hard. It took a lot of push-ups and screaming and emotional calisthenics. I did that a lot. I'd do arm curls, jumping jacks, anything to get the blood flowing, to trigger my throat and face before going in front of the camera. There's something about screaming that actually wakes you up and gets you ready for an action sequence. I developed a bit of a reputation among the other actors. They'd say, "Oh great, there goes Sean, warming up again." Elijah ended up mildly embracing this technique, too, and not just to ridicule me. Action sequences are not as elemental as they might seem. Think about it. You sit around for seven hours and then they call you, and you have to walk in and get all excited and start screaming at the top of your lungs. How do you go from being exhausted to doing *that?* You run around the block, or you do sit-ups or push-ups. You do whatever works. At least I did. My preparatory histrionics became such a source of amusement that someone put together a gag reel of me barking, jumping up and down, screaming like a madman. It was a howl, I have to admit. The Brits would watch me and say, "Excuse me, mate, are you going to be doing that all day? Because it's a bit, well, you know, distracting."

Even more difficult though, are the moments of quiet emotion, for there is an honesty and a rawness to those scenes that require more than just playing. You open your soul when you do work like that—or at least you should. There is a scene near the end of *The Return of the King* in which Sam cradles a weary and wounded Frodo on the side of a volcano, and tries to comfort him with a sweet and simple speech about the land they have left behind and all that it represents. In Sam's tearful words is a tribute to the simple things in life, the things worth fighting for, as well as a recognition of the likelihood that they may not survive their journey: *Do you remember the Shire, Mr. Frodo? It'll be spring soon and the orchards will be in blossom, and the birds will be nesting in the hazel thicket. And they'll be sowing the summer barley in the lower fields. And eating the first of the strawberries with cream . . . Do you remember the taste of strawberries?*

That scene was the single greatest acting experience of my life, and I'll never forget it. But getting there—getting to the point where I was capable of such work, of meeting the standard set by my director, my fellow performers, and the script of a lifetime—was a long process. Roughly twenty-five years.

Here's what I mean. There are four specific scenes in my career that I consider to be the equivalent of a complete educational experience—grade school, high school, college, graduate school—in terms of emotional maturity on screen. The first was in *Please Don't Hit Me, Mom*, when I was eight years old and received a spontaneous acting lesson from my mother. She had asked me if I wanted to be in the movie, and I thought it sounded like fun, even though I'd be playing her abused son. The role wasn't simply handed to me—I had to audition. So I worked on the scenes with my mother at home, and then we taped the audition on the set of the television show *One Day at a Time*. I don't remember feeling stressed or nervous, just comfortable doing the work with my mother. And I got the part.

The challenge came on the day we were supposed to film the most disturbing and emotionally charged scene in the movie: a scene in which the mother attacks her son in the family kitchen. We went at it according to the script. Mom grabbed me and threw me around and started banging my head against the counter, all the while screaming at the top of her lungs. Acting her little heart out. Instead of wailing like a frightened, wounded animal, as the script suggested, I covered my face and started to giggle uncontrollably. It was nervous laughter really, for I couldn't help but think, *Whoa, this is a little too close to home. I've known some of these moments.* We did a few takes, but each time I'd break out laughing, and the director would yell, "Cut," and my mother would walk away, seething. Finally, she pulled me aside, crouched low, and put her face right next to mine.

"Look," she said, and I could tell by her tone that I was in trouble. "I took a chance on you. What do you think you're doing? This is my career; this is my life." She paused, looked back at the cast and crew. "These people are counting on me. They're counting on you!"

With that, I burst into tears.

As soon as I started crying, my mother turned to the director, made a circular motion with her hand, and whispered something that sounded a lot like, "Keep it rolling." And that's what they did. Within seconds my movie mother was beating me about the head and face all over again, shouting her lines, and I was sobbing like a baby. Eventually the scene came to an end, the director yelled, "Cut! Print! That was brilliant!" and my mother wrapped her arms around me, gave me a big kiss on the cheek, messed up my hair, and said, "Now *that's* acting!"

"Yeah?" I sniffed.

"Yes."

Proud and relieved, and maybe just a bit confused, I said, "Uhhhh, okay."

That was my first drama lesson.

The second lesson came a few years later, in a miniseries called *The Rules of Marriage*, starring Elizabeth Montgomery and Elliott Gould, and directed by a man named Milton Catsalas, who later went on to become a world-renowned acting instructor in Beverly Hills. This, for me, was another case of art imitating life, for the movie centered on a couple in the midst of an eroding marriage. My parents were in the process of getting a divorce, just like the couple in the movie. I played their son. The audition included a scene in which the father sits with the boy in the front yard of their lovely home and tells him that he's going to be leaving. Milton played the part of the father in the audition, and when the script called for me to hug him and cry, I did precisely that. I mean, I wasn't really crying, but the feeling I experienced as we embraced was real enough, and he loved it. He noted it, congratulated me on the work, and I got the job.

When we shot the scene, however, something went very wrong.

Elliott Gould, whom I liked and admired, and with whom I established a strong rapport, had some type of problem on the day we filmed that particular scene. I remember it was late in the day, and Elliott was beating himself up because he was having an extremely difficult time working up the requisite emotion. It's a strange and awkward thing when this happens. The director always prefers that an actor summon whatever it is that's required to produce a *real* emotional moment, to open the tear ducts in a manner that is plausible and effective. In other words, don't fake it.

Elliott was giving it his best shot, but nothing seemed to work for him, and with each passing take the anxiety and tension mounted. There were discussions about whether they should resort to using artificial tears, but Elliott balked at that notion. Meanwhile, Milton kept looking at me, the ten-year-old kid on the side, in much the same way that a baseball coach might look at a pitcher in his bullpen. I was the ace reliever, the guy Milton could insert into the lineup if he needed someone to capture the emotion of the scene. But I could feel that pressure, and when we shot the scene, I was just honest and reacted the way I had in the audition with Milton. Or so I thought. It didn't come across that way on camera. Milton had been more committed to me in the audition than Elliott was during the actual filming of the movie, simply because he was thoroughly consumed by his own anxiety over how he was coming across in front of the camera. There was no give-and-take, no partnership, no sharing of the emotional burden. It was almost as if each of us was performing a monologue, which was exactly the opposite of the scene's intent.

We shot the scene a couple of times, but it never really worked the way it should have, which exasperated Milton.

"What's wrong?" he asked me. "Why isn't it like it was the last time, in the audition?"

I had no answer, of course. I was only ten years old and following the lead of the adults. I didn't know what was wrong, but I knew it wasn't my fault, and that awareness caused me to lose respect in that moment for both Milton and Elliott. Over the years, as I matured and learned more about acting, my memory of the incident only intensified; how unfair, I thought, to expect a child to carry the full emotional weight of a scene when he's working alongside a seasoned professional who is having a bad day. Later, I audited Milton's class and reminded him of that incident. I told him how I felt, and he apologized. He didn't realize I had experienced the incident in that way, and he felt bad about it. I was impressed that he was so open to hearing me talk about something that had happened so long ago, and it was important for me to share the memory of that experience, because it really did screw me up for a while; whenever I had a crying scene in a movie, I had tremendous difficulty summoning the requisite emotion to make the scene work.[5]

Crying in front of the camera is an interesting act, one that is often devoid of any real emotion. Most actors have ways of faking it and getting by. They can pinch a tear or two and project emotion that seems to match the quality of the scene, or they can rely on chemical help, a dash of instant tears. Really, though, it's extraordinarily rare that someone is talented enough and emotive enough to cry authentically on cue, in the moment, take after take after take. When it happens, it's no accident; it's usually a marriage of a great performer and the best moment in a great script. Here's the truth: a lot of the time, actors have a hard time crying because the scenes in which they are asked to cry really aren't that good. The writing doesn't facilitate the muse. It's a remarkable thing when you see an actor who is so emotionally available that he can be sitting off camera, eating a burger, waiting for his call, and then moments later, when the director says, "Start crying, please," he does it. I've seen this, and I've often wondered, How can anyone do that? Because I just don't get it. But when it happens naturally, when the drama of the scene lends itself to real emotion—that I understand.

My third acting lesson—college, so to speak—occurred when I was playing a college student: Rudy Reuttiger. *Rudy* is a movie that wants to make its audience cry, which can be a dangerous thing. Done

---

5. I hold nothing against Elliott, either. The fact is, he's a good man and a gifted actor. When we wrapped *The Rules of Marriage*, he presented me with a gift: a tiny mezuzah inscribed with the words, "Forever, Elliott." That, in the end, far outweighed any discomfort I might have experienced on the set.

properly, emotional movies stir something in the viewers and pull them into the experience. Done badly, they become unintentional jokes and black marks on the résumés of everyone involved. *Rudy*, I think, was exceptionally well done. The writer took great care to be faithful to the character's legitimately inspirational story, while refusing to fall prey to the pitfalls of overt sentimentality. That's a roundabout way of saying that Angelo Pizzo wrote a great script. My job was to inject honesty and believability into this blue-collar character, to make him a three-dimensional human being, and not just a sports-movie cliché.

A pivotal scene in the movie, and the most challenging for me as an actor, is one that depicts Rudy's acceptance to Notre Dame, the fulfillment of a lifelong dream. It's a powerful scene, one that begins quietly, with Rudy reading the acceptance letter while sitting on a bench. The director, David Anspaugh, designed the scene beautifully, with a crane shot that pans from humble Holy Cross Junior College, where Rudy is a struggling student working his way through school, to the glistening Golden Dome of Notre Dame. The point of the shot, made with elegance and grace, is to convey a sense of Rudy's journey: he's moving less than a mile away, but his life is about to change forever. The tears shed by Rudy as he opens and reads the letter represent not only an expression of joy over this accomplishment, but an awareness of what it means. It's nearly a perfect scene, one that captures the spirit of the entire movie.

On the day we filmed, David Anspaugh encouraged me to remain isolated from the rest of the cast and crew, which isn't something I normally like to do.

"I don't want you to talk to anybody," he said. "You've got two or three hours before we shoot this thing, so just go away and clear your head. Don't speak to a soul."

I did as instructed. To occupy my time, I read the script again, start to finish. I did that a lot on *Rudy*, partly because I was the star and felt significant pressure to be thoroughly well-versed in the subject matter, but also because I just loved reading the damn story. Anyway, eventually I made my way to the set, and we began rehearsing the sequence. Finally, it was time to shoot the scene. Everything was designed for me to succeed in that moment. I was working with a superbly composed scene and a thoughtful, sympathetic director; I was playing a character with whom I felt an innate connection. So I opened the letter and started to read, and . . .

Nothing. Not a drop. My tear ducts were dry, my heart empty.

We reset the scene. David shouted "Action," and again . . . nothing.

David shuffled over to where I was standing and quietly tried to encourage me. He didn't want to make a big fuss about it, but the truth is, there was a lot riding on this scene. He knew—and I knew—that if I didn't nail that moment emotionally, it was a failure, in a big way, on a big stage. I was the title character in a major studio picture. I was expected to come through. Anything less than an honest, heartfelt rendering of the scene would be viewed as a failure on my part. But I was determined to keep trying. I would rather have failed big than to have faked the tears—a truly ignominious defeat.

"You okay?" David asked calmly. I was at once impressed and amused by the utter lack of urgency in his voice. He had the attitude of a great coach or manager who's dying on the inside, but knows he has to project confidence to his players. And you could tell he was thinking that way. He actually looked like he was playing the part of a coach trying to think of the right thing to say to his athlete.

"I'm fine," I responded, although I really wasn't.

David clapped his hands together. "Good, let's try it again."

So we did a third take, but that one stunk as well.

Now things were getting complicated. The Notre Dame officials and trustees who had been invited to the set were starting to shift uncomfortably in their seats. The crew members were looking at their watches. Most important of all, the sun was falling in the sky, resulting in the real possibility that David's gorgeous shot, so dependent on a sun-drenched Golden Dome, would lose some of its luster—or worse, it would have to be postponed to another day.

Once again David stepped out from behind the monitor and walked over to where I was standing, but now his appearance and demeanor had changed. This time he seemed less like a confident major-league baseball manager than a harried office manager who has to get the completed project to his boss by five o'clock if he wants to save his ass—and his job.

"Sean," he said, with something like panic in his voice, "what's the problem?"

I didn't know what to say, how to explain what I was feeling, when what I was feeling was essentially emptiness. I didn't want to pull a star trip, didn't want to thrash about and make excuses. I didn't want to make a big fuss about my shortcomings as an actor to engender sympathy from the director. Instead I just looked at David and said, "I don't know."

This was not what he wanted to hear. I'm sure he would have preferred that I communicate to him the root of my anxiety, but I had nothing to offer. So we stood there for a moment, the blocked actor and the panic-stricken director, with what seemed to be a giant clock ticking in the sky above us. Finally, after what felt like an eternity, David held up his hands, palms to the sky, and said out of pure exasperation, "What are you afraid of?"

And that was it, the key that opened the lock. I started sobbing hysterically.

Shocked, David put a hand on my back, presumably to console me. But noooooo. Instead he leaned in and whispered into my ear, "Wait! Please . . . wait!" It was a crane shot, see, and they had to set it up, and it just wouldn't have made sense for me to be crying before I even opened the letter.

"Keep it together, Sean," David urged. "Just hang in there for a minute or two."

I choked back the tears and wiped my eyes as David rushed off to the monitor. The rest of the crew jumped to attention, and within a minute or two we were filming the scene. And it was beautiful. One take. Pitch-perfect. The scene ends with Rudy running off in celebration, the acceptance letter in his hand. When David yelled, "Cut!" I fell to the ground, completely exhausted. Fifteen minutes passed before my heart stopped racing and I could catch my breath, so cathartic was the experience. Intentionally or not, David had released something within me, and that fear of crying, of being emotionally naked in front of other people, was gone. Looking back on it, I think the emotion was the result of a confluence of events, like a perfect storm. I'd recently gotten married; we were in Indiana, near Christine's family; my personal life was in place; the ideas of the story were good and right, in line with who I aspired to be. It was just morally right for me to be in that role, trying to embody persistence and determination, and all those things that Rudy is and that I wanted to be. There was no excuse for not doing it right on that particular day, so when David said, "What are you afraid of?" the question was the answer. Simply put, I was afraid. David had struck a nerve, or to risk another metaphor, he pulled my finger out of the dike, allowing the dam to burst.

That was college. Graduate school (in so many ways) was *The Lord of the Rings*, in particular the scene on the side of Mount Doom.

I can't recall for certain, but I think new pages for that scene were handed to us the morning of the shoot. I knew we were getting close to filming the scene, and I understood that it would be one of the most important and emotional moments in the film, but I wasn't quite sure how it would turn out, or even how it was to be depicted. When I looked at the pages that morning and glanced at the dialogue, it seemed at once familiar and fresh. Somehow, it seemed new to me. I read it several times while sitting in the makeup truck, having my feet and ears and hair applied for roughly the three-hundredth time, and I was filled with admiration for the work that the writers had done. Not just because of the way it looked on a cold page, or the way it sounded when I spoke the words, but also because I knew how hard they had worked to get it right. It was impossible, even when I was busy wallowing in self-pity, not to respect Fran and Philippa, for theirs was a never-ending quest. I've written screenplays; to me, even under the best of conditions, it's torture. I can't imagine what this must have been like for them, or how they survived the experience.

This scene was a perfect example of their talent and commitment. It wasn't just good; it was great. As I read my lines aloud to Elijah and my makeup artist, Vivienne "Bliss" Macgillicuddy, I reveled in the poetry. By the time we left the makeup truck, I knew my lines cold and couldn't wait to get started. We took four-wheel-drive vehicles to a base station on Mount Ruapehu, and then hiked twenty minutes to the side of an active volcano that served as a stand-in for Mount

Doom. Along the way, Elijah and I rehearsed our lines over and over, not merely because we wanted to be prepared, but because it was fun. This was exactly the type of work I had hoped to do.

Before we shot the scene, I had a flashback to the first day of principal photography, when the production was blessed by Maori elders in a formal ceremony in Wellington. I had no idea what I was getting into then, but there was something in the earnestness of these men, the way they not only offered their encouragement and support, but also reminded us of our obligation, that struck a chord.

"We hope that the land takes care of you," they had said, "and that you are good stewards of the land. It was here long before you, and it'll be here long after you leave."

I understood what that meant. We were on an island in the South Pacific, filming an epic trilogy that would become a part of cinematic history, an indelible stamp on popular culture. Nevertheless, as with all things human, we were but a footnote. Eventually we would all be gone and the movies would be forgotten, but the mountains would still be there. The desert and the jungle, too. In one form or another that thought stayed with me throughout my time in New Zealand. It helped put things in perspective on the bad days and gave me strength in times of anxiety or crisis. On a purely selfish level, it was comforting when flying by helicopter to the top of a rocky, fog-enshrouded peak to know that the production had been blessed by the Maori elders; somehow their approval made it seem less likely that the chopper would slam into the side of the mountain. We tried to be good stewards, and we—at least, those of us who weren't New Zealanders—tried to be mindful that we were merely visitors.

The thought of that blessing came rushing back to me now as we hiked up Mount Ruapehu, which only a century ago belched ash as far as Wellington. I was in awe of the setting, with its stunning physical beauty, and I was grateful for the opportunity to be there. I felt like I had earned this moment, but I also realized that I was part of something much bigger than myself, and a part of me regretted having indulged the low moments of selfishness and egocentrism (even if they are considered inalienable rights by most members of the acting fraternity). I like to be a good guy, the kind of person who says the right thing and knows the right way to be and doesn't command attention when it's not necessary. I just seem to find lots of situations where I can be polite and still be the center of attention, which helps feed my ego without making me a jerk; I've generally figured out a way to not be unseemly in order to thrive. In New Zealand, however, I'd gotten myself into a situation where what was appropriate was to be patient and quiet. That was hard for me. I was accustomed to getting reams of positive reinforcement for my work, which simply did not and could not happen on *The Lord of the Rings*. Peter Jackson was at the controls of a magnificent, sprawling moviemaking machine, with thousands of workers, each performing at the height of his or her abilities. I wanted a pat on the back, reassurance that my contribution was real and valued, and I wanted it more often than it came. But you know what? The lucidity of hindsight is startling, for I know now that I was treated exactly as I should have been treated. Any more feedback than I received would have been fake, and I'd be horrified now to think I was the one actor on the production who required or received such coddling. Samwise Gamgee neither needed nor deserved that. He wasn't the kind of character who was going to be the focus of the movie. He would have his moments, just like so many other characters—more of them than most, in fact—and a few that were undeniably powerful. Peter knew that and wasn't going to go out of his way to make me feel better. Dealing with that realization, day in and day out, was a challenge; knowing I wasn't the reason people would be flocking to the movie was hard. I had to be a utility player who could score when called upon, but wouldn't be called upon too often.

Now, however, I was getting a chance to score, and after waiting for such a long time, well, it was meaningful. It was important. Having kept a lid on my emotions—both personally and professionally—for so many months, I was eager to do some real *acting*, and when the opportunity finally presented itself, I was relieved to discover that I had a command of the material. There was no reason for it not to be that way, of course. I'd spent months working with dialect coaches. I'd read the books and understood the story. I'd done other crying scenes, so I understood the culture of the set: I knew there would be respect for the actors and the process. I knew Peter would be patient and encouraging. There was nothing precious about it. I simply under-stood on every level what needed to happen at that moment.

There was something else I knew: the crying scene, the tender scene, would be immediately followed by the *heroic* scene, the scene in which Sam hoists a weakened Frodo onto his back and carries him up the side of the mountain ("I can't carry the ring for you, but I can carry you!"). That was my moment to become the Sam I envisioned, the Sam who was strong and noble and not a bumbling buffoon. You can drive yourself crazy if you spend too much time thinking about the implications of a scene like that, but I knew subconsciously that four years hence, when *The Return of the King* was released, that scene would be everywhere. If any scene would get the audience to feel uplifted and satisfied, that was it.

The filming was almost uneventful, which is strange because it was an inherently dangerous sequence. We didn't use stunt doubles. I wore a harness in the event that I slipped and tumbled off a precipice, but Elijah employed no such safety measures. He simply and bravely, maybe even foolishly, climbed onto my back and allowed his body to go limp. As I trudged up the side of the moun-tain, with my prosthetic feet slipping and sliding through the gravel, I remember thinking, *Holy shit! I've got the whole $270 million franchise on my shoulders right now.* Maybe the crew had some sense that if I fell, they'd be able to catch Elijah, but in my estimation, he was in real danger.

Through the fog of memory, however, that scene has faded, while the emotional moment that preceded it has gained even greater clarity. It was a nearly perfect acting experience. I felt like I had complete con-trol over my instrument, that I could cry and quiver and emote, and tears would stream down, and it was real and authentic. When Peter came out from behind the monitors, both Elijah and I realized we had nailed the scene. Peter is so conservative and stoic; I mean, he carries himself lightly. He bounces around the set and gets down on one knee to feel closer to the action, but he's not a guy who is overly dramatic. This is generally an admirable trait in a director. Peter won't panic if he's losing light, or not getting exactly what he wants from an actor, or otherwise suffering the frustrations of a typical movie production.

He uses his language and his actual authority to ask people to do their jobs and to do them well. Simple as that.

There is no hysteria in Peter Jackson, although there probably should be once in a while, if only to strike fear into the hearts of his cast. If you think you're going to piss off the director, and he's going to scream at you and humiliate you in front of everyone, you want to get it right. Intimidation can trigger a performance. Take Oliver Stone, for example. I'm sure crying in front of him is easy, because if you come up empty, he'll make you suffer. Peter will just be disappointed, and then he'll come up with something to take the place of what you didn't deliver. In this case, though, we had delivered. That much was apparent from Peter's reaction. It wasn't so much what he said that was meaningful. (He offered a simple instruction: "Sean, could you move your hand this way a little bit?") It was the fact that his glasses were all fogged up and tears were streaming down his cheeks.

Yes! We did it!

Knowing that we'd reached Peter was galvanizing. I felt like a fighter who sees blood in an opponent: *Time to go in for the kill!* And that's what we did. Elijah and I kept going at it, take after take, and each time it got better. I loved reading the speech and kept doing it over and over, with escalating emotion. It was amazing: I felt like I was crying from the bottom of my soul. It was unlike anything I'd ever experienced on a movie set. It's a rare thing where your expectations are met or exceeded and everything works out exactly as you hoped, and this was such a time. We had peaked at exactly the right moment.

When Peter yelled, "Cut!" I felt a rush of adrenaline. I picked Elijah up and practically lifted him over my head. We hugged and exchanged high fives and pumped our fists. And we weren't alone in exulting. The boom operator came over and told us how moving the scene had been. The camera operator said he was having a hard time looking through the eyepiece because he was crying so hard. Admittedly, movie sets are prone to groupthink, wherein the director or the cinematographer or someone else pays you a compliment, and suddenly everyone jumps on the bandwagon and it's all kind of bullshit. In your heart, you know you've done nothing special. But this was different. This was real. We all recognized the importance of the scene, of getting it just right. This was the climax of the story; done properly, it would serve as a tribute to Tolkien and the fans of Tolkien, and it would honor the studio that had gambled $270 million. Everything pointed to this moment. Either we were going to succeed and thus validate the support of those who had believed in us, or we were going to fail.

And if we failed, I would perceive it as my failure.

So I think everyone on the set that day experienced the scene in much the same way that audiences would experience it later: as a genuinely cathartic moment.

The next day Elijah and I got a fax from Fran and Philippa, saying, in effect, "You guys rock!" I have to say, I didn't get a lot of faxes like that, which only served to make it more meaningful. And for the next three years, regardless of the ups and downs, the anxiety over being in the background at many of the premieres and media functions and awards show that accompanied the first two movies, because Sam wasn't worth much attention, I had this to sustain me. Someday, I knew, audiences would see it. They'd see Sam cradling Frodo, expressing the purest form of love and strength, and they'd hear him talking about springtime in the shire . . . and they would weep.

Someday . . .

That the scenes between Frodo and Sam provoke such a visceral emotional response in audiences speaks volumes about the purity of Tolkien's writing, and the characters he created. There is, after all, an abundance of tenderness and closeness between male characters in *The Lord of the Rings*, more than one might reasonably expect to find in a blockbuster Hollywood epic, a fact that moviegoers have generally accepted without reservation. And yet there exists an ongoing debate, in both critical and casual conversation, over whether there is an undercurrent of homosexuality in both Tolkien's books and Peter Jackson's movies.

Simply and succinctly put: Are Frodo and Sam gay?

I think it's a legitimate question. A lot has been written about homoeroticism throughout the three-year cycle of the movies, and many people on the Internet have had a field day fantasizing about the hobbits or writing humor pieces. I've even been interviewed on this subject by both *The Advocate* and *Out*, two of the most visible and successful publications that cater to a gay audience. So I do think it's a subject worth discussing; in fact, it would be a bit spineless not to.

There was an inordinate amount of male bonding during the filming of *The Lord of the Rings*. When you put a bunch of men together in a relatively confined space, with little female influence to mitigate their bad behavior, things can and do get ugly. Raunch was often the order of the day, and as in any all-male environment (locker rooms, army barracks, prison cell blocks), there was a lot of juvenile behavior: ass grabbing, horrifyingly graphic insults regarding anatomy and sexual proclivities, and various permutations of gay jokes that have been around since the dawn of time. Or at least the dawn of Monty Python.

I'm not talking about making jokes about homosexuals who weren't in our presence, but rather making jokes that centered on the possibility that any one of us might be gay. I think that happens a lot with guys in such circumstances. When you change clothes together, eat meals together, travel together, and get your makeup and hair done together (okay, maybe that's a bad example), you can't help but grow close, and humor, perhaps defensive humor, arises out of that scenario. But when it comes to the actual sexuality of the characters, I don't think there's anything there. I don't believe Sam and Frodo are homosexual. I really don't. That said, I think it's true that if two males live together for a long time, travel together, and share almost every aspect of their lives, it's inevitable that they develop a rapport, and I can see why gay men might identify with their relationship. I've tried to be very careful in interviews not to disavow anyone else's take on it. I'm not bothered in the least that some people—maybe even a lot of people—enjoy the notion of Frodo or Sam as gay.

That's not how I played the character, and it's not how I see the character, but it's okay. To me, *The Lord of the Rings* depicts a powerful bond of love between two male hobbits, with the complete absence of sexuality. In that sense, it's remarkably innocent and pure. Not everyone sees it that way, of course. A New York journalist once told me how angry he had become when he first saw the movie because a small portion of the audience was giggling during some of the tender moments. I want to be careful not to intrude upon anyone's interaction or personal experience with the material. That's their privilege, their right. But this guy was annoyed, and he asked me if I thought there was a lot of cynicism about the relationship between Frodo and Sam. I told him I didn't think so. Some people might not be accustomed to experiencing that level of emotional honesty in their own lives, and they might want to cover up the fact that they felt something by being cynical or irreverent. The giggling, especially among adolescent males—who make up a significant percentage of the audience—is an involuntary response to something that makes them feel awkward. Thus, you could argue that the movie is accomplishing something simply by facilitating that nervous giggle; it's cracked the armor in which some people wrap their emotional lives. Personally, I think that's a great achievement.

Elijah and I never had a serious discussion about this subject. Not one. I must admit, however, that we did engage in a broad range of homosexual humor with each other, and with Billy and Dom. It was just another way of relating that wasn't meant as an affront to anyone. Look, I was raised in Hollywood. I've had, and continue to have, more gay friends than I can count. But we did enjoy the jokes. It was a way to release tension, and to acknowledge what was on everyone's mind in a way that seemed harmless and funny.

Most of the time, while acting, it didn't cross my mind. The scene on Mount Doom, for example, was uncolored by sexuality. Sam is cradling Frodo in his arms, crying over the possible loss of his friend. They are fellow travelers, warriors, brothers. To me, that plays less like a love scene than a battlefield death scene. But there were other times—in scenes when the envelope was pushed in a way that invited not just speculation, but an arched eyebrow as well—when as a male actor working with another male, you couldn't help but think, *Oh, God, that is so gay!*

Near the end of *The Return of the King*, for example, the reunited hobbits gather around a healing Frodo and hug him and hold his hand, and eventually they begin jumping on the bed together, and it's like, *Okay, do you guys want to be alone for a little while?* I think our standard of awkwardness was significantly higher than an adolescent boy's, but there was a standard, and when it was met, either because of a longing look that you could see magnified tenfold on a monitor, or because someone inadvertently touched the backside of a fellow hobbit—well, it provoked laughter.

There was one rather memorable day during the looping phase of the production when Elijah and I were working on a scene in which Sam reaches around Frodo to lift him off the ground. The technicians kept rewinding and playing the scene as we tried to match dialogue to the film—back and forth, back and forth—the result being a slightly porno-graphic image of what appeared to be Sam having his way with Frodo from behind. Elijah and I fell victim to our most sophomoric tendencies in this setting, as we looped dialogue appropriate for the moment.

What can I say? These were the kinds of jokes that sometimes bub-bled to the surface over the course of an eighteen-month shoot. Some-times they helped us get through the day. I'm sure it would be off-putting to some people, but to us it was funny, and it seemed harmless.

To me, though, the emotional scenes involving Sam and Frodo stand on their own merit. Whatever is at stake is what it's about. If you prefer to think of Sam and Frodo as two gay males, that's fine. You could take that reading of the relationship and extend it as long as you want to, and it would sustain that reading. When Frodo says good-bye and kisses Sam on the forehead, it's whatever it is. It's sweet and tender and honest. And that's all that really matters. But don't for-get something. Sam did go on to marry Rosie Cotton. And he was, as it turned out, a rather prolific little hobbit.

As far I'm concerned, it comes down to this: Sam is the best friend anyone could ever hope for. His relationship with Frodo is a perfect study in dedication, devotion, and heartfelt companionship. Despite the hundreds of interactions I've had with folks who prefer to see the bond between Frodo and Sam through a prism of homoeroticism, I remain convinced that the power of their friendship derives primarily from the purity and innocence of their love for one another. As the member of a beautiful if untraditional hodgepodge of a family, and someone who has had connections with and lost touch with more people I consider friends than many folks ever meet in a lifetime, I gain strength from my understanding of the character I got to play.

Sam probably knows that time and experience reveal the true nature of our loyalty, and that even after extraordinary circumstances real friends emerge from the scars they have caused one another with a deeper understanding of just how important they are to each other. Making movies brings you into extremely close contact with tens of thousands of people over the course of a career (a fact that can be simultaneously thrilling and exhausting). It occurs to me that stardom is won oftentimes by the formation and retention of close alliances with those practiced in the art of success through a series of critical decisions. To the extent that cynicism plays a mitigating part in that selection process, I am saddened. Conversely, I love it when strategic interpersonal alliances are formed in organic ways. I usually can't quite help myself when I feel the impulse to "make a new friend," and I'm not above trying to capitalize on the formation of a new friendship with someone who can help me. You see, because I played Sam, a lot of people ask me questions about myself and just what kind of friend I really am. I've gotten the impression from folks that they are looking to me, Sean, as an authority on the nature of friendship. I've worried, frankly, that I'm not worthy.

My personality is such that I try to meet or exceed the positive expectations that many have of me and for me. When I'm traveling, I think sometimes that people are saddened because they realize or sense that I may not be as good a friend as Sam. I am always quick to point out that in fact I am *not* as good a friend as Sam; I couldn't be, because fundamentally I'm too selfish. My wife and others have a hard time understanding what I mean when I tell them that I like to be "used." I'm not going to bore you too much with my half-baked philosophy, but I do think there can be real value to heartfelt, sensitive, respectful engagement in discovering where mutual self-interests can collide when you meet people. But friendship? That is something else. I've come to learn that friendship is more about making an effort to act on your thoughtfulness toward others than trying to get stuff out of them, even when you honestly believe that you give as good as you get.

I guess I'll have a lifetime to consider how playing Sam has affected my life, but at the very least, I'd like to believe that he taught me that it's worth trying to be a better friend than I was before I played him. In that regard, my journey of self-discovery and individual improvement continues.

CHAPTER SIXTEEN

To this day, Elijah insists it was his idea. Given half a chance, though, Orlando will also take credit. Or responsibility. Or blame. And while Viggo has never sought any recognition for his role in the episode, I'm pretty sure he was a major player. Regardless of its origin, I do know that the seed was planted shortly after we arrived in New Zealand and took root in the months that followed. Every so often, someone (usually Elijah) would bring it up, and someone else would second the motion. Then we'd all forget about it. In the final week of principal photography, however, as it finally began to dawn on us that the adventure was really going to come to an end and we'd all be going home, the discussion began anew, this time with an almost religious fervor.

"Let's all get tattoos!"

My initial reaction back in the summer of 1999 was one of self-righteous dismissal: *Ah, that's stupid. I'm not doing that.* To me, the concept lacked an air of authenticity. It felt like Elijah trying a little bit too hard to form a bond among the actors that mirrored the bond between the members of the Fellowship. Not that I doubted his sincerity. Far from it, in fact. I knew Elijah would leave Wellington sporting a fresh tattoo. Not me, though. I would be nearly thirty years old by the time we left, and in all those years I'd never once succumbed to the urge to brand my body. For a kid who had been raised in the bubble of celebrity, who had been hanging out with artists and writers and actors since he was a toddler, I was an unusually conservative fellow. Not politically, perhaps, but certainly in my personal life. Let's put it this way: I was more Ozzie Nelson than Ozzy Osbourne.

The idea of me getting a tattoo seemed patently ridiculous and a little bit pathetic, like a middle-aged man who goes out and buys a flashy sports car, leaves his wife, and begins dating a fitness instructor barely out of her teens. I wasn't that guy. I didn't want to be that guy. Getting a tattoo seemed a tentative step down that slippery slope.

As I said, though, that was in the beginning.

My attitude toward the production improved in its last few months. As Sam's character was presented with exactly the type of heroic moments that Peter had promised, I was filled with pride about the work I had done and more than a little regret over not having handled the setbacks and frustrations with more elegance. Moreover, a closeness had developed between the cast members—the hobbits in particular—that could not be denied. We had spent nearly a year and a half together, living like brothers, working, playing, arguing, and supporting each other through the hard times and celebrating as one in the good times. Regardless of the outcome, we had shared and endured something extraordinary, and the likelihood that any one of us would ever be involved in a similar cinematic experience was remote, to say the least. (Remember, we really didn't know then how the films would be received, and I don't think anyone assumed they would become the worldwide phenomenon that they have.) As the countdown to our day of departure reached single digits, an inevitable and inescapable sadness permeated the air. It was almost as though we couldn't believe that it was really coming to an end. But it was, and that truth prompted another, more serious round of discussions about commemorating our experience with a trip to a local tattoo parlor.

A few days before our scheduled exodus it came to my attention that Viggo had already begun negotiations with the proprietor of a little place on Cuba Street called Roger's Tattoo Art. The idea was to open the shop for a couple hours on a Saturday or Sunday morning, at a time when it would normally be closed and the streets would not yet be flocked with shoppers and tourists. I remember smiling to myself when I heard about this. Somehow, after so much time in New Zealand, working so closely with this group of people, it no longer seemed like such a silly or self-destructive thing to do. It seemed appropriate. It seemed honorable.

"You know what?" I told Christine that night. "If everybody else agrees, I think I'm going to do it."

She gave me a hard look, the kind that only a wife can give a husband, and while she didn't exactly shake her head or roll her eyes, I could tell she wasn't crazy about the idea. Whether her disapproval stemmed from a simple dislike of body art (on her husband, anyway), or from concern that my decision was due to simple, sophomoric peer pressure, I can't be sure. Nevertheless, Christine gave me her blessing.

"If you really want to do this, I'll support you."

My primary concern revolved around my daughter. What if by getting a tattoo I was sending the wrong message to Ali? What would I say, ten or twelve years hence, when she strolled into the house with her navel pierced?

"Ali, you really shouldn't disfigure your body that way. It shows a lack of self-respect."

"Uh, Dad?

"Yes, dear?"

"Don't be such a hypocrite."

In the end, the thought of that exchange, however unpleasant, wasn't enough to dissuade me. Nor was the fact that my own standard for crumbling to the will of the group—"I'll do it if everyone else does"—had failed to hold up. First of all, Sean Bean, who played Boromir, had already departed, so he was out (in fairness, it should be pointed out that Sean eventually joined the off-screen Fellowship by getting a tattoo during a long night in New York or London—I forget which—with Orlando Bloom). Second, John Rhys-Davies steadfastly refused to participate in such shenanigans, in part, he explained (not entirely without irony), because of an epidemic of mad cow disease that was ravaging Europe: "Why, I wouldn't follow an Englishman behind a needle for all the money in the world!" No matter.

In John's stead, an invitation was extended to his scale double, Brett Beattie, who jumped at the opportunity.[6]

In retrospect, I think my primary motivation was fear. I couldn't imagine at that point that the movie (or movies) would ever actually come out. I couldn't imagine the movies being completed or anyone ever seeing them or enjoying them, or me being in them. None of my time in New Zealand seemed real. I was getting on a plane to go home, and soon it would all be a memory. At times, I'd wonder, *Did any of it really happen? It all seems like an illusion, a jumble of images and sound bites that don't quite add up to something whole. Was I really here for eighteen months? Is that possible?* In some ways I felt so disconnected from the whole experience that I legitimately worried about whether the movies would ever be presented to a mass audience. Maybe they'd go straight to video. Maybe they'd sit in a can in Peter's basement. That sounds crazy, I know, but it didn't seem out of the realm of possibility. After all, nothing like this had ever been done—nothing like this had ever been *attempted*. What if the movies disappeared and nobody ever had a chance to see what we did? Or what if the movies were released and still no one *got it*, because even if each of the movies was ten hours long, there still would be a thousand brilliant little moments left on the cutting-room floor?

I knew that when I boarded a plane and looked down at New Zealand fading into the blue Pacific, I wanted to be able to say, "It happened, and here's my own little memorial to it." So it wasn't like I was coerced into getting a tattoo; no one twisted my arm. I went along willingly because I came to believe it was a worthy thing to do, and I don't regret it in the least.

Once we committed to the idea of getting tattoos, the next step was to come up with an interesting design, something cool and interesting and emblematic of our collective experience. It had to be small, too, something that wouldn't call unnecessary attention to itself. We were actors, after all, not bikers, and this act was merely a brief walk on the

---

6. John now claims to have sent his stunt double. He knows, or should know, that he doesn't need a tattoo to be a permanent, deserving, and integral member of our Fellowship—for all time.

wild side. Furthermore, we had agreed ahead of time that a small tattoo would work best because it could be hidden. This wasn't supposed to be a publicity stunt, and we didn't want it to devolve into that. This was about honoring each other and the work we had done, as well as solidifying, in some way, our commitment to remain friends and brothers for life. To that end, we settled on a tattoo that depicts the elvish symbol for the number nine, the number of members of the Fellowship. Deepening the impact of the tattoo is that it was based on a drawing created by Alan Lee specifically for this occasion. In other words, it's an Alan Lee original, and it was a very nice thing for him to do. Alan is a gracious man who was always doing things like that. Before we left New Zealand, Elijah and I wanted to present something to the crew, so we asked Alan to sketch an image of Frodo and Sam turning and waving good-bye. He kindly agreed, of course, and even added Gollum—peering out between our legs. We transferred the image to a card and made hundreds of copies that we signed and distributed as parting gifts.

We arrived at Roger's Tattoo Art on the morning of December 17, 2000. I'd walked by the shop a hundred times before but had never given any thought to opening the door, had in fact barely noticed the place even existed. But now, here I was, surrounded by the Fellowship (as well as Christine and Alexandra), waiting for my turn at the needle. It was almost hard to believe. For Viggo and Orlando, who already had tattoos, I'm sure this was nothing more than a joyous event, a noble salute to friendship and camaraderie. To me it was all of that, as well as a frightening leap into the great unknown. I think the other neophytes—the tattoo virgins—probably felt as I did, although we all did our best to put up a sturdy facade, including the one person I was most shocked to see: Ian McKellen.

I could only imagine what they would think back in England, if they could see Ian now, this giant of the British stage, hanging out at a tattoo parlor. Not that Ian was opposed to getting in touch with his funky side. Ian is an exceptionally hip guy who exists on the cutting edge of culture. He's always finding interesting places to go, and hanging out with the most fascinating people. He's just a very cool guy, the kind of guy I wanted to be when I lived in New York for three months when I was twenty years old and didn't have kids. Ian was sixty, but vigorously protective of his attachment to youth and youth culture. And I'm sure he experienced less trepidation than I did about patronizing Roger's Tattoo Art.

Two major decisions had to be made before the fun could begin: which part of the body to decorate, and who would go first. Each of us made his own decision about where to have the tattoo applied. Billy suggested the ankle, which I thought was perfect, since we hobbits had spent thousands of hours having our feet attended to. Hobbit feet, of course, have long been the subject of conjecture and speculation and armchair psychoanalysis. They're big and hairy and goofy, and Tolkien devotes considerable effort to their description. One of the reasons Tolkien really connected with the people who dominated the counterculture of the 1960s was his apparent agreement with hippie philosophy: not just the environmental treatise and not just his messages of peace and brotherhood, but also the smoking of the pipe weed, and the elves and the barefoot hobbits. There's something about the sacredness of feet that people in the hippie world would understand and appreciate. Tolkien couldn't have known that, of course, since he wrote *The Lord of the Rings* many years earlier. Nevertheless, he knew that by making the feet bigger, he was drawing attention to them. Whether he was making a sexual joke (big feet, big dick), I don't know, although there was certainly no shortage of those during filming, for anyone who chose to reach for that interpretation. Anyway, Billy liked the idea of honoring the hobbit feet by having his ankle tattooed, and I agreed with him, so we became the two members of the Fellowship to have tattoos etched on our ankles.

Billy went first, and while it was obviously not a pleasant experience for him, he had a sense of humor about it. I held his leg down, as Roger Ingerton, the proprietor and tattoo artist, pulled up a chair and went to work. For the next seven or eight minutes, with the needle whining and whirring, Billy grimaced and moaned. Every so often, he shouted, "Oh, man, it hurts!" while the rest of us laughed nervously. Then he jumped off the table, winced dramatically, and gave me a pat on the back.

"Your turn, Sean."

And so it was. I was scared, but also emboldened by adrenaline. As hard as the previous year and a half had been, at that moment, in that setting, all I could think was, *Look how much fun we're having.* So I lay down on the table and presented my ankle to Roger, who wasted no time in getting started. I'd always wondered how it would feel to get a tattoo, and now I knew.

Aaaaaarrrrggghh!

I was shocked by how much it hurt, how quickly the pain shot through my skin and into my anklebone. You see people getting tattoos in the movies, and it never seems to be a big deal. They kind of sit there and laugh or chat casually as the artist dabs ink onto a meaty biceps. Well, maybe that's the way it works when they have some flesh with which to work, but on the ankle? Uh-uh. In a way, this was even worse than when I'd gored my foot. That had been an accident, and the initial pain had subsided quickly. This was self-induced agony, and it wasn't going to end anytime soon.

"Oh, God!" I whined, although I tried to smile as I said it. When Alexandra, clearly frightened, crawled under the table, I realized it might have been a slight miscalculation on my part to bring her along. Just what she needed: a lingering image of her father being tortured like Dustin Hoffman in *Marathon Man.*

I want you to think very carefully, Sean, and tell me, is it safe?

"Do you want to come under here with me, Daddy?"

"No, Ali, I'm okay." I smiled at her, then turned away and clenched my teeth. The other guys were supportive, although they did laugh even as they offered encouragement. Such was the gallows atmosphere that surrounded the event. Toward the end of the procedure, Roger began scraping with the needle, in an effort to spread the ink evenly and deeply. That was the worst part, like having periodontal work without the novocaine. The fact that some people, like Roger, who looked like Ray Bradbury's Illustrated Man, regularly and willingly give themselves over to this kind of pain seemed patently absurd to me. When the needle finally stopped and Roger said, "Done," I breathed a sigh of relief and rolled off the table, as weak in the knees as a seasick tourist returning from a whale watch. Within seconds, though, the pain was gone, replaced by a flush of pride and excitement.

I'd done it! I'd gotten my first tattoo!

Next up was Ian, who chose to have his shoulder tattooed. I held his right arm while Roger snapped on a fresh latex glove and went to work. As we tried to ritualize the experience by simultaneously teasing and comforting each other, the tattoo shop took on the feel of a pirate ship—*Arrh, maties!*—and at the center of it all was Roger, a massively tattooed fifty-something Kiwi with a voice like sandpaper and a fiercely individualistic outlook on the world. Or so he wanted us to believe.

"You know what I am?" Roger growled at one point. "I'm a bloody anarchist!"

"Really?" I said. "How long did you say this shop has been here?"

"About thirty-five years, give or take."

"Oh, no offense, Roger, but after thirty-five years, you're pretty much part of the establishment, aren't you?"

Roger pulled the needle away from Ian's shoulder, cocked his head in my direction, and smiled.

"Well, I'm sort of on the fringe. Know what I mean?"

That was the highlight of the day: the self-proclaimed anarchist tattooing the gay, knighted legend of stage and screen. I just loved that moment. But it was all fun. We stayed for the better part of two hours, until each of us had been stamped. Orlando was tattooed on the right forearm, Viggo and Dom on the shoulder, Elijah on the lower part of his belly, near the hipbone, and Brett on the small of his back.

Afterward, when I proudly showed my tattoo to Peter Jackson, I was surprised and moved by his reaction.

"Wow, that's great," he said, and I could tell by the look in his eyes that he meant it. I would think it pleased Peter to know that our experience had been so profound, and that he had been the man chiefly responsible for that experience. He had inspired us and instilled within us a commitment that was unprecedented and permanent. Not until a year later, however, after the release of the first film, did I realize just how much Peter liked the idea of the Fellowship tattoo. That's when he and producer Mark Ordesky got tattoos of their own: the number 10.

·   ·   ·

We took a vow to keep the bond private and spiritual in nature. Granted, there was no way to prevent the media from revealing that we had gotten tattoos—I think the news had leaked by the time we left Roger's studio—but at least we could maintain a purity of purpose, and prevent hundreds of thousands of *The Lord of the Rings* fans from tattooing themselves with the elvish symbol for 9, by declining to reveal the image in public. We all agreed to that. No going on Leno or Letterman and flashing the tattoo for a national audience. That would cheapen the experience, tarnish the memory.

Ah, the best laid plans . . . The Fellowship tattoo became big news in the entertainment world; everywhere we went, people asked to see it. At first we refused, but we've all cracked at some point. My moment of shame—admittedly, the most egregious and knuckle-headed offense committed by any of us—came with Steve Kmetko of the E! network, during a broadcast of *E! News Live*.

"Hey, you know Ian McKellen showed us his tattoo the other day," Steve said. "We want to see yours, too."

"Really? Ian?"

"He sure did."

"I don't know, Steve. I mean, we made a pact."

"Well, I guess someone forgot to tell Ian, because we saw his tattoo."

Hell, if Ian is going to show his tattoo, I guess I can, too.

With that I rolled up my pants leg and the camera zoomed in and got a nice close-up of my tattoo, which immediately made its way to the Internet, effectively killing the secret we had promised to take to our graves. But at least I wasn't the only person—or even the first person—to have broken the vow.

Or so I thought.

As I walked off the set, I couldn't shake the nagging feeling that I'd been duped, that Steve had tricked me in order to be the first person to broadcast an image of the Fellowship tattoo. So I pulled out my cell phone and placed a call to Ian. I asked him if he had also succumbed to the urges of the wily journalist Steve Kmetko and displayed his tattoo on television.

"No, Sean, I did not," Ian said. In his voice was a hint of condescension, as if this was precisely the sort of gaffe he expected of me. "As a matter of fact, I haven't shown it to anyone, just as we agreed."

I hung up the phone and stood there, shaking.

Kmetko, you son of a bitch!

The next time I saw Steve, I playfully accused him of lying to me, which he denied. And then I got to thinking about it: *Wait a minute. Maybe Ian was lying! Or they were both playing with me.* Anyway, I called Elijah and told him I'd screwed up. He was terribly disappointed in me for being stupid and for giving such a lame excuse. But you know what? He forgave me. And, of course, he later revealed his tattoo as well.

The wrap party is a Hollywood tradition, an opportunity for the studio to thank everyone for all their hard work, a chance for cast and crew to say farewell, and to celebrate the end of the journey. At one point, I went through a phase during which I didn't like wrap parties and often opted to skip town before they were held. Why? Sometimes, I suppose, it was because I didn't feel particularly proud of the work I'd done and thus wasn't interested in paying tribute to it. I simply wanted it in the rearview mirror. Other times, on the better films, I couldn't bring myself to say good-bye. So I'd just leave.

At the end of filming *The Lord of the Rings*, though, I was okay with it. I was happy to be leaving, happy to be saying good-bye to people, happy the movie was over. It felt right, as though we'd all been there long enough and done all that we could to make *The Lord of the Rings* the best it could be. I was proud of what we'd accomplished, but I was also tired and homesick and ready to move on to the next phase of my life, whatever that might mean. (I certainly didn't comprehend just how completely the movies would come to dominate my career, or that the roller-coaster ride was, in fact, just beginning.)

So Christine and I got a babysitter, I pulled on a red Dr. Seuss sweater bearing the words "I am Sam," and we went to the wrap party, which had to be one of the biggest in the history of cinema. By "big," I don't mean lavish. I mean just plain big, as in huge. The party was held at a warehouse in downtown Wellington, near the waterfront.

There were searchlights outside and mountains of food within. Generally speaking, it was a casual and comfortable affair, but sprawling, as well; intimacy is difficult when there are more than a thousand guests.

As always happens at these affairs, great gobs of time were devoted to the exchanging of gifts. The actors, collectively, presented Peter with a mockette, courtesy of the makeup wizards at Weta Workshop. Mockettes are little sculptures used as models for all the different fictional characters in the films. The models would be scanned into a computer and the digital gurus would build off those, so the images that appeared on screen were not just based on drawings, but three-dimensional characters. Anyway, we had a mockette created for Peter, and of course it looked not only like Peter, but also like a hobbit: big feet, wild, unruly hair, and a bemused expression on its face. Peter seemed genuinely touched by the gift, and I remember feeling somewhat disappointed in myself for not putting more effort into the process. Elijah and I had gotten the cards done, and we had written notes to people, but here in the swirl of celebration our efforts seemed insufficient.

Bliss Macgillicuddy, my makeup artist, gave me a rather extraordinary gift, an enormous collage of pictures and images encased in Plexiglas. There was a head shot illustrated by Alan Lee; photos of me with Elijah; me with Peter, Dom, Billy; my scale double and chess partner, Kiran "B. K." Shah; everyone. What struck me about the gift was not just the time and thought that went into it, but that I seemed to be smiling in virtually every photo. Clearly, Bliss was trying to send me a message.

"See, you don't have to be such a sourpuss. You really did have a good time, and you connected with a lot of people in a lot of meaningful ways."

Leave it to the makeup artist to deliver a gentle kick in the ass. Bliss routinely allowed me to go through some of my interior monologue of anguish and insecurity with her; she would let me be grumpy and not hold it against me. She was wonderful, and I appreciated her thoughtfulness as much as her professionalism and attention to detail.

The party went on for hours. There was lots of eating and drinking and dancing, as well as the customary viewing of a gag reel, wherein some of the funniest outtakes of the production were compiled in a single, gut-busting collection. I remember laughing pretty hard at the gag reel, but also feeling sad that I wasn't in more of it; I knew that my absence could be attributed to the fact that I had internalized the process too much and hadn't allowed myself to become part of everyone's fun.

Most of my colleagues, however, were forgiving of my tendency to take things too seriously, and that included Peter and Fran. Although we had several different "good-bye" moments, the official farewell occurred at their house during a dinner for the acting ensemble. Each of us was presented with a green bound yearbook with *The Lord of the Rings* etched into the spine. Between the covers was a collection of beautiful photographs that eloquently told the story of the making of the trilogy. And each book was inscribed with a personalized note. Mine included a few words of thanks for the work I had done, and reassurance that the performance had been meaningful and would one day resonate with audiences. Then came the kicker, the part about my wife and daughter, a reminder of why I had admired Peter and Fran in the first place: they were the coolest couple and the hippest parents on the planet.

"Thank you for giving us Christine and Alexandra," they wrote, "and for bringing them into our lives."

I closed the yearbook and ran my hand over the spine. I looked at Fran and Peter. And then I started to cry.

CHAPTER SEVENTEEN

The veil of secrecy was officially removed on May 10, 2001, at the Cannes Film Festival. Cannes, of course, is the world's biggest movie-related party, a sprawling hedonistic seaside celebration of fame and stardom and wealth, as well as an occasional forum for serious filmmaking. Thanks in no small part to the swelling influence of the Internet, there had been significant buzz about *The Lord of the Rings*, most of it positive. But aside from the occasional screening of an isolated scene or two at Peter Jackson's home in Wellington, nothing had been released for public consumption. That all changed at Cannes, when a montage of scenes—essentially a very long trailer for *The Fellowship of the Ring*—was displayed for the first time.

There had been moments in the past when I had some vague notion that the movie might accomplish precisely what Peter had set out to accomplish. Whenever we'd come back from a short hiatus, for example, Peter would try to get everyone back in the proper frame of mind by showing us some rough footage accompanied by temp music. On those occasions I'd be reminded of Peter's awesome talent and the potential for the trilogy to be everything fans hoped it would be. Unfortunately, for me the impact of those brief glimpses quickly faded. I'm embarrassed now to think about how easily I slipped back into the drudgery of moviemaking, of putting on the makeup and the ears and soldiering on day after day, while failing to recognize the scope of the achievement. The excitement would wear off, and I'd forget about the big picture—or maybe I just couldn't *see* the big picture.

At Cannes, however, it began to come into focus. This was the first time I realized that *The Lord of the Rings* was going to be something truly extraordinary; it was also the beginning of the "rock star" phase of our lives.

The special screening, a brilliantly conceived marketing gambit by New Line, gave journalists from around the world their first big taste of *The Fellowship of the Ring*, and the resulting publicity nearly overshadowed the movies ostensibly at the center of the festival. Running for twenty-six minutes, the footage opened with the elegant wizard Gandalf arriving in Hobbiton at the home of Bilbo Baggins, whose dramatic birthday disappearance (through the use of the ring) preceded a swift and efficient introduction of the members of the Fellowship. Then came the centerpiece of the footage: a fourteen-minute sequence depicting the Fellowship's harrowing trek through the Mines of Moria that climaxed, as the movie does, with a thrilling battle against an army of orcs and a harrowing encounter with a giant cave troll. The footage concluded with the appearance of a flying dragon (a Balrog), and Gandalf bravely standing between the Fellowship and the fiery beast.

When the screen went dark and the lights came up, the theater erupted with applause. Like everyone else, I was awestruck. Digital characters had blended seamlessly with human actors to create a cinematic experience like nothing that had come before it. The media gushed over the quasi-premiere, noting that it bore Peter's unmistakable stamp and suggesting strongly that the film promised to deliver on New Line's huge investment. I knew then that *The Lord of the Rings*, or at least the first installment of the trilogy, was going to be huge, and that life was about to change for all of us. This was the beginning of the endless ride of parties and premieres and public relations.

It was also the start of me losing my mind, fretting constantly about what *The Lord of the Rings* would mean to me, worrying about whether I was in a horse race with other actors, trying to figure out who I was and what I wanted, instead of just relaxing and enjoying the experience.

That same week, for example, I had a regrettable interaction with one of my costars, Orlando Bloom, who had already been plucked out of the ensemble and targeted for stardom. Not that there was anything remotely surprising about that. Orlando was so talented and appealing, so ridiculously good-looking, that there was never any doubt about what lay ahead for him. He had "movie star" written all over him.

From the very beginning, I found Orlando likable. He wasn't a hobbit, but he was part of the hobbit group, and we all connected right away. More than most of us, Orlando was excited about the physical work involved in the films, and his attitude was terrific. He was fresh out of drama school and incredibly happy to be in New Zealand, working on a big-budget movie. There were times when Orlando would get selfish and try to take advantage of the production assistants—"Hey, baby, could you go get me something to eat, please?"—but it wasn't the sort of behavior emblematic of movie star entitlement; it was just lazy guy stuff, and it was harmless and even kind of endearing. We ridiculed him mercilessly whenever he did it, and he weathered that ridicule pretty well, which only added to his appeal.

Like Legolas and like some of the characters he has played since, Orlando is legitimately dashing and swashbuckling. He's an extreme sort of guy who doesn't mind breaking an occasional bone in the pursuit of adventure and thrills. We rented motorcycles one day and did some off-road biking in the hills of Queenstown. I was relatively cautious, but Orlando was utterly fearless, at one point opening the throttle and charging to the top of a steep incline against the advice of our guide.

"I wouldn't do that," he yelled as Orlando leaned into the handlebars and gunned the engine. A few minutes later there was Orlando, sitting proudly atop his bike at the summit. Then he turned the bike around and prepared to descend. There was just one problem: it was too steep. Facing the very real possibility of flying over the handlebars and getting seriously injured, Orlando removed his helmet and yelled to us at the bottom.

"How do I get down?"

The guide laughed. "Hey, mate, you found your way up there, you're gonna have to figure out how to get down."

Which he did. After all, this is a guy who broke his back and somehow escaped any long-term disability or pain. He's got nine lives, and he's living each of them to the fullest.

Orlando and I talked a few times about the business of movies and the stardom that was destined to come his way. We talked about money, and I remember being somewhat amused by the realization that I was probably making a lot more than he was, because that certainly wouldn't be the case in the very near future. Orlando didn't much care about any of that. He was just so happy and easygoing, and it was screamingly obvious what the industry had in store for him.

"You have a chance to be a major star," I said at one point. Orlando just shrugged and smiled, like someone who either didn't care or had just heard something he already knew. I gave him advice about agents and managers, and he went off and made a lot of decisions that I wouldn't have made—decisions that have since proved to be a hell of a lot smarter than decisions I would have made. But there were times when I ran into Orlando, or read some story about him, and thought, *Oh, my God, it's gone to his head, and he's become a cataclysmic jerk!*

That's what happened in Cannes, when I approached Orlando while he was chatting with Barry Diller, one of the more powerful and influential men in Hollywood. I got the feeling that Orlando was blowing me off, that he wasn't about to waste time embracing a friend when there was an opportunity to cultivate a business relationship. And I got mad at him. After Barry left, I gave Orlando a little shove in the chest and said, "Who the hell do you think you are? We're supposed to be friends." He was shocked and sort of apologized, but he also made it clear that he had intended no disrespect at all. When I thought about it afterward, when I really analyzed what had happened, I came to the conclusion that I was the one who had behaved badly. I had misread the situation and overreacted. Envy and insecurity had gotten the better of me, and I'd briefly lost it. Orlando, to his great credit, was instantly forgiving, and we got through it with no discernible fallout.

Since then Orlando has risen to the top of the food chain, and it's hard not to be impressed by the way he's weathering his stardom. He's a good guy and he has talent. I don't know if he'll earn the respect of his fellow actors in the British theater, at least for a while, simply because it's difficult to be taken seriously in those circles when you're making great gobs of money in mainstream movies, while also enjoying the status of international sex symbol. It's astounding to travel with Orlando, to see how many women—from teenagers to grandmothers—fall at his feet. Everywhere I go, fans of *The Lord of the Rings* give me things. Before I can even say, "Thank you," they ask me to please make sure the gift is presented to Orlando.

"I'll see what I can do."

It's a tough job to be adored by millions of women, but I somehow think Orlando is equal to the task.

The Lord of the Rings: The Fellowship of the Ring debuted in December 2001 to overwhelming critical praise and commercial success. After twenty years of hard and sometimes brilliant work on small movies, Peter Jackson was an overnight sensation. The bosses at New Line, considered by many to be foolish for having gambled so heavily on a project that had been rejected by every other studio in town, were suddenly geniuses. Such are the vagaries of the movie business.

For me, the success of the first film was less palpable. Sam was a peripheral character, and so my role in the promotion of the movie was to be a sturdy member of the ensemble, available for interviews and parties, and preferably armed with an assortment of cogent observations and pleasant anecdotes. This was a role I was generally happy to play, for I really was proud of the movie and my work in it, and I was legitimately happy for Peter and Fran. Nevertheless, I can't deny that there were some awkward moments, such as the time I ran into Ian Holm at the London premiere of *The Fellowship of the Ring*.

First, though, a few words about Ian. When this guy showed up in New Zealand to play Bilbo Baggins, he carried himself with a kind of seriousness and elegance that commanded attention, maybe even more so than did the other Ian in the cast. Ian McKellen was playing Gandalf, and thus had to wear a beard and a nose and a hat. Something about the makeup and costume—the hat in particular—took the edge off his presence as an authoritative man of the stage, a grand

Shakespearean actor. Ian Holm, conversely, only worked on the films for a short period of time, and you always got the feeling when you saw him that he was, well, Ian Holm. That's not to say he didn't inhabit the character. He did, of course, and he played Bilbo beautifully. But I was intimidated by him.

There's a feeling you get before you meet an actor of note, an excitement and nervousness and a resolve to work through that transition, and I certainly experienced that with Ian. I had admired his work in so many films, from the duplicitous android in *Alien* to the tough but sensitive coach in *Chariots of Fire*, to the damaged, ambulance-chasing attorney in *The Sweet Hereafter*. That last performance was especially fresh in my mind when Ian arrived in New Zealand, and it fueled my desire to get to know him better. But the opportunity never presented itself. We worked together in only a few scenes and never had any substantive conversations. On the day Ian left, I asked him to sign my single-volume edition of *The Lord of the Rings* (we all did this, much as high school seniors autograph each other's yearbook). Ian smiled, took the book, and wrote, "Sean: Finally, my boy, we meet."

It was kind of tongue-in-cheek, but also a little removed, as if to say, *Why are you having me sign this thing? We barely know each other.* I remember feeling a bit disappointed that we hadn't connected in some other way. Really, though, that wasn't possible. The only extended time we shared—and calling it "shared" is a stretch—occurred when Ian was having his makeup applied and I was sitting there watching him endure the transformation into a hundred-year-old hobbit. Face work is infinitely more difficult and uncomfortable than having prosthetic ears and feet applied. In fact, after watching Ian and John and some of the other actors on *The Lord of the Rings*, I'd have to think long and hard before I'd accept a role that required that kind of daily torture. Anyway, Ian and I shared a small amount of time while he was a prisoner, and I don't think my attempts to converse were unwelcome. I'm aware of those dynamics, too. I used to glad-hand with everybody, but I've developed some restraint over time. You can't necessarily get in someone's face just because you admire his or her work. So I tried to be respectful of Ian's space.

At the London premiere, however, Ian and I had a chance to chat. Typically, there's no real communication at these events, just a lot of awkward, superficial small talk. But I wanted to take a moment to congratulate Ian on his performance, which I thought was just superb. The transformation that suddenly takes place when Bilbo tries to take the ring one last time from Frodo is among the highlights of the movie. And I wanted to share that sentiment with Ian. So I paid him a compliment, after which there was a pregnant pause. Now, actor protocol dictates that a compliment be repaid in kind. But that didn't happen. Instead, Ian said, "Thank you," and we sort of stood there, enveloped in an awkward silence. Honestly, I admired the fact that Ian wasn't going to say something nice just for the sake of saying it, but eventually he relented.

Sort of.

"You don't really do anything, do you?" he said.

"Nope. Not really."

"But it's just fucking brilliant the way you do it. Isn't it?"

Oh, you have no idea.

Ian obviously hadn't really thought about it and wasn't particularly moved by my performance. Admittedly, though, there hadn't been much to elicit a reaction. There is an attractive shot at the end of the film, with Sam and Frodo looking off into the distance, where the viewer is left with the sense that these two characters are destined for greatness, so at least I didn't feel like an interloper at the party. It had been my job to be small and subtle in the first film, and I think I did that reasonably well.

I once did a movie called *Boy Meets Girl*, where I walked with a swagger, smoked a cigar, drank too much, and spewed a lot of self-important nonsense: *"I'm gonna travel, Jack! Gonna see the world!"* It was almost like an homage to my dad's character in *The Addams Family*: everything about it facilitated a *big* performance. *The Lord of the Rings* was just the opposite of that. Sam is so subtle. He doesn't have the showstopper lines, except at the end of the third movie. For much of the trilogy he's quiet and stoic. Earnest. So, in a sense, Ian's observation was astute, not just something born of panic or desperation or even politeness. It was honest, and you can't help but admire that.

．．．

Because *The Lord of the Rings* was designed and marketed as three separate films, yet shot as one very long film, the studio had great chunks of time with which to work following the completion of principal photography. We finished shooting in December 2000; then they (I'm talking primarily about Peter and Fran) had a full year to deliver *The Fellowship of the Ring*, followed by another year to deliver the second installment, *The Two Towers*, and a third year to deliver *The Return of the King*. Each year they would assemble the film and look at it and think about it and be afforded the opportunity to entertain new ideas, to see things in a different light. A year is a long time. Three years is a really long time, especially in the entertainment business. A lot can change. To their credit, they allowed themselves to be responsive to some of the things that fans would say or write. The scene with Orlando sliding down the trunk of the oliphant at the end of the third film, for instance, reflects everybody's understanding of what a matinee idol he'd become. That would not likely have been in the third film initially. It's an amazing thing, actually, that a movie with that kind of an outrageous "wink" in it can also be perceived as serious filmmaking; it's a testament to how broad an experience it is, and how flexible the filmmakers were.

As we all know, the world changed on September 11, 2001, and I think *The Fellowship of the Ring* became even more resonant with people in the wake of the attacks on the United States. As Gandalf says to Frodo in the Mines of Moria, "All we have to decide is what to do with the time that is given to us. There are other forces at work in this world, Frodo, besides the will of evil." I think that sentiment was poignant to a lot of people. I also think that when *The Fellowship of the Ring* was released, it was welcomed almost as a gift by people who had been worn out by the endless media coverage of the sadness and violence of September 11, by the harsh reality of life and death. To be able to disappear into the fantasy world of hobbits and elves and wizards, a world in which courage matters and good triumphs over evil, was a sweet and wonderful respite. In an interview with *USA Today*, I was asked whether I thought *The Fellowship of the Ring* represented a healthy opportunity for people to escape for three hours. Here's the truth: my livelihood depended on the success of these movies, and like anyone else, after the shock of September 11 began to wear off, my mind slowly turned to the pragmatics of life. I remember thinking how great it was that we'd be able to bring *The Lord of the Rings* out in the aftermath of September 11, and how people might be inspired by it.

People all over the world, but especially in the United States, were reeling from the tragedy, and it wasn't as easy to be cynical anymore. Something about being able to play with your kids and enjoy the things in life that are at once simple and fantastic. *The Lord of the Rings* is all about that, really—about being able to give yourself over to those fantastical elements. It's easy to satirize, as *South Park*, *Saturday Night Live*, *National Lampoon*, the *Onion*, and *Mad*, just to name a few, have demonstrated. But the trilogy is still revered. For some reason, people don't get sick of *The Lord of the Rings*, and I think it has a lot to do with the nobility of the characters and their quest for a better world.

The impact of September 11 is most evident in *The Two Towers*. As far as I know, no one blinked at the title (it was Tolkien's, after all), and no real consideration was ever given to changing it out of defer-ence to the victims of the World Trade Center disaster. That would have been a meaningless gesture, I think, and one that betrayed the purity of Tolkien's vision. Better to have handled it the way it was ulti-mately handled: with a thoughtful and eloquent speech delivered at the climax of the movie.

After the success of the first film I think everyone involved was looking for a way to say something meaningful with *The Two Towers*. Peter repeatedly voiced his concern that the movie "didn't have enough heart yet," that perhaps action overwhelmed human emotion, and I know that after the way audiences responded to Sam wading into the water in pursuit of Frodo at the conclusion of *The Fellowship of the Ring*, Peter began looking at me as a guy he could turn to if he wanted to tug on a heartstring. But it was more than just that. Who wasn't questioning the meaning of life in those days? Imagine what it must have been like for Peter, who went from being a relatively obscure director (outside New Zealand, anyway) entrusted with the future of an entire studio to a bona fide man of wealth. What an awesome, complex series of emotions.

I found out that the ending to the second film had been dramatically altered in May 2002, when the fax machine in my house began to ring. I'd had a couple of good conversations with Peter about what he hoped to do in the coming months, when he got us back down to New Zealand for reshoots. *The Two Towers*, he explained, would end with a stirring speech delivered by Sam, one that summed up the mood of the entire trilogy.

"We'll be sending the pages soon," he said. "Let me know what you think."

When the fax came through, I was stunned by the power of the words. Certain moments, certain scenes, are so good that you can almost do them on the spot, without any rehearsal whatsoever. You don't even have to memorize them. That's the way this felt. I was standing in my bathrobe, reading the scene aloud, practically weeping at the clarity and power of it.

> *"It's like the great tales, Mr. Frodo, the ones that really matter. Folk in those stories had lots of chances to turn back, only they didn't. They kept going, because they were holding onto something."*
> *"What are we holding onto, Sam?"*
> *"That there's some good left in this world, and it's worth fighting for."*

I got right back on the phone with Peter, thanked him (and Fran and Philippa) profusely for writing such a beautiful scene, and for giving me a chance to act in it. I couldn't wait to get back to New Zealand, for this was yet another chance to do something important. I just felt so excited about it. It seemed as though the writers had somehow assimilated the mood of the planet and reflected it in this particular scene; it was almost like an homage to the value of the source material in modern society: *Why is it worth watching this fantasy at a time when we're fighting in Afghanistan and you never know when the next terrorist attack will come? Why even go to the movies? Why not stay home with your family and try to learn from history and hold your political leaders accountable for their ability to keep you safe? What's the point of stories anymore?*

By using Sam, the simplest and one of the noblest of Tolkien's characters, as a vessel, the filmmakers tried to answer those questions. They said, in effect, *Thank you for loving and supporting the first film, and this is why the second film is worthy of your attention; this is why you ought to let yourself enjoy the story without a shred of guilt.*

It felt important to me, as if the movie was more than just a movie now. If there was a point to *The Two Towers*, it was summed up in this speech, and I was the one who would get to do it. That recognition, which was instantaneous, brought a sense of pressure, but mainly it brought excitement and enthusiasm. After I got off the phone with Peter, I showed the scene to Christine, who loved it. Then I called my father and read it to him over the phone. Dad can be a harsh critic, but he was blown away by this scene.

"Wow!" he said, almost breathlessly. "That's great, Sean. And you can do it."

That much I already knew: I could do it. But then again, anyone could do it, because it was that good a scene.

Less than three weeks later I found myself back in Wellington, this time without Christine or Alexandra. I stayed for about a month, and during that time I encountered just about every significant member of the cast. That's the way the movies were made: we were constantly fixing and changing and adapting, right up until the release date. Interestingly, each time we saw each other, it was as if no time had passed. There were countless occasions for reunions: premieres, publicity tours, awards shows. For more than three years it was a cycle that would not end. Funny thing, too. People change over the course of two or three years. They look different. But when you put on a wig and makeup and costume, somehow the time dissolves and you melt into the character all over again, to the point where even the camera can't distinguish between scenes shot in 1999 and those shot in 2002. There are some logistical problems, however, such as the issue of my weight. I'd lost most of the fat I'd gained to play Sam shortly after the end of principal photography. By the summer of 2002, however, I'd started to balloon all over again, which made the physical work during reshoots more difficult than it might have been. And more humiliating. Consider the moment when we shot a scene in which Frodo, straining against the power of the ring, pulls his sword on Sam.

"Okay, now put the blade under his chin," Peter yelled to Elijah, who was kneeling over my prone, lumpen form.

Elijah smiled. "Which one?"

That cracked up everyone on the set, including me, although the truth of it hurt a little because I was mad at myself for getting that fat again. And I think the additional weight might have hindered my performance. I'd nailed the speech in rehearsal, but for some reason, when we went to shoot the scene, we needed twenty-five takes to get it right. Ultimately I think the scene met the expectations I had had when the fax came through; I mean, it was so well-written that there really was almost no way to blow it. Even so, I was a little concerned that I felt more emotionally connected to the scene in my bathrobe in Los Angeles, and when I was rehearsing it alone with Elijah, than I did when we actually shot it. I honestly believe it plays well in the movie, and I'm not disappointed with the finished product in any way, but somehow it wasn't the perfect acting experience I had anticipated. But then maybe there's no such thing. When we finally finished, Elijah gave me a hug and said, "That was hard, wasn't it?" But he was so patient. It was a strong Sam moment, and I needed his help and inspiration to get through it.

When I saw the final version of *The Two Towers*, I felt really good about it, better than I had felt about the first film. Naturally, this was partly due to the scene that was written for Sam, but it was also because I was so impressed that Peter and Fran had figured out how to start and end the movie without it being the beginning or ending of the trilogy. *The Two Towers* is a bridge, a link between the setup of *The Fellowship of the Ring* and the denouement of *The Return of the King*, and as such it presents a unique challenge to the director. When most people think of *The Two Towers*, they think of the battle of Helm's Deep, a titanic standoff between ten thousand digital orcs and a far smaller army of men. It's an amazing, visceral sequence, and the indisputable highlight of the film, if not the entire trilogy. Audiences reacted that way when they saw the movie in theaters, and I felt that way when we were making the movies. Even though I had absolutely nothing to do with the battle of Helm's Deep (Frodo and Sam were off on an adventure of their own), it always felt like the most important thing about *The Two Towers*.

But *The Two Towers* succeeds on so many levels: as pure adventure, as epic storytelling, and most notably, as an examination of evil, as personified by Saruman and Wormtongue, and the courage required to stand up against it. Like the entire trilogy, I suppose it also says something about the value of brotherhood. Good triumphs over evil in *The Lord of the Rings* primarily because characters of different races, even different species, are willing to set aside their innate differences, and even their dislike for each other, in pursuit of a common goal.

It was related to the sentiment that I tried to capture, at least in some small way, when I made my short film, *The Long and the Short of It*, during our return trip to New Zealand in the summer of 2002. The idea came to me early in the production, and Dominic Monaghan helped me flesh it out. We ended up with a sweet and simple five-minute film about a man who gets some unexpected assistance while trying to paste a large poster on a wall. Really, though, it's about people silently joining forces to complete a task. Each has some talent, some ability that makes him or her uniquely suited to the job. Simply put, it's a tribute to teamwork, and thus a tribute to *The Lord of the Rings*.

There were twenty-four cameras available during the production, and Peter's attitude was, *Hey, if you can find the time, go ahead and take one of them and do your short film*. Remarkably enough, though, there was never a single camera available during principal photography. We were just too busy. Every camera was in use every day, and nobody had a minute to spare. When we returned for pickups, however, the opportunity presented itself.

A couple of guys from Panavision were on the set demonstrating for Peter the new digital technology that George Lucas had used on *Star Wars*. As soon as I learned of their presence, I leaped into action. All of the thousands of hours of muted frustration that I experienced wishing I could be directing came pouring out in a rush of excitement. Peter, Barrie, Elijah, and everyone around was gracious and supportive. Peter, in particular, had always honored my passion as a filmmaker, in theory and in practice, so long as I demonstrated the right level of respect to the *Lord of the Rings* process. It was during principal photography, while filming the Bridge of Khazad-Dum sequence, that I was originally inspired with the idea for the short film. Actually, the first seeds were planted on the first day in New Zealand and then again on the first day of principal photography. During the tour on the first day in New Zealand, Peter mentioned that he would be using all of these cameras, and he didn't blanch for a moment when I suggested I could do a side project. The only time I ever acted on that impulse was years later during pickups, and Peter was instantly and characteristically supportive.

On the first day of filming, Brian Bansgrove, our gaffer, first came to my attention. Elijah was reading aloft and I was cooking the tomatoes and potatoes and mushrooms and ham, when we heard the most singular and gravelly Australian voice proclaim, "Why don't you point some light at the little bloke in the *trayee?*" I looked at his leathery face and instantly thought, *Man, would he be compelling to watch on screen.* I ruminated that I should try to come up with a way to showcase his charisma and individuality in a short film. Much later in the filming, during Gandalf the Grey's clash with Balrog, and the Fellowship's horrified witnessing of Gandalf's apparent demise, I was noodling the idea of finding some way to showcase in a short film the beauty of a woman named Praphaphorn "Fon" Chansantor. As noted, all of the hobbits had scale doubles who endured so much and evinced remarkable patience in the seemingly thankless task of helping convey the notion of relative height without the promise of future glory. They were bona fide, legitimate members of the Fellowship, and yet few people outside production were likely to ever know that they existed. Fon, who primarily doubled Billy Boyd, was one of the most exquisitely beautiful creatures anyone had ever seen. In her late twenties, she stood about three and a half feet tall, and on her arrival from Thailand, where she'd been discovered for this job, she spoke not a single word of English. Well, besides forming a lifelong friendship with Billy and enjoying a lovely rapport with my wife and daughter, Fon taught herself English over the course of the shoot and now speaks the language fluently. I wanted to do something to celebrate her beauty.

As I stood off to the side of the set watching Fon and Brian (who has since tragically taken his own life), I started cooking up an idea to make a short film about the two of them. I started talking aloud to everyone, and Dom jumped in the most enthusiastically and helped me fashion a story. I walked over to Peter, who was waiting for something to be done, and told him the story. He said it sounded cool and asked if he could be in it. I was thrilled. He asked if he could play the part of a bus driver. I hadn't thought about a bus driver, but if that's what Peter wanted to be, by Jove, I was going to adjust the story to ensure that a bus driver was included! I went home that night and wrote the script. Three pages long, it took me about twenty-five minutes to write. Then nothing happened with it for years. Oh, sure, I thought about it and looked for an opportunity when it might be done, but as I've said, one just didn't present itself. Until the summer of 2002, that is.

So there I was in the makeup bus for the umpteenth time, having ears and wig applied, when I was told by Zane Weiner, our unit production manager, that the Panavision guys would be performing a test of their equipment. As it turned out, the actual body of the camera they were testing was one that George Lucas had used on *Phantom Menace.* Anyway, I jumped out of my chair, and within fifteen minutes I had secured not only the commitment of the Panavision guys to extend their visit over the weekend, but also Peter's agreement to come in on Sunday, and Barrie and Zane's agreement to help me put the project together.

That was just fine, because it was only Wednesday and we weren't going to shoot until Sunday. Never mind that this would be everyone's first day off in weeks. I was a man on a mission. Andrew Lesnie, our now legendary cinematographer, graciously agreed to replace his late gaffer as the star of the picture. I didn't have to ask Paul Randall, our seven-foot-tall elf, human-scale double, and all-around utility crew member, to round out the trifecta of my cast. To my extraordinary benefit, everyone I asked for assistance instantly accommodated my every request.

Without going into too much more detail (the film and its "making of" documentary can be seen on *The Two Towers* DVD), I had an absolute ball. The film was accepted at the Sundance Film Festival and went on to win several film festival prizes. None of that would have happened if I wasn't in *The Lord of the Rings*. It never ceases to amaze me that out of hardship or perceived hardship comes the most glorious of rewards.

To my utter astonishment and great relief, quite a few people turned out for the shoot even though most of them had been out partying until two or three in the morning. They staggered in, bleary-eyed, and volunteered their services. I'll never forget it. At one point, I thought we were going to have to cancel the shoot because of the weather—steady rain and gale-force winds—but no one begged off. We put in a six-hour day and got it done. If you've seen the DVD, you know how it turned out. You also know that Peter Jackson is quite a capable actor. But that's not the point. The point is this: he showed up to do a cameo in my short film, and he treated the job with respect and seriousness. He figured out how to work the bus within a few minutes, and he looked totally authentic. Unlike me, he didn't complain. Not once.

It's fair to say that Peter the actor was a director's dream.

And you know what? I'm not sure I deserved that kind of treatment.

CHAPTER EIGHTEEN

In September 2003 I found myself at a postproduction sound facility in London, doing work on the final installment of the trilogy, *The Lord of the Rings: The Return of the King*. As with each of the first two films, this one was completed under enormous deadline pressure. I wonder sometimes how Peter handled it. There was so much at stake, and yet he seemed unfazed by it all. Here we were, less than three months before the film's scheduled release date, and still there was an enormous amount of work to be done: the looping of dialogue, the refining of computer animation, the musical score (which is an awesome task in itself, and the importance of which can't be overlooked). All of these things had to be in order by December. There were, after all, publicity and marketing schedules to be met, and premiere dates that had been set in stone. To be even one day late would have serious repercussions.

Not that there was any cause for concern, as it turned out. I was granted the privilege of screening an early cut of a large portion of *The Return of the King* in London, and was utterly mesmerized by what I saw. The movie was astonishingly good—a nearly perfect conclusion to the trilogy. On a more personal level, it represented Samwise Gamgee as everything I hoped he would be. Philippa was in charge of the screening. She came to me after a week of looping, before we got to the final reels involving all of the heavy crying scenes, and explained that Fran and Peter had agreed to let me watch the movie to help facilitate the emotion required to recreate the climactic scenes on Mount Doom. In other words, to put me in the proper frame of mind.

So I sat on a couch in front of the mixing board, with only Philippa and a couple of technicians in the room, and I watched. To say I was moved would be the understatement of my career. I started bawling about halfway through the footage and didn't stop until well after it had ended. I cried when Sam was on-screen, and I cried when he wasn't on-screen. I cried when Gollum tricked Frodo into believing that Sam had betrayed him, and I cried when Sam cradled Frodo on the side of Mount Doom, as a river of lava threatened to sweep them away "at the end of all things." When Alexandra appeared at my side, playing the role of Sam's daughter, and I heard her tiny whisper of a voice (her lines had not yet been dubbed over by Frodo's narration), I could barely see the screen through the haze of my tears. I don't think I've ever cried that hard in my entire life.

The anxiety and tension, the doubt and disappointment, the pride and gratification—all were mixed together and flooded out, and I became this throbbing, sobbing mass. For me, *The Lord of the Rings* had been like a five-year period of psychoanalysis. Now it was over.

And Peter had done right by me.

In April 2000, some eighteen months before the first film hit the theaters, an online preview trailer for *The Fellowship of the Ring* drew approximately 1.7 million hits in less than twenty-four hours. In January 2001, the official *Lord of the Rings* website was launched. In its first week, the site attracted an astounding forty-one million visitors! And this was still ten months prior to the film's release. Small wonder that Gordon Paddison, senior vice president in New Line's marketing department, felt like he had one of the best jobs in the world.

"*The Lord of the Rings* has a global prebuilt fan base," Paddison said. "We just embraced that community."

Fans repeatedly and overwhelmingly returned the embrace. *The Fellowship of the Ring* grossed more than $860 million worldwide. *The Two*

Towers earned in excess of $910 million. Both are among the top ten grossing films in history.

But *The Lord of the Rings* proved to be more than just a commercial success. It was that rarest of Hollywood creatures: a film (or in this case, films) that was warmly received by both critics and moviegoers. *The Fellowship of the Ring*, in fact, was one of the most decorated films released in 2001, earning not only rave reviews from critics across the country but also thirteen Academy Award nominations, including best picture. *The Two Towers* was similarly lauded, and also was nominated for an Academy Award, as the best film of 2002.

I've agreed not to talk about my finances with regard to the success of the pictures. But suffice it to say that in the fall of 2003, for the first time in my life, I had a pretty good sense that if I played my cards right with my career, I would be able to support my family and live comfortably for the foreseeable future. So I sat there, as the lights came up, utterly drained. When the film ended, Philippa wrapped her arms around me and let me cry on her shoulder for a few minutes. After I collected myself, I left the studio and got in my car. On the way back to my hotel I called Peter and thanked him. Later I called my agent and manager and told them that everything I had hinted at, everything I believed would happen once people saw the third movie, was about to come true.

"Will there be Oscar talk?" the agent asked.

I thought about it for only a second or two.

"You know what? I think I might get nominated."

To be honest, in the afterglow of that screening, I didn't see how I could miss.

My attitude changed in late November when I saw the movie in its final version, the version that would be released to the public. A private screening had been arranged in Wellington prior to the official world premiere and the tidal wave of publicity that would follow. This was a different experience, one that left me feeling vaguely uneasy and even a bit disappointed. Liv Tyler was sitting next to me, and she seemed delighted with it. So did Andy Serkis, and with good reason.

The movie, of course, opens with Andy in hobbit form, as Smeagol, and becomes a showcase for the character's split personality and the talent of the actor behind it. I remember feeling thrilled for Andy, but it was weird: I wasn't really drawn into the movie, mainly because I was too focused on the ways in which it differed from the version I had seen in London. Once I realized that a particular scene had come and gone—or just "gone," since it had been cut from the final version—I started getting a negative feeling that I couldn't shake. I just didn't like the movie as much.

Since then, I've come to my senses. Fans loved *The Return of the King*, probably more than either of the first two films. I've seen it six times now, and my enjoyment and appreciation have increased with each viewing. But I'm trying to be honest about how I felt, and I can't deny that when I saw the movie in New Zealand in its completed form, I was disappointed. Granted, it was a selfish reaction, one that stemmed primarily from the fact that Sam's screen time had been reduced. There was, for example, a scene right before Gollum tricks Frodo into believing that Sam has eaten the last of their dwindling supply of food. Sam grabs Gollum by the throat and warns the creature, "If one hair is out of place on his head . . . no more Slinker, no more Stinker. You're gone!" Gollum looks at Sam with fear in his eyes, and it's a moment of real strength and heroism, so that the swing from tough guy to sniveling, crying victim ("Don't send me away, Mr. Frodo; it's not true!") is so much stronger. When I realized that scene had been cut, the excitement and enthusiasm were sucked out of me, replaced by sadness.

The orc encampment is another example. Frodo and Sam don armor and say, "We've done it; they're moving off. A bit of luck at last." And then all of a sudden there's this whole sequence where the orcs come around the corner, and they slap us and whip us and put us in their column, and we're marching with the bad guys. Then I pick a mock fight with Frodo to distract the orcs so that we can escape. That's followed by an incredible scene on the Gorgoroth plains, where an exhausted Frodo and Sam are slumped against each other, looking up at the night sky. Sam sees a star and observes, "In the end, a shadow is only a passing thing, Mr. Frodo. Darkness will fade." Basically, it's an echo of Sam's speech at the end of the second film, and almost as good. It was beautifully written and sensitively directed by Fran, with a violin concerto providing accompaniment. I think people were crying as we performed that scene, and I was so happy with the way it turned out in the film. But now it was gone, along with the miles and miles of walking and suffering endured by Sam and Frodo in their march to Morder. Now I thought, *The orc armor is on, it's off, they're at the top of the mountain . . . what? How did that happen?*

It just felt truncated to me. It felt like something less than what it had been.

And yet . . .

The Return of the King was a three-hour-and-fifteen-minute movie, and a very good one at that. I'm sure every director would like to present to the public a five-hour version of his movie, a version that is true to his artistic vision. But that's just not possible. And it wasn't possible in the case of *The Return of the King.* I know that now, and I knew it then. Nevertheless, each time I noticed a scene had been the slightest bit altered from my expectations, it felt wrong to me, and I began to wonder if others noticed, if they were enjoying the film or suffering from the same doubts that I experienced.

Simply put, I lost touch.

Christine was also sitting near me at the screening in New Zealand, and she was obviously and visibly moved by it. Unfortunately, I ruined it for her. We went right from the screening over to a little gathering at Philippa's house (which is adjacent to Peter and Fran's), and as soon as I got Christine alone, I dumped all my doubt and anxiety on her. I was so upset and uncomfortable that I couldn't think of anything positive to say. The idea of doing publicity, which would begin with a round of interviews that very night, was daunting. What would I say? "You should have seen the other version—now *that* was a movie!" Somehow I don't think that would have gone over well.

"They've ruined it!" I whined to Christine. "How am I going to get through this?"

To which she replied, in not so many words, "What is wrong with you?"

Christine thought I was an idiot; she thought I was completely out of my mind, that *The Return of the King* represented the best work I had ever done, and that only someone with an egregiously distorted view of reality would recognize it as anything else. Her response was not without merit. You can see how the film turned out. Certainly I wasn't going to get any sympathy from the other actors, all of whom felt the sting of the editor's shears more acutely than I had. I'd have to be blind not to recognize that Sam's is one of the best roles in the third movie, that he is in some sense the hero of the film, and that I am allowed to shine as an actor as much as anyone in the ensemble. I was going to be disappointed about that!? How ungrateful could I be? But I couldn't keep my mouth shut.

"Am I crazy?" I whispered to Elijah at one point, hoping that he might sympathize, since he, too, had seen an earlier version of the film. "I feel heartbroken."

"Heartbroken? That's a little strong, don't you think? It's a great movie."

"Is it?"

"Uhhhh, yeah. It is."

"Because I didn't care as much this time. I didn't *feel*."

As was often the case, Elijah's grasp on objectivity was superior to mine. Eventually, after some relentless prodding on my part, he agreed that the emotional impact of our scenes on the side of Mount Doom was slightly diminished. But only slightly, and not to a degree that bothered him. Elijah was able to see the movie for what it was: a brilliant piece of filmmaking and a technological marvel. I saw it as a slap in the face. How warped is that? In retrospect, I can identify that day as a rite of passage: I'd finally gotten too close to have any perspective whatsoever.

Now, Christopher Lee? There's a man who had reason to be disappointed. Saruman, the embodiment of evil and arguably the most compelling character in *The Two Towers*, was nowhere to be found in *The Return of the King*. Scenes depicting Saruman's downfall were filmed, of course, but in the end, Peter explained, they didn't work in the third film, and so Saruman's departure occurred off-screen, as mere backstory. And Christopher was left on the cutting-room floor. Such is the business of making movies. Tough, sometimes brutal decisions must be made.

Nevertheless, I felt truly bad for Christopher, with whom I'd developed an extraordinarily strong friendship on the set, a friendship cemented during one particularly long flight from Auckland to Los Angeles. Christopher is a talker like I'm a talker. Maybe even more so, if that's possible. He's got unbelievable stories to tell, and I enjoyed quizzing him on his past and his experiences, and listening to him and learning from him. I think he was happy to have me feeling that way. At one point he even showed me a script because he thought I was perfect for the lead. The project ultimately wound up in limbo, as so many do, but I appreciated Christopher's effort. That's the way it's supposed to work: the older actor reaches out to the younger actor. He recognized that I could do the role, the leading-man part, which was flattering and appreciated.

When Christopher discovered that he had been cut from *The Return of the King*, he called me in South Africa, where I was filming another movie. Listening to him, I realized that I had no reason to be upset about what had happened to Sam. Christopher was crestfallen and offended and pissed off, largely because the decision had been made so late and he'd already gone out publicly in support of the movie. Now he had egg on his face.

Me? I was a supporting character thrust into a starring role. I was one of the heroes of the third film. I was the actor who, as Peter often noted, was making audiences cry. Sam would have been ashamed of my thoughts and feelings.

The seemingly endless series of premieres helped knock a little sense into me. Appropriately enough, the world premiere was held in New Zealand on December 1, 2003, a day that remains one of the most memorable of my life. It included a parade through the streets of Wellington in front of more than a hundred thousand screaming fans. Granted, roughly ninety thousand of them were girls pleading with Orlando to remove some article of clothing or to autograph a portion of their suddenly bared anatomy, but still it was a great experience. I sat next to John Rhys-Davies during the parade, and at one point we spotted Orlando's mother in the crowd and invited her to jump in with us. She sat almost on John's lap as we passed countless throngs of adoring female fans, some of them lifting their skirts or lowering their blouses in the hope of attracting Orlando's attention.

"Now, now!" John would shout. "Please, ladies, this is Orlando's *mum* here. Have a bit of respect!"

The parade automatically put me in the proper frame of mind. Thankfully, I am not so self-involved as to be oblivious to the people who matter: the fans who buy tickets and make it possible for me to earn a living as an actor. It would have been a total disavowal of their feelings not to match their enthusiasm. I watched the movie that night and actually enjoyed it; mainly, I enjoyed their reaction to it. When I felt their positive response to the story, and to the character of Sam in particular, I was genuinely moved, and slowly I began to see things from Peter's perspective.

Hmmmm, maybe that's why he cut the scene, because it connects the story in a certain way.

The doubt wasn't erased all at once, mind you. It happened over the course of several weeks and repeated viewings, and endless hours sitting in the dark, listening to the snivels and sobs of both casual fans and hardened Tolkien critics. In the end, it was the fans who won me over, who embraced the movie and Sam and helped me realize how silly and self-centered I'd been. The changes that Peter had made left me concerned that fans would be disappointed, but they weren't. Far, far from it. When I saw the premiere in Wellington, I began to understand that the fans of the movie, and the feelings of the fans, were bigger than the movie itself. That understanding deepened with each viewing. The third time I saw the movie, at the Los Angeles premiere, I gave myself over to the experience. This was at the Mann Village Theater in Westwood Village, not far from the Bruin Theater, where I had worked as a kid. It was a friendly, hometown kind of crowd— they were applauding for my character, crying with the character— and I just sat back and went along for the ride. For the first time since London, I was happy with what I saw on the screen.

None of the reviews had come in at that point, so I wasn't sure what critics would think (aside from the obvious—that they would express overwhelming appreciation for the directorial skill of Peter Jackson). But when we started doing interviews, there was a rhythm of positive energy, especially as it applied to the character of Sam and my work in the film. After a while, I almost became skeptical, like I was waiting for the other shoe to drop, for someone to rip me apart: "The Return of the King *is a brilliant example of modern cinema, a sweeping epic that seamlessly blends live action and computer-generated effects like no film in history . . . a film so powerful that not even the melodramatic Sean Astin, as a weepy Samwise Gamgee, can ruin the experience.*"

Something like that.

But it didn't happen. Audiences adored the film. Critics were kind. Within a few weeks after the movie's release, it was clear that there would be no backlash, that a broad cross section of people had voiced their approval, and most of the meaningful votes were in. I don't know if I had any conception of how the ensemble would be acknowledged. I'd be lying if I said I didn't want to be recognized for my work. But I did not want that recognition at the expense of any of the other actors, so I found myself getting really uncomfortable if someone, especially a journalist, said, "Hey, you're the guy!" I liked it and sort of wanted it to continue, but in a slightly different way, because it almost felt as if I were stealing the thunder of other performers. Maybe I'd earned that moment by standing patiently in the shadows for the better part of four years, but it still made me a bit queasy.

Bernard Hill (who played Theodin) and I have had some moments where I could tell he was no less affectionate or caring—he's been extraordinarily complimentary—but I could read the disappointment on his face when the attention turned my way. English actors, in my experience, are great at handling that sort of thing. Their reaction is, *Yeah, that hurts. Now let's move on.* I honestly believe that Bernard did some of the best work in *The Lord of the Rings*, and so it feels lousy to have contributed to his disappointment in some way.

I've been on both sides of the equation, so I know how uncomfortable it can be for everyone involved when a member of an ensemble is suddenly singled out. It happened in front of the French press corps, when Liv Tyler became the center of attention, with everyone taking pictures of her, screaming, "Liv, Liv, Liv!" She was surrounded by a dozen actors who had invested infinitely more blood, sweat, and tears, but because Liv is a superstar, a beautiful young woman, and a huge, bankable commodity in the European and Asian markets, she naturally outshines most mere mortals. On a night intended to honor the film as a collaborative venture, even Peter Jackson was eclipsed by her. None of this was Liv's fault. She's a delightful woman who has earned her stardom and success. But the response was disproportionate with people's excitement, simply because of their preconceived notions of fame and celebrity.

Imagine Orlando at ... well, imagine Orlando almost anywhere. Chances are, eighty percent of the crowd is there to see him. Everyone has developed a sense of humor about that, and we all have pride in his success, but there's also a part of you that sometimes says, *What the hell am I doing here?* A lot of people have had moments to shine throughout the process, but there have been a few people who have been allowed to shine more than others. With the release of *The Return of the King*, the spotlight fell on me, and while I won't deny enjoying its warmth, I can also say that there were times when it made me uncomfortable. The moments I enjoyed most were the public appearances that ended with a giant curtain call, with each member of the acting ensemble taking a turn onstage and basking in the applause of the audience.

Nowhere was this type of response more gratifying and enlightening than at New York's Lincoln Center, where more than a thousand people paid one hundred dollars apiece for the chance to take part in a tribute to *The Lord of the Rings*. All three films were screened in a single day, each one introduced by members of the ensemble. Every time we took the stage, we received a standing ovation. I was absolutely blown away by this response. Because I'd been reading scripts and going to meetings and doing interviews—and because I had flown in just a few hours before the event—I hadn't slept for the better part of two days, so my senses were slightly dulled. But somewhere between the hotel and the big SUV in which we were shuttled around, I wiped the sand from my eyes and prepared for what I suspected would be a meaningful event. It was much more than that. The crowd didn't want us to leave. And what a crowd it was! Teenage boys, infatuated girls, fifty-something hippies—an incredibly broad spectrum. One of the first things we did was ask for a show of hands.

"How many of you have already seen the third movie?"

To my astonishment, virtually every person in the room raised his or her hand. These people were so enamored of *The Lord of the Rings* that they were willing to pay a hundred bucks to see the entire trilogy—even though they'd already seen it! That's how much it meant to them. That's how much *we* meant to them.

An actor should never take that sort of loyal support for granted. On some level, of course, it's ludicrous. At least with athletes and dancers and musicians, there is a moment of expertise, something that happens right before the eyes of the audience in real time that merits a response—a slam dunk, a home run, a perfectly executed concerto. But with us, well, we had done the work so long ago. So to be given an ovation for it—well, sometimes you just feel unworthy of the adulation. And yet it happened. Over and over. People rose out of their seats and roared their approval. It was profoundly moving for me as a performer.

And more than a little overwhelming . . .

CHAPTER NINETEEN

"No more being overshadowed by glam-boy elves and hunksome warriors . . . Sean Astin's moment to shine is here."

—USA Today

"Sean Astin comes into his own with this brave, questing performance."

—Rolling Stone

"Sam is played so well by Sean Astin that this affectingly loyal hobbit seems the most human figure on screen."

—The New York Times

Maybe they just ran out of other things to write about. Maybe, after four years and three movies—during which hundreds, if not thousands, of stories were devoted to the vision and talent of Peter Jackson, the rugged good looks of Viggo Mortensen, the shimmering beauty of Liv Tyler, the haunting, luminescent eyes of Elijah Wood, the split personality of Andy Serkis, the musical genius of Howard Shore, the artistic brilliance of Richard Taylor, and so on—maybe it was simply my turn.

The Lord of the Rings: The Return of the King had been unleashed upon the world, and it was met with at least as much critical and commercial enthusiasm as either of the first two films. This was a movie that would become one of the biggest box-office hits in the history of cinema, and it would go on to receive eleven Academy Awards. There was no getting away from it. The entire trilogy had become a pop culture phenomenon, and it was now reaching a climax. The question was this: had the media well run dry? The answer was an emphatic "no!"

But where to train the eye? The media likes a hook, something that will quickly and easily capture the public's fancy. In the winter of 2003, to my own amazement, I became that hook.

There are two distinct threads to discuss here. One is the story of Sean Astin, a Hollywood brat (and I mean that in the military sense, not the derogatory sense) and journeyman actor who finally gets a chance at stardom. The other is the work of Sean Astin in *The Return of the King*. The two threads inevitably became entangled, because that is the nature of celebrity, and it's easy, if you're not careful, to lose yourself in the vortex of hype, to start believing your own press clippings and equating fame with success. I've been around long enough to know the difference between art and commerce, and to maintain a sense of amused detachment when the machinery of publicity begins working in my favor.

I knew what was happening. I understood the angle. People identify with someone who's been around awhile, who's plugged away at his job, generally without complaint, year after year, and then finally gets some supposedly long overdue attention and respect. Fine. I don't disagree with the notion that mine was a nice story, and I didn't mind sharing it. Similarly, I'm proud of the work I did in *The Lord of the Rings*, and I think it's worthy of scrutiny. Somehow, though, it didn't feel like I'd earned the praise quite as much as some other actors.

Like Eugene Levy, for example, who won the New York Film Critics Circle Award for his performance in *A Mighty Wind*. Here's a guy who is old enough to be my father, and whose body of work includes everything from slapstick humor to brilliantly subtle improvisation. Regardless of the film, his work is always interesting. The same is true of Philip Seymour Hoffman, whose name you might know, but whose face you would surely recognize. Philip is a character actor in the truest sense of the word, and his commitment to honest empathetic portrayals of offbeat downtrodden characters—from the late rock critic Lester Bangs in *Almost Famous* to the lovesick friend of porn star Mark Wahlberg in *Boogie Nights*—is admirable. He is justifiably and understandably a critic's darling. I'm not, and to suddenly be placed in that category was at once flattering and disorienting. I've been prolific. My filmography includes a lot of "okay" work punctuated by the occasional outstanding film, but it's not comparable to the work of Philip Seymour Hoffman or Eugene Levy. I get the difference between my career and those kinds of careers. I'd like to think that everything up to this point has been a prologue for me, and maybe with a bit more luck I can have a career like that. But I don't have it yet, and I know it.

So it was odd to hear my name mentioned in the same breath as some of the best actors in the business, which was what happened after the release of *The Return of the King*, when the 2004 Oscar campaign got under way. The 2004 awards season coincided almost exactly with the publicity tour for *The Return of the King*, and I found myself out in front, driving the PR bandwagon for the better part of two months, from the first premiere in Wellington to the day, in late January, when the Academy Award nominations were revealed. It was an exhausting, sometimes hypnotic adventure into the surreal heart of our celebrity culture, one that left me alternately exhilarated and depressed, but ultimately emboldened by the knowledge that I am, at my core, a father and a husband who happens to have an interesting job. I'm luckier than most.

Academy Award nominations do not fall haphazardly and unexpectedly from the sky. The recipients typically are good actors in good parts (as Samwise Gamgee was for me), deserving of praise and recognition. But there are only five nominations in each acting category, and so some deserving performers routinely are overlooked. It's up to the studio to determine which actors it wants to support in the Oscar campaign. To a large extent, this decision is made by answering a pragmatic question: Who has the best chance to win? More often than not, it's the actor whose performance has been singled out and applauded by the broadest range of critics. But there are other criteria: the popularity of the movie in which the performance is embedded; the critical response to that movie; the date the film was released (have people forgotten about it?); and perhaps most important of all, the actor's personal backstory.

In my case, it was an easy call. I think New Line had a sense that as an Academy legacy I might be an attractive candidate for the category formally known as "outstanding performance by an actor in a supporting role," and more colloquially referred to as best supporting actor. For one thing, the studio desperately wanted to win the Academy Award for outstanding motion picture (also known as "best movie"), and historically it's been demonstrated that in order for a film to be so honored, it helps to be viewed as a movie that showcases great acting. Spectacles and fantasies, especially those laden with special effects, have often been denied on Oscar night. Indeed, not since *Braveheart* in 1995 had a film received the Academy Award for outstanding motion picture without receiving at least one nomination in the five acting categories. So you can understand the sense of urgency at New Line to make sure that someone in *The Return of the King* be plucked from the acting ensemble and given an opportunity to sample the heady elixir that produces something known as "Oscar buzz."

Although advertisements were taken out promoting several members of the cast—including Ian McKellen, Viggo Mortensen, Elijah Wood, and me—it soon became apparent that the studio would throw its considerable muscle behind the character of Sam and the story of Sean Astin. Why? Well, probably because Ian, the most logical candidate given his impeccable credentials, had been previously nominated (for *The Fellowship of the Ring*). And also because critics were uniformly generous in their response to my portrayal of Sam. Whatever the reason, I became Oscar boy for New Line.

The way New Line managed the campaign was impressive and relentless, calling feature writers and critics and saying things like, "Have you *really* looked at the performance, because we think it's pretty special." The respected critics from major publications set the tone. If they like the movie and make particular note of your performance, there's a spark of interest. A thumbs-up from Roger Ebert is worth countless millions of dollars. It sells tickets to the movie and provokes interest in the performers from other media outlets. So it's a very conscious, determined campaign that the studio attempts to cultivate. I knew all of this before *The Return of the King*, before I'd even signed onto *The Lord of the Rings*, but it's still a weird thing when it happens to you.

I know that Peter tried valiantly to be evenhanded, to balance all the different performances and not let anybody "steal" anything—the one obvious exception being Andy Serkis. People can't seem to get enough of Gollum/Smeagol (and who can blame them?), so there are moments in each film where Andy nearly does steal the movie. He's that good. Ultimately, though, the thing with which audiences identified most strongly was *the story*. For Peter it always came back to the spine of the narrative: Frodo's quest to destroy the ring and all it represents. The emotion of that quest, the purity of purpose, is at the heart of *The Lord of the Rings*, and Peter never lost sight of that fact. I'm sure he knew that audiences would be awed by the antics of Gollum and thrilled by the swashbuckling heroics of Aragorn and Legolas. In the end, though, they wanted to be with Sam as he reached out and grasped Frodo's bloody hand and pulled him back from the Crack of Doom. They wanted to cry, and they wanted to exult.

Although I wasn't surprised that fans reacted in this manner (I do remain humbled by the *intensity* of their reaction), I was surprised to learn that members of the media, including hardened, cynical critics, seemed similarly captivated. Because of that, there were times when I dropped my guard and became too playful with the media, too comfortable with the setting and my new role as ambassador for *The Lord of the Rings*.

I like to talk, and sometimes words pass my lips without first being edited by my brain, which can lead to trouble and hurt feelings. And you never know when it will happen. Regis Philbin, a self-professed Notre Dame nut and a big fan of *Rudy*, introduced me as "Sean Austin." Kind of funny, I thought, and endearing in that bumbling sort of way that has become a Regis trademark. I was comfortable on that show, so comfortable that when Regis started asking me questions about the actors' ongoing negotiations with New Line regarding bonus payments, I talked a little too freely. I've skimmed that issue in this book for only one reason: I promised my fellow actors that I would not talk about it in detail, and yet there I was, making jokes about buying a new house with my bonus money. I was stupid and insensitive, and I felt terrible about it afterward.

Then there was the brief but unfortunate interview with *People*, in which the reporter engaged me in a game of free association. It was supposed to be one of those benign little pieces, less than a hundred words in length, that showcase the celebrity's ability to be glib and irreverent. Not exactly heavy lifting. I enjoy this sort of sparring, and I'm usually pretty good at it. Take a look:

People: "The Atkins diet."
Astin: "The body needs carbs."

People: "Groupies."
Astin: "Okay, but be cool."

People: "Wacky celebrity baby names."
Astin: "My daughters' names are Alexandra and Elizabeth. I wasn't confident enough to go for Banjo or Pizza."

So far, so good. Right? Everything was basically fine, right up until—

People: "Prenuptial agreements."
Astin: "Am I still eligible?"

What? Excuse me? Are you out of your mind?
Christine thought so, and I can't say I blame her. Here's my lame excuse: when the reporter asked the question, I thought, *I'm the old married guy. Why would you ask me that question?* But that's not the way it was received. Not by casual, barely interested readers, and certainly not by the people who mean the most to me, Christine being at the head of that list. She was deeply and understandably wounded by my response, so I did what any husband in the doghouse would do: I apologized in front of a national television audience.

The forum for this mea culpa, appropriately enough, was the ultimate morning coffee-klatsch, *The View.* The setup for my apology was perfect. We talked about finding joy in life, and in the simple pleasures of love and family and children. For me, personally, it was an illuminating experience, because I know that *The View* is an accurate reflection of the way my wife, my mother-in-law, and a lot of other women think and talk and communicate. I needed to hear it, and I understood it. So I espoused my love for Christine and acknowledged having been an idiot in *People*. I took the sword and fell right on it, and the hosts were instantly forgiving, as was the studio audience. And Christine was happy, which was the most important thing.

But I wasn't through wreaking havoc. Oh, no. Not by a long shot. In an ostensibly sweet-natured *Time* magazine story about previously little-known actors in breakthrough roles, I managed to take a big chunk out of the hand that fed me.

Sam's fiercest moment comes when he leans over his friend, ailing and bearing the deadly Ring, and declares, "Come on, Mr. Frodo. I can't carry it for you. But I can carry you." The scene has evoked tears from strong men and yanked Astin into the awards limelight. Yet as much as he reveres Jackson, Astin believes the wrong take is in the film. "I know the way I delivered the line was so much more powerful than what the audience sees. That was one of the great acting achievements of my life, and I feel only 20% is on the screen."

I regretted that comment almost as soon as it came out of my mouth. A few days after the story appeared, as I was getting ready to board a plane for Hawaii, I got an e-mail from Fran Walsh saying, in essence, "I think you should know how hurt Peter was by what you said in *Time*, and how unfair it was that you said that."

Mortified that I had insulted Peter (and implied that he had failed in some way), I quickly composed a response to Fran. I told her the journalist got it wrong, that I was describing an esoteric dynamic about being able to hear the difference between the postproduction looping session and the emotion that was present on the day we filmed the actual scene. The bottom line, however, is that Fran was right. I'd appeared ungrateful in a national magazine, and I'd said something that had caused Peter (and her) pain. I should have discussed it with them first or, better yet, kept my mouth shut. It's one thing to express your joy and frustration in a book, where you have control over the way it turns out; it's quite another to speak carelessly to a reporter for *Time*. My fault. I should have known better. And, oh my God, I was heartsick about it.

Eventually, before I boarded the plane, I got in touch with Peter and Fran's assistant and said, "Please, please tell Fran and Peter how sorry I am. This is one of the greatest moments in cinema history, and it looks like I just took a giant crap on it. That's not what I meant; that's not how I feel." I also said something about how my senses had been dimmed and dulled, and my wit numbed during the two months of publicity. "I'm sorry," I said again. And once more for good measure: "I'm sorry."

I hit the wall during the Christmas holiday. For nearly two months I'd been promoting the movie nonstop, with all the energy I could muster, all the enthusiasm it deserved. When we were given a few weeks to recharge the batteries, I crashed. I just sat around all day, sleeping and watching television and playing video games. I'd say I was depressed, except that's not a word I liked to throw around casually, not with my family history. Christine was worried about me, as was my mom, but really I was just exhausted. I could barely summon the strength for Christmas dinner at my father's house. I went, but it was an odd experience: everyone was so complimentary of my success, which was very nice, of course, but being the center of attention in my own family was something I had never experienced before. All I wanted to do was talk to them about their kids and their jobs and their lives, and all they wanted to do was talk about *The Lord of the Rings*. That's the way it was for a while: with every human interaction there was a moment where we had to talk about the movie, because it was so ubiquitous. It got so bad that I didn't want to leave the house or even answer the phone. It was all I could do to not be so catatonic that Christine would think I was unsafe around my own children.

And yet, she was really supportive, as she's always been. She gave me space for a week or two, and then started to nudge me toward the door, eventually kicking me in the butt, encouraging me to join the ranks of the living again. After a while the haze lifted. I started reading the paper for a couple of hours each morning, getting back in touch with the real world, the one that exists outside Middle-earth. I started running. I played with Alexandra and cuddled with the baby, and as I held them I was reminded of what's important in life.

I hadn't been fair to the kids and I hadn't been fair to Christine, but I didn't know what to do. It wasn't as if we could go on a hike or a drive. Any experience we had in public—any museum, amusement park, theater, or shopping mall—was going to be informed with *The Lord of the Rings*. It was number one at the box office all over the world, and everyone was going to recognize Samwise Gamgee. Stardom was now covering me like a blanket, and I was thoroughly ambivalent about it.

I know exactly how that sounds: pathetic and shallow. Who the hell wants to hear a movie star complain about the very things that provide him with such a wonderful life? Not me. And so I won't belabor the point. I recognize it as a character flaw, and so I don't surrender to it without a fight. For a brief time, though, it was a battle I nearly lost. For one thing, I realized that during November, when I had been traveling on my own, promoting the movie, Christine and I had grown apart. And in December, when my family joined me at the premieres in New Zealand and Europe, and then at home, I'd been a self-involved jerk. Christine and the kids had a great time sightseeing in Berlin, London, and Paris, and I was happy they had fun, but as she pointed out, "None of our great time was because of you—you were miserable." And she was right. At moments when I was receiving adulation, I honored it by being up and happy and genuinely satisfied with it. At home, however, I withdrew.

Maybe it was just too much. You know what they say: *Be careful what you wish for. You might just get it.* The attention was overwhelming, and my response to it was not what I had anticipated. When I think of a movie star—a *real* movie star—I think of Joan Crawford shouting, "I need to be with my *public!*" as if there was something in her that craved the spotlight, that needed it. To me it was different; it was almost like the process forced me to be a star, and I was out there every day, answering questions, shaking hands, signing autographs, and smiling for the cameras, and all of a sudden I thought, *Oh, God! I'm Joan fucking Crawford!*

A result of my brief taste of stardom has been a greater appreciation for the skill and style of those who live in the goldfish bowl—the people who run for the highest levels of public office, for example, who have to be smart and focused and tireless and gracious twenty-four hours a day.

There was one night in early January 2004, when Christine and I stayed up all night talking. I had put a bunch of logs in the fireplace and forgotten about it, and Christine smelled the smoke and came down to make sure everything was okay. And we just started talking. I suspect that every marriage must have a bunch of low moments, where something's got to give, or change. We had one of those moments, and we talked our way through it. Christine told me how horrible she was feeling because of my withdrawal and apparent unhappiness at a time when I should have been proud and happy and satisfied; I shared the same with her. We held hands and watched the sun rise, and then the kids woke up and the house filled with life, and we moved on.

By the time the nominations for the Academy Awards were announced, I simply wanted it to be over. I'd experienced an incredible spectrum of emotions: from wanting a nomination, to feeling guilty and shallow for wanting a nomination, to not caring about a nomination—and finally to just wanting to put the disappointment of not getting a nomination behind me. As for whether I had a legitimate shot at a nomination, I really didn't know what to think. My work had been noted and praised by many respected critics, and I'd been nominated by a handful of organizations. The "real" awards season, however, brought mostly disappointment and only served to cloud the issue.

The first of the major contests to announce its nominees was the

Golden Globe Awards, generally regarded as a reasonably accurate barometer of the Oscar climate, if not exactly a predictor of the Academy Awards themselves. I was in the middle of a live interview on ABC's *Good Morning America* when the announcement was made.

"Wait a minute," said the woman who was interviewing me. "We have breaking news. The Golden Globe nominations just came in."

"Oh, yeah?" I tried not to betray a hint of nervousness, even though I could feel my heart suddenly racing.

Through her earpiece the news was delivered, and she repeated it back to me (and an audience of a couple of million viewers), reciting the nominations for *The Return of the King*.

"Best picture, best director, best song . . . and . . . best musical score! So, four! Four nominations."

She smiled at me. I smiled back.

"Wow, that's great. I mean, best director—that's the one we all really wanted. We're pulling for Peter. He deserves this more than anyone."

Meanwhile, inside, I was dying. I was surprised by how much it hurt. I could feel the blood rising in my face, the hair rising on the back of my neck. I think I recovered pretty well, though. I've analyzed the tape and thought, *Man, that was a tough moment.* I can detect a subtle change in my demeanor, a slight dip in the shoulders, a little twitch in the eyebrow, but I don't think it was noticeable to the viewers. When the segment ended, the interviewer was thrilled. She shook my hand and thanked me.

"Hey, Sean, nice job! That was great live television, huh?"

Oh, yeah, just terrific.

But it *was* great television. It was honest and dramatic, and as a moment of masochistic self-discovery, it was meaningful. It made me wonder, *What am I really about? What do I want out of life?* The marketing folks at New Line were somewhat less philosophical and introspective.

"Those fucking assholes!" one of them said later that morning, referring to the mysterious Hollywood Foreign Press Association, which chooses the Golden Globe nominees and winners. "How dare they!"

Yeah, he was pretty pissed off. And legitimately surprised. New Line executives thought I was a shoo-in for a Golden Globe nomination, especially since they had been told that I was runner-up to Eugene Levy in the arguably far more prestigious and competitive New York Film Critics Circle Awards. I still don't know if that was true or not. I know only that the Golden Globes came and went, and the Oscar buzz began to diminish.

Next came the nominations for the Screen Actors Guild Awards. This was vastly more important to me because the nominees were selected by my peers in the union. Christine set the alarm for 6 A.M. and we got up together and watched the announcements live on television. I was groggy and tired, and I kept telling Christine, "Honey, it's not going to happen," not because I was hypersensitive or because I was trying to dilute the potential disappointment. I just had a feeling it wasn't going to happen. And it didn't. Although *The Return of the King* was nominated for best acting by an ensemble, the film received no individual acting nominations, which left me feeling somewhat conflicted: I was happy for the cast, and disappointed for myself. We deserved recognition in the ensemble category, of course, but I had clung to an unspoken hope that I'd get singled out and that perhaps a SAG nomination would start the trend toward an Academy Award nomination.

Christine gave me a hug and we walked together into the kitchen, where Ali was busily eating her cinnamon toast.

"Hey, guess what?" Christine said. "The nominations for the Screen Actors Guild Awards were just announced, and Daddy and the rest of the cast got nominated for the ensemble award."

Ali looked up, fork in hand. "What does 'ensemble' mean?"

Christine smiled. "It means you're part of a big group."

Ali glanced at me and nodded soberly. "Oh," she said, a trace of disdain in her voice. "It's so nice to be part of a *group*."

We were floored. Here was my seven-year-old daughter, reflecting my disappointment. So we laughed it off, and that was that. I took Ali to school and along the way reiterated my pleasure with the SAG ensemble award. That was important, I told her. It was meaningful. And this time she agreed.

. . .

The Academy Award nominations were announced on January 26. I did nothing special to prepare, nothing to sway the Oscar karma. More than a decade earlier, when I discovered that my first short film was being considered for a nomination, I had driven up into the Hollywood hills with a couple of colleagues and sat there in front of the Hollywood sign and swore to the movie gods. "I promise to use an Academy Award for good, not for ill!" The nomination was really meaningful to me then. It was important, and the next morning when the announcements came out and I wasn't nominated, I was really disappointed. I moved on, and two years later I got nominated for *Kangaroo Court*, and that was a great moment. But it was funny. Weeks before that nomination, I wasn't even thinking about it. Christine and I were in college, working hard. My mind was elsewhere. I found out about the nomination through a phone call from the writer of the film. And that led me to wonder, Is there a moral here? Like, if you're thinking about it and hoping for it, it won't happen, but if you're really about the business of doing something more meaningful and valuable with your life, then that kind of acknowledgment will come to you.

It's like watching a sporting event. You sometimes wonder if you can have an impact on the outcome simply by watching it or not watching it. It's about superstition, and it's fundamentally ridiculous, although I think we all fall prey to it once in a while. Maybe I did. More than just a little bit. But I wouldn't call it more than a recurring fantasy. I tried as much as possible to divest myself of the speculation and oddsmaking, although the barrage of information was hard to avoid. I received dozens of calls and messages saying, "You deserve a nomination." Online polls were enthusiastic in their support of Sam. Critics were divided. There seemed a reasonable chance. The night before the nominations were announced brought more phone calls: from studio executives, family members, agents and managers and publicists. Joel Stevens, my manager, wanted to know where I'd be in the morning, when the nominations came in, so that he could get in touch with me immediately.

"Don't worry," I said. "I'll call you."

I made no specific plans. The nominations were to be announced on live television at 5:30 A.M. Pacific Standard Time. There was no need to set the alarm. I figured if I woke up comfortably and the sun was already rising in the sky, I'd have my answer: no nomination. If there was a nomination, someone would call. Either way, I wouldn't have to live through it in real time.

I woke up a few times during the night, and as dawn approached I began actively dreaming. I was in that fugue state where you're half asleep, half awake. I dreamed that I got nominated; then I dreamed that I didn't get nominated. When the cycle completed itself, I opened my eyes, lifted my head, and saw that the room was empty. The house was quiet. Outside, darkness had given way to light. I looked at the clock: it was 6:53.

And I knew.

I rolled out of bed, put on my bathrobe, and wandered downstairs and into the kitchen, where Christine was standing at the center island, looking over some paperwork, sipping a cup of coffee. Our eyes met for just a second. Christine shook her head. I nodded, smiled, and walked into another room, my office, and turned on the TV. The pain was not acute. It was more like, *Okay, well, let's see who got nominated.*

You know what? They were all good. Really good and deserving actors in strong, memorable performances: Djimon Hounsou (*In America*), Tim Robbins (*Mystic River*), Benicio Del Toro (*21 Grams*), Ken Watanabe (*The Last Samurai*), and Alec Baldwin (*The Cooler*). Can I honestly say that my work was any more deserving of recognition than theirs? Can I point to one of those men and say, *Why him and not me?* Absolutely not. In fact, I could look at that list and ask, Where is Eugene Levy? Where is Paul Bettany (*Master and Commander*)? That's the thing about the Academy Awards: they are almost by definition unfair. There is no objective standard by which to measure great acting. Never has been, never will be. Most actors understand the inherent flaw of the Oscars, but give themselves over to it anyway—especially if they're lucky enough to get nominated. I won't lie: it would have been a kick to sit there in the Kodak Theater on Oscar night and hear my name read aloud, to hold my breath and try to maintain my composure as the envelope was opened. That's a dream for any actor. But now that it hadn't come true, well, I was oddly unaffected.

Time to get on with the business of life.

Others in my orbit were less sanguine. That day brought dozens of sympathetic phone calls from friends and relatives and business associates. My mother was the most persistent. She was in Los Angeles working on a movie, and she left a bunch of messages on my cell phone. Mom was all wrapped up in the Oscar race, far more than I was. I later found out that there was even a story in Mom's local newspaper detailing her efforts to bring good fortune my way. She'd purchased a statue of Sam from Weta, and in the days leading up to the unveiling of the nominations, she'd placed the statue just inches from the Oscar she'd won decades earlier for *The Miracle Worker,* in the hope that it would bring good luck. Not surprisingly, Mom was a wreck when she learned I hadn't been nominated. She hadn't slept all night and had stood in front of the television at 5:30 in the morning screaming her lungs out as the nominations were announced.

"Your mother has called eight or nine times," Christine said. "You'd better get in touch with her."

So I phoned her, and of course she was devastated. "I'm sorry, honey. It's so unfair. Are you all right?"

"I'm fine, Mom. Don't worry."

The truth is, I didn't value the nomination to the extent that she did. In my heart of hearts, I was okay. The Academy snub, as it was sometimes called, became a big subject of discussion in my corner of the universe, primarily because the studio had invested a lot of money in its Oscar campaign, and because there were legitimate career ramifications. Ultimately, though, in terms of what's really important, I discovered that it wasn't all that valuable to me; it wasn't that big a deal. All of this I communicated to my mother, who seemed at once bewildered and relieved.

"Oh, Sean," she responded proudly, "you're so well adjusted."

I'm trying, Mom . . . I'm trying.

EPILOGUE

As I write this in the early spring of 2004, I can honestly say that my life has never been better, never more filled with hope and promise. The awards season came and went, and I found myself taking great pride in the accomplishments of everyone involved in *The Lord of the Rings*. We won the acting ensemble award at the SAG (Screen Actors Guild) Awards, and I was almost surprised by how good it felt to stand there on the stage, to be part of a team and to be recognized as a team. There was legitimate honor to it. And there was dignity in the sharing of it.

Bernard Hill spoke first on our behalf, and then introduced me as "the next president of the United States." I used my brief time at the microphone to implore my fellow SAG members to put aside the bickering and partisanship that too often divide a labor movement, and that threaten the core of SAG. It didn't come across too well on television, but I was challenging the stars in the room to be more involved. Before I could complete that sentiment, however, I was nudged out of the way by John Rhys-Davies. A few media accounts focused on that event, as if it signified a rift in the Fellowship. But it didn't. John sometimes referred to us as the "dysfunctional ensemble," and he was right. To an extent we were a family, and I don't know of any family that isn't dysfunctional. John was just being John, and I love him. (Although not evident in the broadcast, it was amusing the way John bumped me; it was the perfect bookend to Bernard's introduction of me, and I responded well. Off camera, but well.)

But that's not what I will remember about the night. I will remember holding the award and carrying it around all night, and remarking on how heavy it was, and thinking that it represented the exact weight of the accomplishment. There was no regret or sadness about the Oscars, only satisfaction that we had been honored as a group, which was precisely the way it should have been.

If John hadn't bumped me offstage, here's what I would have added: "To the fans who were disappointed that I personally didn't get nominated for an Oscar, please understand that given the disparate talents that came together in the making of *The Lord of the Rings*, nothing could be more meaningful to me than a Screen Actors Guild Award in the ensemble category."

Granted, it would be nice if ensemble performances were recognized at the Academy Awards, and perhaps that will happen in the future. Still, it's hard to imagine Oscar night being any more rewarding than it was on February 29, 2004, when *The Return of the King* won eleven awards, tying the all-time record. And unlike *The Return of the King*, neither of the previous record holders, *Ben Hur* (1959) and *Titanic* (1997), had the distinction of winning in every category in which it was nominated.

The parade of Kiwis began early, with predictable and entirely deserved recognition in a host of technical categories. This didn't surprise anyone. Whatever else one might have thought about the trilogy, it was hard, if not impossible, to deny that it was a triumph of technological and design achievement. Not until the award for best adapted screenplay did I start to get nervous. You could feel the room starting to get sick of everyone associated with *The Lord of the Rings* about two awards before that, and as the nominees were read, I looked over at Philippa Boyens. Philippa is such a rock; she's so emotionally strong and stable that it's easy to take her for granted. Now, though, as we reached the category in which she personally was nominated, I had this horrible sinking feeling that the night was going to shift and it would all come down on her head. Philippa's category would represent a sea change, and from that point on, with the technical awards behind us, the night would belong to one of the other nominated films, either *Mystic River* or *Lost in Translation*.

I reached over and held Philippa's hand. She smiled, but I could tell she was nervous. Then they announced her name (as well as the names of her cowriters, Peter and Fran), and I thought, *My God, it's going to be a sweep!* I think everybody felt that way. It was like watching a no-hitter in baseball: in a way, it's boring as hell, but then in the last two innings it gets really exciting because you don't want anyone to get a hit.

In accepting the award, Peter mentioned his two children, Billy and Katie; he thanked them, in essence, for their patience, because "Mommy and Daddy have been working on this movie for their entire lives." With those words, I think, Peter won the room. You could see the heads bobbing in agreement, as if the magnitude of the effort and accomplishment had been driven home: *You know what? He deserves it.*

Peter shambled to the stage again a few minutes later to accept the award for directing, and then once more at the end of the night when *The Return of the King* was honored as best picture. I held my breath before the last of the awards, worrying for just a moment or two that something freakish might happen, and the perfect game would come to an end. But that didn't happen. When the winner was announced, Peter and Fran and producer Barrie Osborne rose from their seats. I was sitting between Billy Boyd and Dominic Monaghan; at the end of the row, closest to the aisle, was Elijah Wood. Before walking to the stage, Fran turned to me and said, "Let's go; the hobbits have to come with us."

Elijah raised his hands in protest. "No, no. This is yours. I can't go up there."

But then Peter got into the act. And Fran and Philippa and half of New Zealand, it seemed, and suddenly there we all were, up on stage, crying and laughing and hugging. It's hard to explain how it felt to climb the stairs and stand on that stage. It was an electric moment of arrival. It felt important. But it wasn't about me. It was about being part of something much bigger: the idea that when you walk into the Kodak Theater, you pass these massive pillars on which is inscribed the name of each film that has been honored with an Academy Award for best picture. As long as that building survives, *The Lord of the Rings: The Return of the King,* of which I am a not insignificant part, will be on those pillars.

I exited the stage alongside Steven Spielberg, who had presented the award for best picture. Don't ask me why, but for some reason this is what I said to him: "You know how many people want us to make *Goonies II*?"

Steven shook his head and laughed. "Come on, Sean, you guys just made history tonight. Let's not talk about *The Goonies* right now."

A few seconds later, my cell phone rang.

"Hi, Mom."

"Honey, I'm so proud of you. You were the heart of that movie, and you were the heart of the awards show tonight."

"Oh, Mom, stop!"

"No, really. You were!"

"I love you, Mom. I'll call you later."

In the middle of the chaos, Steven Spielberg began talking to Liv Tyler and me. He said something I will never forget.

"You know how many kids around the world are happy right now, because the Academy finally agrees with them and has the same sensibilities? They wanted it for *Star Wars*; they wanted it for *Raiders*." He paused for a second.

"And now the Academy has graduated in its thinking?" I interjected. "And they'll honor fantasy and science fiction?"

Steven nodded. A smile crossed his bearded face; even now, in his mid-fifties, he looked like a kid.

"Yeah. I hope so."

After both the SAG Awards and the Oscars, when we met the media backstage, we were asked whether the on-screen friendships in *The Lord of the Rings* had been mirrored in real life. Everyone nodded and offered their own take on the subject. I thought about what Elijah had said years earlier, when we first arrived in New Zealand for preproduction training.

"Friends for life."

At the time I had dismissed his comment as the product of youthful optimism and naïveté. But now I wondered whether he was right after all. It's nice to think so, anyway.

Time has a way of distorting memory, of amplifying the good things and muting the bad; nostalgia replaces clear recollection. With each passing year my time in New Zealand seems less arduous, less painful. Every once in a while I'll pull out a scrapbook and flip through the pages, and I'm surprised at how happy everyone seems to be. The exhaustion and boredom and frustration that were so much a part of the experience—or at least of my experience—are not readily evident. There's a lesson there, I guess.

I owe everything to *The Lord of the Rings*—and to Peter Jackson.

In the past six months I've had a few nice roles: first, in a hugely successful romantic comedy called *Fifty First Dates*, starring Adam Sandler and Drew Barrymore. I also worked for a month in South Africa on David Van Eyssen's *Slipstream*, which is a low-budget but innovative project worthy of the time invested. Most recently, I filmed a coming-of-age drama called *Smile*, about the relationship between an American teen who travels to China with a charitable organization, and a Chinese counterpart who receives surgery to correct a facial deformity. The film, written and directed by Jeff Kramer, a journeyman actor and first-time screenwriter, is based on his daughter's experiences with Operation Smile, an organization that helps provide funding and services for children who need reconstructive facial surgery. Jeff started out a quarter century ago in the touring company of *Grease* and has done a lot of television and theater work through the years. He never quite made it big as an actor, but now, through optimism and persistence, he's done this film, and it's the realization of a lifelong dream. His daughter was there on the set, and the righteousness of why he was doing it permeated our experience. It was only a few days of work for me, playing a teacher who inspires and encourages the young woman to get involved in volunteerism, to follow her passion.

The role, you might say, was in my wheelhouse. In fact, as I review the last few pages of this manuscript, I'm standing in the customs section of Los Angeles International Airport. Christine is waiting for the luggage. Ali and Elizabeth are with us. We've just returned from a weekend visiting Jeff in Shanghai.

What's next? I don't really know. There have been other offers, lots of them. I'm trying to wade through the scripts and make smart decisions. I might get a chance to direct, which would be cool. Or I might just focus on acting (but I doubt it). I look ahead and see nothing but blinking lights. Some will turn red; some will turn green. Either way, this much is certain:

The road goes ever on.